THE WAR OF 1812 JOURNAL OF
LIEUTENANT JOHN LE COUTEUR, 104TH FOOT

# MERRY HEARTS MAKE LIGHT DAYS

EDITED BY
DONALD E. GRAVES

Battle of Niagara 25 July 1814

The Glengarry Light Infantry who had been covering the extreme right, were recalled into line - Suddenly our line [illegible] black line rising over the hill in our front, when we poured in a rolling volley on them - Col Battersby in the most daring manner rode down and shouted were British! happily the rise of the hill and the darkness favored them, and few if any were hurt. Immediately after this, the enemy having reformed, and obtained Reinforcements came forward in great strength continuing his efforts to take the hill till midnight. The Centre of the 89th was literally charged five times - Capt Spunner, on seeing Lieutt Latham fall, seized the Kings Color which He had carried - and shouted! My boys would you desert this color? the fine fellows rallied to their colour - but, poor Spunner was killed. The heavy Columns which crossed our front, I heard receive the word, form Subdivisions - and the Officers repeating their words - into which we poured some heavy volleys till they retreated. Two Officers were taken Prisoners in our front, by the Americans on being questioned - answering "we are the Glengarry and the Royals" and walking up to them did not return.

One circumstance I shall never forget, was a lesson in war - Genl Drummond rode up to the 103rd - "My lads will you charge the Americans? He put a question instead of giving the order - they fired instead of charging. About Midnight the whole of the American army had retired. While we kept the field - as there was a rumour that General Brown was coming to renew his attack on our Small but victorious army 2500 to 3000 at first - Col Drummond made us draw all the dead horses into a line, on the crest of our position - and if attacked to kneel behind them as a breastwork, a capital one it would have proved. I was on duty that night - what a dismal night - there were 300 dead on the Niagara side of the hillock, and about a hundred of ours - besides several hundred wounded - the miserable badly wounded were groaning and imploring us for water - the Indians prowling about them and scalping or plundering - Close by me lay a fine young man the son of the American general Hull - He was mortally wounded, and I gave Him some Brandy and Water - and wished Him to give me his watch, rings and anything He wished sent to his family. He told me much about Himself, and to come to Him in the morning when He would give them to me in charge: when I got to Him, He was a beautiful Corpse, stripped stark naked - amidst a host of friends and foes. Our Mens heads and those of the Americans were within a few yards of each other, at this spot - so close had been the deadly strife at this point - A magnificent man a field Officer of the Yankee army lay close by Him. One old Yankee who I relieved much, told me it was a judgment on Him for leaving his happy home, wife and children. I sent an American Captain to the rear, in a litter shot through both legs. The scene of the morning was not more pleasant, than the nights horrors - we had to wait on our slaughter house till clean before we got a mouthful - when a great Camp Kettle full of thick chocolate, revived us surprisingly - though we devoured it among dead bodies in all directions.

*Sample page from Le Couteur's journal describing the battle of Lundy's Lane, 25 July 1814.*

THE WAR OF 1812 JOURNAL OF
LIEUTENANT JOHN LE COUTEUR, 104TH FOOT

# MERRY HEARTS MAKE LIGHT DAYS

EDITED BY
DONALD E. GRAVES

CARLETON UNIVERSITY PRESS
OTTAWA, CANADA
1994

Published with the assistance of the Ontario Heritage Foundation

Second Printing 1994
Printed and bound in Canada

---

CANADIAN CATALOGUING IN PUBLICATION DATA

Le Couteur, John, Sir, 1794-1874
Merry hearts make light days: the War of 1812 journal of Lieutenant John Le Couteur, 104th Foot

Includes bibliographical references and index.
ISBN 0-88629-224-7 (bound) -
ISBN 0-88629-225-5 (pbk.)

1. Le Couteur, John, Sir, 1794-1874—Diaries.
2. Canada—History—War of 1812—Personal narratives. I. Graves, Donald E. (Donald Edward), 1949- . II. Title.

E361.L43A3 1993 971.03'4 C93-090643-8

---

Carleton University Press
160 Paterson Hall, 1125 Colonel By Dr.
Ottawa K1S 5B6 Canada
(613) 788-3740

Distributed in Canada by:
Oxford University Press Canada
70 Wynford Dr., Don Mills, ON M3C 1J9
(416) 441-2941

Cover Design: Karen Temple Design
Cover illustrations: Portrait of Lieutenant John Le Couteur, artist unknown, courtesy of the Société Jersiaise, St. Helier, Jersey. Sketch of the American attack on Fort George, artist unknown/National Archives of Canada/C-23675.
Interior: Xpressive Designs, Ottawa. Typeset in Optima and Century Oldstyle

Acknowledgements

Carleton University Press gratefully acknowledges the support extended to its publishing programme by the Canada Council and the Ontario Arts Council.

The Press would also like to thank the Department of Communications, Government of Canada, and the Government of Ontario through the Ministry of Culture, Tourism and Recreation, for their assistance.

This book has been published with the assistance of the Ontario Heritage Foundation.

*For S.D.G.*
*who had the misfortune to live, not only with me,*
*but also with the ghostly tramp of long-dead legions.*

*D.G.*

# *Table of Contents*

# *Illustrations*

Acknowledgments

The editing of Sir John Le Couteur's Journal of his experiences in Canada during the War of 1812 has been a lengthy but enjoyable process. It would never have been completed without the assistance of the following persons and institutions.

First of all, I would like to thank Mrs. Nancy V. Agate of Berkhamsted, United Kingdom, for her gracious permission, on the part of the descendants of Sir John Le Couteur, to prepare his Journal for publication.

Second, I must thank the staff of the Lord Coutanche Library, Société Jersiaise, St. Helier, Jersey, who have patiently done their best for six years to answer my numerous requests for information and photocopies. Without the generous and professional assistance of Miss Catherine Buddin, Miss Jean McDougall and the late Miss Joan de la Haye, it would have been impossible for a Canadian to conduct research into the Le Couteur-Sumner Archives, a complex and extensive collection of family papers located in Jersey.

Next, I owe a special debt of gratitude to Dr. John C. Fredriksen of Warwick, Rhode Island, who set me on the path that led to my discovery of Le Couteur's Journal and who, on the basis of his nationality, stepped aside to let me prepare it for publication. Those privileged to know John personally are aware that, not only is he one of the leading experts on the manuscript sources of the War of 1812, but that he is also an extremely generous and helpful person.

I have received much advice and help from four valued friends and colleagues. Mr. René Chartrand of the Canadian Parks Service made available material from his own research on the Royal Military College and the 104th Foot, while Mr. Timothy Dubé of the Manuscript Division, National Archives of Canada, provided his usual expert guidance through the maze of that institution's collection of British military documents. Professor Wesley Turner of Brock University brought to my attention Le Couteur's letter to William Robison which is in the holdings of the Clements Library, University of Michigan. Finally, Mr. Stewart Sutherland of the Dictionary of Canadian Biography read the entire manuscript, corrected several embarrassing factual errors, and generously allowed me to make use of the results of his own personal research into the British officer corps in Canada during the War of 1812.

Dr. Margaret Angus of Kingston, that city's prominent local historian, helped me sort out the Robison-Cartwright connection and the intricacies of Kingston society during the War of 1812 period. I am also indebted to Mr. John Grenville of Kingston for answering questions concerning local matters.

Two of my colleagues at the Directorate of History deserve special mention. Mr. Brereton Greenhous cast his well-honed critical eye over portions of the manuscript, while Lieutenant Commander W.R. Glover, CD, officer and scholar, provided useful and helpful commentary.

I would also like to thank the following individuals and institutions: the staff of the National Library of Canada who, unfailingly, traced obscure publications and located the sources of some very esoteric quotations; Dr. John Dann and Mr. John Harrigan of the Clements Library, University of Michigan, Ann Arbor, for permission to reprint Le Couteur's letter to William Robison; Mr. Douglas Hendry for some very thorough research at the Public Record Office in London; Mr. John Marteinson, editor, *Canadian Defence Quarterly*, and Dr. W.A.B. Douglas, Director-General, Directorate General of History, Department of National Defence, for permission to reprint Le Couteur's account of the winter march of the 104th; Mr. A.A. Orgill, Senior Librarian, Royal Military College, Sandhurst, United Kingdom, for information regarding Le Couteur's cadet days at that institution; and Ms. Ruth Isaacs of the Woodland Cultural Centre in Brantford, Ontario, for assistance with questions regarding native languages.

At Carleton University Press, I am indebted to the assistance rendered to me in the preparation of the manuscript by Professor Michael Gnarowski, General Editior, and Professor S.F. Wise, History Editor. I must also record my thanks to Ms. Diane Mew of Toronto for her thorough editing of the final product.

Finally, I have to acknowledge my great debt to two authors whose books have been fixtures on my desk these past six years. W. Austin Squires's *The 104th Regiment of Foot (The New Brunswick Regiment). 1803-1817* answered many questions I had concerning Le Couteur's regiment while Joan Stevens's *Victorian Voices. An Introduction to the Papers of Sir John Le Couteur, Q.A.D.C., F.R.S.* was indispensable for unravelling the complexities of Le Couteur's geneology and understanding his later life. The following manuscript is built upon the firm scholarly foundations first put in place by these two historians.

*Donald E. Graves*
*Almonte, Ontario*
*Canada, 1993*

# *Introduction*

## I

At half past nine in the "balmy, soft evening" of 21 June 1812, a young British officer stood on the deck of the brig *Anns* as it "glided gently into Halifax Harbour."[1] Eighteen-year-old Lieutenant John Le Couteur of the British army had arrived in Canada to join his regiment, the 104th Foot, stationed in New Brunswick. Three days before, unknown to Le Couteur or anyone else in Halifax, the United States had declared war on Great Britain, setting the stage for a series of battles and campaigns along the Canadian border and the eastern seaboard of the United States. The most active theatre of operations proved to be Upper Canada (present-day Ontario) where Le Couteur would serve and where he would suffer sickness, inclement weather, short rations and other privations, endure an epic winter march from Fredericton to Kingston, and fight in countless skirmishes and six major engagements. In February 1815, as an older, wiser and more experienced officer, he would rejoice at the "blessed news of Peace" and "the close of a hot war and unnatural war between kindred people."[2]

John Le Couteur would have been just another faceless British soldier who served in Canada during the War of 1812 but for one important difference — he left a lengthy record of his experiences in a manuscript Journal. Today, this Journal is part of a collection of Le Couteur family papers, some "one hundred closely written books and many documents,"[3] held by the Lord Coutanche Library of the Société Jersiaise, St. Helier, Jersey. This important collection, which has already formed the subject of one specialized study, contains not only Le Couteur's personal papers but also those of his maternal grandfather, his parents and his children, and spans the period from 1770 to 1890.[4] It was preserved from the vicissitudes of fate (including the German occupation of Jersey during the Second World War) by the foresight of his descendants and, in 1970, was donated by the family to the Société.

Document M-10 of the Le Couteur papers is described in the collection finding aid as "Diary My Journal. (largely in Canada 1820-1851)."[5] It is primarily an account of Le Couteur's early life and his military career including his service in North America from 1812 to 1817, and Le Couteur apparently intended it to be his autobiography. Judging by the marginal notes on the original manuscript, he worked steadily on it from 1821 to 1851, and less frequently thereafter. Although historians of Jersey have made use of the Journal, its existence was unsuspected outside the island until the publication of Joan Stevens's biography of Le Couteur in 1969. Unknown in Canada and the United States, it is an important historical source for students both of Canadian and American history and of the War of 1812.

John Le Couteur inherited a family penchant for keeping diaries, beginning his first in 1812 and continuing this activity almost to the day of his death.[6] Unfortunately his diary for the important years 1812-1815 has not survived, although a second for 1815-1817 has, and this was used to check the accuracy of the statements in his Journal for those years. Close examination of the Journal reveals that Le Couteur based it primarily on transcriptions from his daily diaries, fleshed out with anecdotes, correspondence, official documents and excerpts from his mother's diary. Many passages remain bare daily entries from the diaries, others have been extensively reworked and the manuscript includes many crossed-out or corrected sections.

As reproduced here, the Journal recounts Le Couteur's childhood, his experiences at the Royal Military College, his garrison service in Jersey and his wartime experiences in Canada. It also contains several letters and loose documents that the author placed between its pages, as well as an additional letter from Le Couteur to William Robison describing the battle of Lundy's Lane, 1814. It must be noted that the contents of the Journal are not reproduced below exactly as Le Couteur had intended they should be. A small portion of the original, a repetitious and invented dialogue that repeats a considerable portion of the material contained in chapter 1, has been omitted. In addition, the material in chapters 1, 2, 12 and 14 has been rearranged to place it in chronological order — a process fully described in the notes. Chapter 4 is based on the one part of the Journal that did see publication, an account of the march of the 104th Foot from New Brunswick to Upper Canada in 1813, and has been reassembled from three different versions: Le Couteur's original draft, the first publication in 1830, and the second in 1930. After some deliberation it was decided not to reproduce the diary for 1815-1817 as to do so would have expanded what is an already lengthy manuscript.

Le Couteur's Journal falls squarely within a genre that can best be categorized by the classification "the young subaltern abroad." This type of memoir blossomed during the first half of the nineteenth century, a result of the tremendous expansion of the British army during the Napoleonic wars which brought into its ranks many educated and literate young men who were determined to leave a record of their experiences for posterity. In 1912 the military historian Sir Charles Oman identified over a hundred such published memoirs and many more have since appeared in print.[7] Le Couteur's Journal is, therefore, contemporary with such well-known reminiscences as those of Cadell, Costello, Grattan, Gronow, Kincaid, Leeke and Mercer.[8] It is interesting to note that if his original intention to join a regiment earmarked for service with Wellington in Spain had been approved, Le Couteur's Journal might have become another title in that voluminous literature, and instead of learning about the battle of Beaver Dams, we would have read of the siege of Badajos; instead of Conjocta Creek, perhaps Quatre Bras.

In the event, John Le Couteur joined the 104th Foot, a regiment stationed in North America, and fought throughout the War of 1812. His Journal is therefore best compared with the published and unpublished accounts by British and Canadian participants of that conflict. They are not many and the comparison works in Le Couteur's favour. Most are by Canadians and most of them only fragmentary in nature.[9] Accounts by British regulars, including both published[10] and unpublished material,[11] are much rarer — only two works, both published, are equivalent in historical value with Le Couteur — the journal of the Mohawk war chief, John Norton,[12] and the memoir of William Dunlop of the 89th Foot.[13]

Surgeon William Dunlop compiled an informative, perceptive and humorous account of his military services in Upper Canada in 1813-1815 that first saw publication in 1847. A polished and witty raconteur, he produced an entertaining memoir that still provides easy and enjoyable reading. Unlike Le Couteur, whose diary formed the basis of his Journal, Dunlop wrote from memory thirty-three years after the events he is describing, and although his Recollections are informative, they cannot be compared with the historical quality of Le Couteur's account.

Le Couteur's work compares less well with that of John Norton. Norton's manuscript was written to give readers an accurate history of the native tribes he had visited during his voyage to the territory of the Cherokees in 1810-1811, and with whom he was associated as a war chief in the War of 1812. The result is possibly the best personal account of the War of 1812 from the British side and certainly the best from the native point of view. In terms of historical value it is superior to Le Couteur's Journal, but this is understandable as Norton was an older and more experienced man who occupied a position that gave him access to the councils of senior officers. Although they fought side by side in the Niagara in 1813 and 1814, as far as we know, the two men never met.

*Lieutenant John Le Couteur, 104th Foot. Portrait painted between 1811 and 1816.* Artist unknown. Courtesy of the Société Jersiaise, St. Helier, Jersey

A keen observer, committed recorder and gifted writer, Le Couteur followed his mother's *dictum* that "a great deal of the elegance of writing consists not only in the choice of expression, but in the use of those words only which are necessary."[14] He loved a good story and sometimes included one in his text even though it did not personally happen to him. These anecdotes have been identified (where they can be) in the textual notes. Le Couteur was also a linguist, with the musical ear that those proficient in languages often possess, a characteristic that allowed him to catch not only the particular vernacular but the rhythm of the speaker as well. In sum, Le Couteur possessed such obvious talents that, had he not chosen a military career, he might have enjoyed success as an author.

## II

Who was this literary young officer? What was his background? John Le Couteur was born in 1794 at St. Helier, Jersey. The largest of the Channel Islands, Jersey is located in the Gulf of Avranches, fifteen miles from the coast of France. Blessed with a mild climate and fertile soil, but with few good harbours, Jersey's forty-five square miles contained about twenty-six thousand residents in Le Couteur's time.[15] Originally part of the Duchy of Normandy, it passed, with the other French territories of William the Conqueror, to the English crown in 1066 and has remained a British possession ever since. Throughout their long association with Britain the inhabitants of the island have demonstrated two outstanding attributes: loyalty to the Crown and a fierce independence where their island customs and traditions (especially exemption from British customs duties) are concerned.

Jersey's strategic, and precarious, location close to France led to the construction of fortifications, the presence of large permanent garrisons and the early creation of a local defence force, the island militia. Organized on a permanent basis during the Hundred Years' War, by the end of the eighteenth century, the Jersey militia consisted of five regiments composed of all able-bodied males over the age of seventeen, who were required to serve unpaid as required. There was little complaint and commissions in the militia were eagerly sought after because they brought social distinction.[16]

This was the Jersey into which John Le Couteur was born into on 21 October 1794. It was a small, closely-knit community whose social and political organization was based on the island's twelve church parishes. The common people spoke a Norman patois although this was starting to die out; the gentry spoke both French and English and were heavily intermarried among similar families on

Jersey and the other Channel islands. They eagerly sought commissions in the British army or Royal Navy. The name of Major General Sir Isaac Brock is well known in Canadian history, what is less well known is that he was only one of four brothers who served in either the British army or Royal Navy during the Napoleonic period. The Brocks of Guernsey, like the Le Marchant and Saumarez families of the same island, the Le Mesurier family of Alderney and the Carteret, Durell, Le Breton, Lemprière, Pipon and Dumaresq clans of Jersey, provided an unduly large number of officers for the forces of the Crown during the eighteenth and nineteenth centuries.

Le Couteur's father, General John Le Couteur (1760-1835), was a member of this group of prominent Channel Islanders who entered the King's service. The family name had been recorded on Jersey since the fourteenth century and the ancestral home was traditionally located at Les Buttes, in St. John's parish in the northern part of the island.[17] Le Couteur's father was born in 1760 and baptised Jean but preferred the anglicized John. Little is known about his parents. His father, also Jean Le Couteur, was born in 1716, and was Constable of St. John's parish in 1776-1778 but died during a trip to Paris in 1794.[18] His mother, the former Marie Bertault, married his father in 1753 and had two other children, both daughters, who died young.

In 1780, Le Couteur's father purchased an ensign's commission in the 95th Regiment of Foot, then stationed in Jersey. The following year he saw action when he participated in the defeat of a French landing force and, perhaps as a result, was promoted a lieutenant in the 100th Foot. He campaigned with his regiment on the Malabar coast of India but was captured by native forces at the surrender of Chittledroog in April 1783, and endured nearly a year of harsh imprisonment before being released at the end of the war. Promoted captain, he was placed on half-pay when his regiment was disbanded in 1785. He returned home to take an active part in local political and militia activities and, displaying the literary bent that was a family trait, published two accounts of his experiences in India and helped to establish the first island newspaper, the *Gazette de Jersey*.[19] In 1792, Captain Le Couteur purchased the manor of Belle Vue, near the village of St. Aubin's, from Jean Dumaresq and the following year he married that gentleman's daughter, Marie.[20]

Le Couteur's maternal grandfather, Jean Dumaresq (1749-1819) was one of the most prominent islanders of his time. Educated at Winchester, Dumaresq read law and represented Jersey's claims before the English parliament on numerous occasions. He led the political faction known as the "Magots" who emphasized self-government against the claims of an opposing faction, the "Charlots," who wanted to keep political control of Jersey in the hands of an autocracy composed of a few inter-related families. A quarter of a century of strife between these two bitterly opposed parties ended in 1802 when Dumaresq was appointed Lieutenant Bailiff of Jersey, a post which combined the functions of chief magistrate and president of the States, the island's legislative assembly.[21]

Jean Dumaresq married Marie Le Mesurier (1748-1787), daughter of the hereditary governor of Alderney, a neighbouring Channel Island, and they had ten children. Their eldest daughter, Marie (1774-1845), was only thirteen when her mother died, and she raised her nine siblings. Marie Dumaresq possessed a lively sense of humour, a love of society and an artistic bent that found its outlet in watercolours and the keeping of a diary. She was nineteen in 1793 when she married Captain John Le Couteur in an elaborate wedding at the home of her father. The couple set up house in their newly-purchased manor at Belle Vue and in October 1794 had their first child, a son whom they christened John.[22] A second son, Gordon, was born in 1801.

The coming of war with France led to the recall of Le Couteur's father to active service in 1793 and he was appointed to the staff of the large Jersey garrison. In 1797 he purchased a majority in the 16th Foot, then stationed at Aberdeen, and the following year the couple travelled to Scotland with their four-year-old child when Major Le Couteur joined his unit for a spell of regimental duty. The family returned to Jersey in 1799 when John's father was promoted lieutenant-colonel and appointed Inspecting Field Officer of the island militia, a position that he held for twelve years. This post was no sinecure as Jersey was under constant threat of attack and the militia were almost permanently on duty. Against strong opposition, Colonel Le Couteur introduced compulsory daily drill beginning at 6 A.M. for all the boys of the island aged thirteen and over. He usually attended these drills and may have watched his son John with some pride as young Le Couteur was one of the more proficient recruits.[23]

The Le Couteurs were a closely-knit family. The parents enjoyed a lively social life among their large circle of acquaintances. They were fond of artistic pursuits, including writing, painting and the theatre, a fondness that was passed on to their son. They were not wealthy people (although Marie Le Couteur seems to have had some private income), but they did not want. Devout Anglicans, the Le Couteurs were religious without being oppressively so and Marie devoted much of her later years to the work of the British and Foreign Bible Society. In a word, they were "gentry," with all the privileges and responsibilities attendant on their station in the early nineteenth century.

Young John Le Couteur received his early education at home under his mother's direction. He could read and write English by the age of five and French by the age of seven. Tutors then coached him in German and the higher branches of mathematics. He grew into a handsome young man of slightly smaller than average stature but with a wiry, athletic frame. At age seventeen his portrait shows an intelligent and sensitive face already stamped with a certain measure of self-assurance. He worshipped his mother and treated his father, who was a somewhat stern and distant figure, with an obedience appropriate to a military family. It is not surprising that it was early decided that John would follow his father's profession. In 1807 he was sent to William Sproston's academy at High Wycombe, the preparatory school for the Royal Military College.

This newly-founded institution was an outgrowth of the increasing professionalism that the British army experienced during the tenure of the Duke of York as commander-in-chief from 1795 to 1809. Determined to render the army fit for combat against a well-trained French foe, York revised almost every aspect of the military machinery of Great Britain including the education of officers. While the technical corps of the army, the Royal Artillery and Royal Engineers, already possessed their own training establishment for junior officers — the Royal Military Academy at Woolwich — there was no provision for the training of junior officers for the infantry and cavalry or for the higher levels of staff work. In 1801 the Senior Department of the Royal Military College, organized to instruct officers in staff duties, was founded at High Wycombe in Buckinghamshire.[24]

This was followed in 1802 by the creation of the Junior Department, intended for the education of prospective officers. Because of a shortage of accommodation at High Wycombe, it was located at Marlow, five miles away. The first class began its studies in May 1802; by Le Couteur's time, three hundred cadets were enrolled. Military instruction was in the hands of officers seconded from the army, while scholastic teaching was the business of civilian instructors. The curriculum consisted of courses in mathematics, fortification, gunnery and artillery service, drawing, military movements and perspectives, tactics, geography, history, French, German and Latin. The cadet's day was long, beginning with reveille at 5.15 A.M. and included six and a half hours of classes, ninety minutes of drill, and at least an hour of prayer before lights out at 10 P.M.[25]

Thirteen years old and four feet seven inches tall, John Le Couteur entered this institution in February 1808 to remain for nearly three years.[26] His time at the college marked Le Couteur and he often referred to himself in later years simply as a "G.C." (Gentleman Cadet). Although he participated in his share of pranks and misadventures, young Le Couteur gained steady promotion within the cadet ranks until he achieved the rank of senior under-officer (cadet commander) of the college. His enthusiasm for both his military and scholastic studies and his qualities of leadership and maturity earned him the approbation of the college staff and he was entrusted with the protection and guidance of a royal prince, the son of the future William IV. It was at Marlow that Le Couteur began to formulate his concept of leadership that "Persuasion and esprit de corps do more than Punishments."[27] He passed his graduation examination in 1810. That November, having just turned sixteen, the minimum age for holding a commission, he was appointed an ensign in the 96th Regiment of Foot. He thus became a member of a small and select group, as only one in every twenty-five newly-commissioned officers in the army were Royal Military College graduates.[28]

The 2nd Battalion of the 96th Foot was part of the garrison of Jersey and Le Couteur's appointment to this unit was no accident. His father, who regarded his son as "too young for immediate active service," had successfully petitioned to have Le Couteur stationed close to his family.[29] Small, agile and an accomplished athlete, Le Couteur was assigned to the elite light infantry company of his battalion which he remembered as being composed of "Welshmen, as active as Goats, very smart, nice fellows but quarrelsome."[30] Throughout his military career Le Couteur served as a light infantryman and liked to describe himself as a "light Bob."[31]

Le Couteur did not stay with the 96th for long. In November 1811, after only one year of service, he gained an unusually accelerated promotion to the rank of lieutenant, rather than the two that this step usually required.[32] He was anxious to see active service and wanted to join the 77th Foot, under orders for Wellington's army in Spain, but in dutiful response to his father's wishes he exchanged instead into the 104th Foot, stationed in Canada. At this time, Le Couteur's family was also preparing to leave Jersey as his father, recently promoted to major general, was under orders to join the staff in Ireland. His wife and younger son were planning to accompany him and it was with great regret that young John watched the "Break up of the Establishment in old Belle Vue."[33]

In June 1812, after a period of waiting in the Army Depot on the Isle of Wight where he experienced some comic misadventures, Le Couteur sailed for North America. His new regiment was unique in the British army as it was the only line infantry unit recruited outside the United Kingdom. The 104th Foot had begun life in 1803-1805 as the New Brunswick Fencibles. Fencible regiments were units that were only required to serve locally — in the case of the New Brunswick Fencibles, this meant British North America —and were not liable for worldwide service. Most of the enlisted ranks were recruited in New Brunswick and Lower Canada, although some recruits joined in the United Kingdom, notably Scotland.[34]

In 1810 the officers of the regiment (but not the other ranks) had volunteered for general service and the regiment was brought into the regular army list the following year as the 104th Foot. In the summer of 1812, when Le Couteur joined, it was serving as the garrison of New Brunswick and Prince Edward Island.[35]

Le Couteur's fellow officers were a mixed lot. The regiment was commanded by Lieutenant Colonel Alexander Halkett, an amiable and sociable nonentity who would not remain long with it. The second-in-command, Major William Drummond, was quite another matter. Drummond had spent fourteen years in the West Indies before joining the 104th in 1809 and was a veteran light infantryman who trained the entire regiment as skirmishers. Honest, upright, approachable and good-humoured, William Drummond impressed all who met him, and he was worshipped by Le Couteur and the other junior officers of the 104th. The rest of Le Couteur's fellows were a lively collection of veterans and neophytes: "Old Dick" (Captain Richard Leonard), the commander of the grenadier company; bald "Woody" (Assistant Surgeon William Woodford), "Bass" (Lieutenant R.L. Basserer); the "Irish Sub" (Lieutenant Michael Considine) and the remainder of a set of "frank, friendly-hearted Young Men"[36] with whom John Le Couteur was to spend five years of war and peace.

Le Couteur is less informative about the enlisted men of the regiment. At best he provides only their surnames and some indication of their function. Thus, we have Woodward,"a New Brunswick canoeman"; Brisland, the regimental fiddler; Nickerson, "a short active Highlander"; and Sergeant Lamery, "a handsome, gay, chattering humbug." This seeming lack of interest in the lower ranks is not surprising given the great gulf that existed between officers and enlisted men during the period. The close relationship that exists between the modern officer and his subordinates was not possible in Le Couteur's time because of the rigidly stratified hierarchy of the society from which both groups came. An additional element in maintaining this gulf was the officer's power to impose corporal punishment on his men which was far greater in 1812 than in any western army today.

"The punishments at this period," Le Couteur remembered, "were tremendous in the extreme."[37] The standard disciplinary response was flogging, and regimental courts martial had the power to award up to three hundred lashes while garrison or general courts martial could impose up to one thousand. Witnessing his first flogging, Le Couteur "fainted away like a Sick girl to my own great horror and Confusion" when the drummer wielding the lash "switched a quantity of ... blood over my Face and Belts."[38] His brother officers laughed but "the men did not." Unwilling to resort to such a drastic means of discipline, Le Couteur preferred to devise milder forms of punishments rather than report his men to higher authorities and subject them to courts martial. His good sense paid dividends as his "kind and devoted Soldiers ... understood my meaning perfectly and appreciated it — their honor was mine."[39] The test of such (for the time) novel methods of leadership came in the field in the autumn of 1813. Le Couteur remembers with obvious pride that when he called for a few volunteers to accompany him on a particularly hazardous mission, every one of his men stepped forward.

From the day he joined the 104th, Le Couteur's Journal betrays his single-minded determination to gain a captaincy. This determination was possibly fuelled by money, for Le Couteur's parents could only provide him an allowance of a guinea a week to add to his pay.[40] As an infantry lieutenant with under seven years of service, Le Couteur was paid six shillings, sixpence a day, with an additional foreign service allowance of sixpence per day towards forage for the horses to carry his baggage in the field.[41] Unfortunately, there were also deductions which amounted to about a fifth of his gross pay and included "poundage," a primitive form of income tax; "agency," or fees paid to the army agent for the administration of his accounts; and a day's pay a year for the support of military hospitals. Finally, the regimental band of the 104th, which Le Couteur admired so much, was financed by sums levied on each officer.

Even with the guinea a week from his parents and his extra allowances, Le Couteur would have had only about six shillings a day disposable income, about the same as a small farmer or minor clergyman.[42] From this, he had to provide not only his uniforms and equipment but also pay for his rations and mess bill when not serving in the field. Small wonder he complains bitterly about being charged three shillings for a dozen eggs in wartime Kingston. Small wonder that, in 1814, the half-starved subalterns of the Kingston garrison mount a midnight raid that decimates the commanding general's prized flock of turkeys! Promotion would nearly double his income, as captains were paid ten shillings, sixpence per day, plus the foreign service allowance and an additional £20 annual allowance for administrative costs involved in commanding a company.[43]

Simply said, but not simply done. The promotion system of the British army at this time was complicated and convoluted. There were three ways for a regimental officer to advance in rank: by seniority, by patronage or by purchase. Promotion by seniority depended on the amount of time an officer had been in the regiment at his current rank. By tradition, if not regulation, all vacancies caused by combat deaths were filled by seniority; if a captain was killed then the most senior lieutenant in the regiment was promoted, his position in turn being filled by the most senior ensign. Patronage was a promotion gained through the intervention of the Duke of York, the commander-in-chief. In theory, he had the right to appoint officers to any vacancy, but in practice he filled only those vacancies caused by deaths other than combat, the creation of new units or the augmentation of old ones, and disciplinary measures resulting from courts martial. Usually, the duke used this power only in cases involving officers with long and outstanding service or who had displayed extreme merit or gallantry.[44]

Purchase was, as it implies, simply buying the next rank — a procedure that sounds strange to the modern reader but one that prevailed in the British army until 1870. But purchase also went by seniority; when a vacancy occurred among the captains that could be filled by purchase, it was offered to the most senior lieutenant of the regiment. The purchase system was under rigorous control by 1812 and officers had to serve a certain amount of time in each rank before they were eligible for promotion by purchase (at least three years for a captaincy and seven years for a majority).[45] Purchase, therefore, did not mean accelerated promotion, and as most wartime officer vacancies were not fillable by purchase there was a decreasing number of promotions that could be obtained by this method. By 1814 it has been estimated that only two of every ten promotions in the army were gained by purchase, whereas seven went by seniority and one by patronage.[46]

By any means, promotion was slow. Even in wartime, a line infantry lieutenant could expect to serve an average of seven years for promotion to captain.[47] Le Couteur would thus have to wait until November 1813 before he was even eligible for this rank. His best hope was to gain promotion by merit. One way to do this would be serve on the staff of the army, or as the personal aide-de-camp of a general officer, where it would be easier to attract the notice of his superiors. Here again, the regulations demanded at least one year's service with a regiment to be considered as an aide-de-camp and a minimum of three years and "a perfect knowledge of ... Regimental duties" to receive a junior staff appointment.[48] There was no way out — Le Couteur would have to serve a minimum of a year of the "fated Regimental service"[49] before he was even eligible for the staff.

As his Journal reveals, this service was not all that dreadful. Although war broke out only a few days after he arrived in Canada, the 104th Foot remained in garrison in New Brunswick throughout the winter of 1812-1813. Le Couteur fully enjoyed the leisure activities available: fishing, shooting, canoeing, snowshoeing and skating, as well as the benefits of local society in Fredericton, his garrison post. As a British officer, he had an instant entrée into the highest levels of colonial society, and the coming of war did nothing to dampen its rather frenetic pace. Between September and December 1812 Le Couteur records that he attended "Thirty five dinners, evening parties or balls."[50]

He continued this busy schedule throughout his service in Canada whenever he was not actually in the field, but such popularity could not be solely based on Le Couteur's officer status. His engaging personality must have played some part, for he was a warm and outgoing young man with a sense of humour that won him many friends from such "big wigs" (as he privately called them) as Lieutenant General Sir George Prevost, the Governor General of British North America, on down. In Lower Canada his fluent French was an additional asset that gained him entrance to francophone circles that were closed to most British officers.

Le Couteur loved this active social life, which went a long way towards easing his time in the rather primitive conditions of British North America; and he was such a relentless recorder of the names of those with whom he socialized that his Journal sometimes runs the danger of becoming a directory of Canadian high society as it existed in 1812-1817.

He did not, however, follow the example of so many of his fellow officers and marry a Canadian. Not that he wasn't attracted to the opposite sex — quite the opposite. John Le Couteur was a very romantic young man and his Journal contains so many affairs of the youthful heart that it risks straining the reader's patience. But he was always too aware of his financial condition to think of contracting a permanent relationship with any of the many young ladies he so fervently admired. Regarding himself as a poor, penniless "soldier of fortune," Le Couteur kept his distance even as, in the privacy of his quarters, he devoured romantic novels.

He was a prodigious reader and his taste ran mainly to historical fiction. Like many another adolescent, Le Couteur viewed the world through the prism of his favourite authors and behaved accordingly. His hero, Major William Drummond of the 104th, was the personification of Roderick Dhu, one of Sir Walter Scott's characters — "a kind-hearted, noble sort of liberal Scotchman".[51] And, like Scott's heroes, Le Couteur was protective of women. In 1814, he gets "a fair Lady Captain — of the 100th Reg[imen]t, wife" across a muddy stream in Kingston by providing his well-polished boot as a stepping stone.[52] During his time in Canada, however, Lieutenant John Le Couteur was a soldier at war and it is as a soldier's memoir that his Journal must be read.

## III

On 26 June 1812 Le Couteur was dining in the gunroom of HMS *Africa*, the flagship of the commander of the America and West Indies squadron of the Royal Navy, when an excited officer burst in to announce that the frigate *Belvidera* was entering the harbour with "no boats, no anchors, and shot holes through her sails!"[53] The *Belvidera* had just escaped an American squadron to bring news of the declaration of war between the United States and Great Britain in a most dramatic fashion. Thus, after only five days in Canada, Le Couteur found himself in the middle of a hot war. On his way across the Bay of Fundy to join his regiment, he experienced an exciting episode when the warship he was on attempted to capture an American privateer, and for the first time, as he triumphantly recorded, he saw "wounds and death in real war!"[54]

New Brunswick was not in any great danger of invasion and "although duty was hard," the 104th Foot endured none of "its horrors" in that province.[55] Matters changed in February 1813, when the regiment was ordered to Upper Canada, an active theatre, and marched overland for Quebec. This march, in the middle of a severe winter which was seeing greater snowfall and lower temperatures than normal, was a spectacular feat of soldiering and Le Couteur leaves us with a detailed account. After nearly two months and hundreds of miles of hard marching, the 104th reached Kingston, Upper Canada to view "magnificent Lake Ontario, and ... a squadron of ships-of-war frozen on its bosom."[56]

Shortly after its arrival in Upper Canada, the 104th fought its first action. On the afternoon of 27 May 1813 the British commander in North America, Lieutenant General Sir George Prevost, loaded all available troops in Kingston, about nine hundred men, in the ships of Captain Sir James Lucas Yeo's naval squadron and set sail for Sackets Harbor, located on the south shore of Lake Ontario. The next morning, the British force was off the Harbor but contrary winds prevented it from landing as an alerted American garrison prepared to meet the attack. While Prevost and Yeo hesitated for an entire day, a frustrated Major William Drummond, whose men had been embarked in small boats in preparation for landing, began to row into the harbour "to practice pulling."[57]

A curt and peremptory order from Prevost brought a furious Drummond back to the squadron. After nearly twenty-four hours of indecision, the landing was made about 5 A.M. on the morning of 29 May 1813. Le Couteur gives us an exciting account of his first main battle. We read of Drummond "running sword in hand, like Roderick Dhu in a fray" leading the attack along with Sir James Yeo, who was "waving his cap, cheering the men on, without sword or pistol."[58] Yeo would have been better advised to have remained on his flagship to co-ordinate a naval bombardment in support of the troops on shore, as their advance was stopped dead by Americans firing from behind fieldworks. A nervous Prevost then ordered a retreat although, at the same time, he permitted Drummond to summon the defenders to surrender. But, as Le Couteur recorded, the Americans were "too grass sharp. 'Why do you retreat, if you wish us to surrender?'", they inquired.[59] Drummond had no good answer and the assault force re-embarked having suffered over two hundred casualties to no purpose. "It was," in Le Couteur's opinion, "a scandalously managed affair."

After a further month of garrison duty in Kingston, the 104th received orders in early June 1813 to join the army fighting in the Niagara peninsula. The war in this area had degenerated into a loose British blockade of the American army in and around the Canadian town of Newark (modern Niagara-on-the-Lake). As soon as it arrived, Le Couteur's light infantry company joined the "light division" of the army, an ad hoc formation under the command of Major Peter De Haren. Here he gained the first major step in his quest for promotion when De Haren appointed him adjutant at the age of eighteen. From mid-June until early October the light division was involved in the ceaseless round of skirmishing that took place between the two armies and it was here, for the first time, that Le Couteur witnessed the use of the scalping knife, that "nasty adjunct" to North American warfare.

Just before dawn on 24 June 1813 Le Couteur was awakened by an Indian messenger informing him that an enemy force had been spotted moving towards the light division's position. He immediately alerted De Haren and the division was put under arms. Not long afterwards, the noise of musketry and artillery was heard from the vicinity of the beech woods a few miles away and Le Couteur was sent to investigate. He thus became the first non-participant to arrive at the scene of the battle of Beaver Dams, and he witnessed the surrender of an American force to a much smaller British and native force under the command of Lieutenant Edward Fitzgibbon of the 49th Foot.

For Le Couteur, the victory was marred by the behaviour of the Indian warriors who scalped most of the American dead. In his feelings towards the "Nitchies," the native auxiliaries, whom he described as "ticklish friends to deal with,"[60] Le Couteur echoed the sentiments of many of the British army who were quite incapable of appreciating the independent attitude of these warriors who fought when, how, and where they chose. Some regular officers, notably William Drummond, had a different attitude and forged a special relationship with the natives; but to Le Couteur and most British soldiers, the Indians' reluctance to suffer heavy casualties in gaining an objective that could be better won by stealth simply confirmed them in the opinion that the tribesmen were "cunning, cowardly and revengeful in the highest degree, brave only when their enemy is Broken or flying."[61] Le Couteur had little contact with the natives of Upper Canada and knew little about them. In March 1814 he attended services in the Mohawk

Chapel at Deseronto and found it "striking and imposing" to watch warriors he had seen "scalping, looting, Yelling and carousing" in the Niagara listen to the Gospel of St. John read in the Mohawk language.[62] He did not realize that the man who had translated those gospels was John Norton, the war chief of these same warriors.

One aspect of the war that the Journal brings home to the modern reader is the high rate of sickness among the soldiers. Stationed for nearly two months in the Black Swamp area west of Niagara-on-the-Lake, the 104th Foot suffered dreadfully from disease; on one day in September, they reported 62 men sick from a total of 194 posted at the Four-Mile Creek.[63] Le Couteur was spared a major illness during his first campaign in the autumn of 1813, an escape he attributes to his "temperance and early habits."[64] On his return to Kingston, however, he suffered a bad attack of boils, almost certainly caused by poor diet, and the following winter he was smitten with rheumatism, fever and a case of dysentery that lasted more three months.

Certainly, the 104th never recovered its health and, after 1813, did not serve again in the field as a complete unit. In early July 1814, however, the grenadier and light infantry companies were sent back to the Niagara in a convoy of small boats. This was not the first major troop movement by boat Le Couteur participated in, and his Journal sheds much light on the use of inland maritime transport during the war. Le Couteur had both a healthy respect for, and a hearty dislike of, waterborne travel — with good reason, for his Journal recounts several nautical misadventures. He was no fonder of inland waters as "the seas" of Lake Ontario, "if not mountainous in the sense of those of the Atlantic, were quite so for the description of vessels we were scudding with."[65] Besides the danger of capture by American warships, there was inclement weather and "nothing could be more uncomfortable than our open flat-bottomed boats ... with the cold at freezing."[66]

John Le Couteur fought in four of the six major actions that comprised the Niagara campaign of 1814, the longest and bloodiest military operation of the war. The two companies of the 104th joined the main army just in time to participate in the latter part of the confusing and sanguinary night action at Lundy's Lane. The next morning, Le Couteur records, "was not more pleasant, than the night's horrors"[67] as dawn revealed a field covered with hundreds of dead and wounded men lying in and around a pleasant, tree-shrouded country lane. Nonetheless, "a great Camp Kettle full of thick chocolate, revived us surprisingly, though we devoured it among dead bodies in all directions."[68]

Following the battle, the American army retreated to Fort Erie but the British commander, Lieutenant General Gordon Drummond (no relation to William Drummond of the 104th) did not mount a very active pursuit and it was only five days later that Le Couteur and the rest of the light infantry of the army moved south, up the Niagara river. On 2 August 1814, they were dispatched across the river to raid the American depots at Black Rock and Buffalo. Embarking in boats at night, "in expectation of making lots of prize money, *plunder*, etc.,"[69] the British encountered a battalion of American regular riflemen dug in behind log earthworks along the Conjocta Creek. The result was a fiasco that was largely the result of the incompetence of the British commander, Colonel John Tucker of the 41st Foot (known in the army as "Brigadier Shindy").[70] It was a thoroughly disgruntled light force that rejoined the main army before Fort Erie.

General Drummond's tardy pursuit after Lundy's Lane had allowed the Americans to strengthen and extend the original small Fort Erie into a well-fortified position that Le Couteur thought "an ugly Customer."[71] Le Couteur, who, it will be remembered, had been trained in field engineering at the Royal Military College, was seconded to the engineer department to construct siege batteries. After spending five days working "in my shirt like the men,"[72] he had a disagreement with the command engineer and returned to his regiment. Much to his chagrin, he later learned that this cost him a staff position, which Drummond awarded to another officer, and the loss of an additional £250 per year.

Early in the morning of 15 August 1814, after a rather desultory bombardment which had little effect, the British army mounted an assault on Fort Erie. Le Couteur and the 104th were assigned to the column commanded by Lieutenant Colonel William Drummond who, having a presentiment of his mortality, bid them goodbye, asking them to "Remember the honor of the Regiment."[73] At 3 A.M. this column penetrated one of the bastions of the fort but was unable to clear a large stone barrack building from which the American defenders taunted them. Le Couteur was just climbing into the bastion when "a black volume"[74] rose from the earth and he lost consciousness. When he regained it, he was lying among the stunned, burned and mangled survivors from the explosion of a magazine located beneath the bastion. Determined not to be taken prisoner, Le Couteur ran back to the British lines "under such a roar of voices, Musquetry & Artillery as I never desire to run from again."[75] Safe at last, he gave way to a natural despair, threw his sword down and exclaimed: "This is a disgraceful day for Old England!"[76] And it was, for the British army had just lost over one thousand men (including Le Couteur's beloved commander, William Drummond), the second greatest loss in a single engagement that it suffered during the entire war.[77] When the roll was called in the 104th Foot that evening and only twenty-three answered of the seventy-seven soldiers who had been present in the morning, the survivors, to a man, "burst into tears."[78]

Another three weeks of almost constant skirmishing followed before the 104th were withdrawn to Queenston to guard the lines of communication. On 21 September, following an American sortie that destroyed some of his artillery, General Drummond lifted the siege of Fort Erie and withdrew to the line of the Chippawa River. The remnants of the 104th were now placed in a brigade commanded by Lieutenant Colonel George Hay, the Marquis of Tweeddale. On the eve of his twentieth birthday, Le Couteur was routed from a sound sleep to march "knee deep in mud in a pitch dark night ... an exquisite enjoyment for those who have never tried it"[79] some fifteen miles to intercept an attempted American flanking movement. The next day, 20 October, 1814, he fought his last engagement — "the prettiest little affair any of us had ever seen"[80] — at Cook's Mills. Four days later he left the Niagara, never to return.

The 104th remained in Kingston over the winter of 1814-1815 and suffered much from sickness. In March 1815 Le Couteur was chosen to take the official announcement of the Treaty of Ghent to Montreal. He was no longer the naive young subaltern who, thirty-three months before, had proudly recorded witnessing "wounds and death in real war." Le Couteur had seen enough. He had also gained respect for his foes. In the early stages of the war, he had described the Americans as "rascals" who "are worse than Frenchmen,"[81] but his attitude had begun to change during his first campaign in the Niagara when he was sent into American-occupied Fort George under a flag of truce. There he met a young American officer and the two "got to be friends in a Jiffy for I talked to Him as if He had been one of our mess."[82] Once Le Couteur begins to realize that there are more similarities than differences between him and his enemies, he muses that the conflict is "uncomfortably like a civil war."[83] By 1815 he is praising the Americans as being "old anglo-Saxons" who "had turned out very good soldiers" and were led by "gallant and enterprizing" officers.[84]

By and large, John Le Couteur's Journal is an entertaining and historically valuable description of the War of 1812 in Upper Canada from the viewpoint of a junior officer. He gives us little about higher policy or strategy because he had little knowledge of it (although he, like many on both sides, was puzzled by the half-hearted way the war appeared to be prosecuted). Le Couteur's war was a subaltern's war and a light infantryman's war; he leaves us with valuable first-hand accounts of some of the major battles along the frontier but he cannot tell us much about the higher military decisions that caused those actions. What this naturally gifted writer does provide is an eyewitness account of Canada at war,

1812-1815, that is a testament to the courage and discipline of the forgotten victor of that forgotten struggle — the regular British soldier. It is also a testament to a high-spirited young man whose Journal underscores the fact that he followed his own credo: "Merry hearts make light days!"[85]

## IV

Following the war, Le Couteur remained in North America. Peace brought a period of intense social activity when he was stationed in Montreal and was patronized by Sir John and Lady Johnson and other members of that city's elite. Le Couteur's interest in Canada, however, "abated with the declaration of peace"[86] and he longed to be reunited with his family. His wish was granted when he received permission to join his father's staff as an aide-de-camp. In January 1816 he travelled overland to New York and took ship for Curaçao, the Caribbean island where his father was serving as governor. The reunion with his family was touching: "What a rush of joy to meet, all in health, after so many Scenes of War, Pestilence, climates and Storms!"[87]

When General Le Couteur's term of office came to an end, the family returned to England. After a long and tedious voyage, they reached Jersey in May 1816, to rejoin "our Beloved circle and happy land, at old Belle Vue." A few weeks later Le Couteur became engaged to his first cousin, Harriet Janvrin, and the couple planned to marry when he obtained his captaincy.

It was Le Couteur's understanding that the 104th Foot was to be disbanded and that he would not have to return to North America. But after six short weeks of leave, orders arrived for him to take passage to Quebec. Following another tiresome sea voyage, he rejoined his regiment in October 1816. Older and more mature, Le Couteur now put his spare time to good use studying military authors such as Jomini and Tielke. When the 104th was finally dissolved in May 1817, he returned to Europe. On 23 June he landed in England to learn that he had at long last obtained his captaincy.

The British army, however, was about to lose a good officer. Le Couteur's parents asked him to resign his commission and reside in Jersey "never to leave them again."[88] Ever the dutiful son, he obeyed and, in 1818, he married Harriet.[89] Theirs was a happy union that produced five children, two boys and three girls.

John Le Couteur went on to live a wonderfully active Victorian life, dedicated to public and private improvement. For more than half a century he was prominent in the political, social, religious, economic and intellectual life of Jersey and he held almost every major public office. He was instrumental in the construction of a college, prison and asylum; he helped to establish a postal system and regulate weights and measures; was the prime mover behind the construction of Jersey's first railroad and the erection of telegraph links with England; the dredging and extension of harbours; the paving of roads and the completion of proper tidal and navigation surveys. It would seem that there was no part of his beloved Jersey that Le Couteur did not influence for the better.[90]

His intelligent, observant and curious mind, so evident in the pages of his Journal, found a multitude of outlets. His interest in agriculture and horticulture led him to create new strains of wheat which he described in scientific monographs and exhibited at the Crystal Palace Exhibition of 1851.[91] He helped to found the Royal Jersey Agricultural and Horticultural Society and established the breeding points for the Jersey cow. He was a prominent member of his parish church and worked hard to improve the lot of the island poor while maintaining a life-long interest in history. He wrote several unpublished histories of the island and assisted authors working on topics related to Jersey.

Le Couteur served in progressively higher positions in the island militia until he became adjutant-general, a post he held for nineteen years until 1872. In 1830, as a reward for services he had performed at the Royal Military College over twenty years before, he was made Jersey militia aide-de-camp to William IV and continued as such under Victoria. He used the patronage that came with this honorary but prestigious position to secure improvements to the island's military institutions. At his instigation, drill sheds and arsenals were constructed on Jersey and he was constantly suggesting improvements to its coastal defences. Le Couteur served as aide-de-camp to Queen Victoria when she visited Jersey in 1846 and was the island's representative to the funeral of the Duke of Wellington in 1852. He invented a new and improved buckle for the standard service belt and experimented with the design of a rifle bullet which was tested by the army on the ranges at Enfield and Hythe in 1855. In 1872, after a lifetime of service, Colonel John Le Couteur was knighted.

Like many another veteran, Le Couteur remembered with pride the days of his youth and constantly harked back to his wartime experiences in North America. Visits from old campaign comrades or their children were noted with great satisfaction in his diaries, as were the anniversaries of important battles and events. An 1853 visit to a yacht drew forth memories of the American schooner, *Lady of the Lake*, "which beat all our fleet" on Lake Ontario.[92] Asked to provide a brief biography for *Hart's Army List* in 1847, Le Couteur listed his proudest achievements as being adjutant to De Haren's light division in 1813, having fought at the battle of Niagara and being "blown up by the springing of a mine" at Fort Erie.[93] When his son, John Halkett, who rose to command a battalion of the Coldstream Guards before dying prematurely from diabetes at the age of forty-six, wrote in 1869 to tell him that he had met the son of Colonel Hercules Scott, killed with William Drummond that fateful night at Fort Erie, the response was a long letter of reminiscences.[94] The margins of the wartime passages of his Journal are filled with notes dated as much as forty years after the events described, explaining that he had just read these passages again to his wife.

The old soldier's last years were troubled with blindness and he was forced to ask family members to make entries in the daily diaries which he kept almost to the end. He suffered the loss of his wife in 1865 and his son, John Halkett, three years later, but his final days were gladdened by his grandchildren and great-grandchildren, who were delighted with "Grampy's" long white beard and loved to hear stories from his soldier youth. These tales must have appealed to at least one young listener, as in 1874 some of Le Couteur's last official correspondence was concerned with procuring his grandson, Charles Maunoir Summer, a commission in the army. This was Le Couteur's final connection with the military. On Christmas Eve, 1875, at the age of eighty-two, Colonel Sir John Le Couteur, Queen's Aide de Camp, Fellow of the Royal Society, gentleman cadet, light infantryman, and veteran of the War of 1812, died peacefully in his home at Belle Vue, Jersey.

# *Editor's Note*

The editor's task of preparing John Le Couteur's Journal for publication without damaging either the historical value or flavour of the original was made simpler by the fact that Le Couteur was a natural writer with a relaxed and fluid style. Editorial work was therefore restricted to putting a readable early nineteenth century text into a form readily intelligible to the modern reader and none of the resulting changes have altered the original in any substantive way.

The major editorial function was to divide the Journal into chapters and provide better paragraphing to break up the manuscript's density and to give the narrative increased movement. In terms of text changes, major errors or inconsistencies in fact have been indicated in the notes, while simple errors in dates and the spelling of proper and place names have been silently corrected.

Le Couteur's use of punctuation defies intelligent analysis. In the original text, periods, commas and apostrophes are rare, while dashes, colons and semi-colons are scattered with liberal generosity and confusing logic. While the author's original sentence structure has generally been retained, this bewildering array of punctuation has been made to conform with modern standards.

A similar inconsistency is evident in his use of capitalization and spelling. All proper names have been put in upper case but all other nineteenth century capitalization has been retained. With the exception of proper and place names, the original spelling has been left unchanged. Words and phrases in French have been reproduced as they were in the original.

The author had a gifted ear for dialogue and would often catch not only a good turn of phrase but also the speaker's vernacular. Unfortunately, he rarely saw reason to use quotation marks to set off spoken words and these have been supplied by the editor.

Le Couteur was somewhat careless in his presentation of dates and times and in his use of abbreviations for ranks, titles, units, measurements, weights and coinage. These have been made consistent and modern military abbreviations have been substituted for the wildly variant rank abbreviations in the original. One frequent period abbreviation has been retained — the use of "Sub." or "Sub" for subaltern, a junior officer below the rank of captain. Other period abbreviations have been filled out with the missing letters in square brackets. Ampersands and "&c." have been kept for flavour but the frequent superscripts have been omitted.

Le Couteur left blanks in his original text where he could not supply, or did not want to supply, missing information. Where this information is available it has been provided within square brackets; where it is not, a base line has been utilized. Square brackets have also been used to supply missing letters, words or phrases that clarify the author's meaning and to indicate words that are illegible in the original text.

The text notes are intended to clarify and complement the Journal, not to lengthen it. These notes indicate any major changes in the organization of the original manuscript and provide additional information on the persons, places and events mentioned in the Journal. Although every effort was made to make these notes as complete as possible, where no such identification is contained in a note, either insufficient direction was given in the original text to find the relevant information, or it was not available. The reference works used to compile these notes will be found in the bibliography appended to the Journal.

Editing is a laborious and thankless but necessary task. In the case of John Le Couteur's Journal, this task was lessened by the author's natural talent; Le Couteur's prose is as alive today as when it was first written. Having lived with the man for six years, I have come to like John Le Couteur very much and it is hoped that, after meeting the young officer who emerges from the following pages, the reader will experience a similar feeling.

*D.G.*

# *List of Abbreviations Used in Notes*

| | |
|---|---|
| ADC | Aide de camp |
| CO | Colonial Office |
| DCB | *Dictionary of Canadian Biography*, followed by relevant volume and page number. |
| *Doc. Hist.* | Ernest Cruikshank, *Documentary History of the Campaigns on the Niagara Frontier in the Years 1812 to 1814*, 9 vols., Welland, Ontario, 1896-1908, followed by relevant volume and page number. |
| HMS | His Majesty's Ship |
| MG | Manuscript Group |
| NAC | National Archives of Canada |
| PRO | Public Record Office, Great Britain |
| RA | Royal Artillery |
| RE | Royal Engineers |
| RN | Royal Navy |
| RG | Record Group |
| USN | United States Navy |
| USS | United States Ship |
| WO | War Office |

## Notes

[1] Le Couteur's Journal, entry for 21 June 1812.

[2] Journal, 25 February 1814.

[3] Joan Stevens, *Victorian Voices. An Introduction to the Papers of Sir John Le Couteur, Q.A.D.C., F.R.S.* (St. Helier, 1969), xi.

[4] Stevens, *Victorian Voices,* xi.

[5] Finding Aid to the Le Couteur-Sumner Collection, Lord Coutanche Library, Société Jersiaise, St. Helier, Jersey.

[6] Stevens, *Victorian Voices,* 253.

[7] Sir Charles Oman, *Wellington's Army, 1809-1814* (London, 1912), Appendix III, "Peninsular Autobiographies, Journals, Letters, etc.".

[8] Lieutenant Charles Cadell, 28th Foot, *Narrative of the Campaigns of the Twenty-Eighth Regiment* (London, 1835); Lieutenant Edward Costello, 95th Rifles, *Memoirs of Edward Costello of the Rifle Brigade, comprising a Narrative of Wellington's Campaigns in the Peninsula* (London, 1857; reprinted 1967); Lieutenant William Grattan, 88th Foot, *Adventures with the Connaught Rangers, 1809-1814* (London, 1902); Captain Rees Howell Gronow, *The Reminiscences and Recollections of Captain Gronow* (4 vols., London, 1889); Lieutenant John Kincaid, *Adventures in the Rifle-Brigade, in the Peninsula, France, and the Netherlands, 1810-1815* (London, 1830); Lieutenant William Leeke, *The History of Lord Seaton's Regiment (52nd Light Infantry)* (London, 1866); and Captain Cavalie Mercer, *Journal of the Waterloo Campaign* (London, 1927).

[9] See, for example, the memoir of Ensign John Kilborn, Incorporated Militia, in Thaddeus Leavitt, *History of Leeds and Grenville* (Belleville, 1879; reprinted 1972); the memoir of Lieutenant Henry Ruttan, Incorporated Militia, in J.J. Talman, ed., *Loyalist Narratives from Upper Canada* (Toronto, 1946); and Ernest A. Cruikshank, ed., *Campaigns of 1812-1814: Contemporary Narratives by Captain W.H. Merritt, Colonel William Claus, Lieutenant Colonel Matthew and Captain John Elliot* (Niagara-on-the-Lake, 1902). There is also Captain Jacques Viger of the Canadian Voltiguers, whose "Saberdache," a comprehensive archive of his wartime experiences, is found in the Archives du Séminaire de Québec in Quebec City and has seen partial publication in J.L.H. Neilson, ed. *Reminiscences of the War of 1812* (Kingston, 1895) and the Watertown *Daily Times,* May and June 1963. Unpublished diaries include that of Ensign Andrew Warffe, Incorporated Militia, for 1814-1815, contained in the Burton Historical Library, Detroit, and Christopher Hagerman, Staff of Upper Canada, Metropolitan Toronto Library.

[10] See, for examples: Robert S. Allen, ed., "The Bisshopp Papers during the War of 1812," *Journal of the Society for Army Historical Research* 61, 22-29; Lewis

Einstein, ed., "Recollections of the War of 1812 by George Hay, Eighth Marquis of Tweeddale," *American Historical Review*, XXXII (1926-1927), 69-78; C.P. Stacey, "Upper Canada at War, 1814: Captain Armstrong Reports", *Ontario History*, XLVIII (1956), 37-42; [Arthur Brymner, ed.] , *Excerpts from Letters from Lieutenant and Adjutant William MacEwen, 1st Battalion, Royal Scots, to his Wife, Canada, 1813-1814* (n.p., n.d.); Norman C. Lord, ed., "The War on the Canadian Frontier, 1812-1814. Letters Written by Sergt. James Commins, 8th Foot," *Journal of the Society for Army Historical Research*, XVIII (1939), 199-211; and the Memoir of Private Shadrach Byfield in John Gellner, ed., *Recollections of the War of 1812. Three Eye-witness Accounts* (Toronto, 1964).

[11] Unpublished sources include: the 1813-1815 diary of Major General Louis de Watteville, NAC, MG 24, F96; correspondence of Colonel Hercules Scott, 103rd Foot, 1814, NAC, MG 24, F15; memoir of the Niagara campaign of 1813 by Colonel Sir John Harvey, Ontario Archives, MU 2037; correspondence of Lieutenant Colonel Cecil Bisshopp, 49th Foot, NAC, MG 24, F4; correspondence of Lieutenant Maurice Nowlan, 100th Foot, Archives Nationales du Québec, XXXIV; the memoir of Midshipman David Wingfield, Royal Navy, NAC, MG 24, F18; the memoir of Private George Ferguson, 100th Foot, United Church Archives, Victoria College, Toronto; and the Diary of Lieutenant John Lang, 19th Light Dragoons, 1814, Perkins Library, Duke University, Durham, NC.

[12] Carl F. Klinck and James J. Talman, eds., *The Journal of Major John Norton, 1816* (Toronto, 1970).

[13] William Dunlop, *Tiger Dunlop's Upper Canada* (Toronto, 1967). This contains Dunlop's "Recollections of the American War" first published serially in the periodical *Literary Garland* in 1847 and reprinted in 1905, with an introduction by A.H.U. Colquhoun. Throughout the text, all references will be to the 1967 edition.

[14] Stevens, *Victorian Voices*, 25.

[15] Stevens, *Victorian Voices*, iii.

[16] A. C. Saunders, *Jersey in the 18th and 19th Centuries* (Jersey, 1930), 60.

[17] Stevens, *Victorian Voices*, 2. According to Stevens, the name originated in medieval times from the office of "le Cousteur" or sexton, the parish functionary charged with calculating or "costing" the sums to be paid for tithes, funerals, baptisms and other church functions.

[18] There were, in all, six generations of Le Couteur males, from 1661 to 1875, who bore the name Jean or John.

[19] John Le Couteur, *Lettre d'un Officier du Centieme Régiment* (Jersey, 1787) and *Letters, chiefly from India, giving an Account of the Military Transactions on the Coast of Malabar during the Late War ...* (London, 1790).

[20] The career of John Le Couteur, the elder, is extracted from Stevens, *Victorian Voices*, 10-11; G.R. Balleine, *A Biographical Dictionary of Jersey* (London, n.d.),

378-379; *Dictionary of National Biography*, vol. XXXIII (London, 1892); John Philipart, *The Royal Military Calendar* (2 vols., London, 1815) II: 23.

[21] Balleine, *Dictionary of Jersey*, 240-245.

[22] Details of Marie Le Couteur's early life from Stevens, *Victorian Voices*, 22-23.

[23] Stevens, *Victorian Voices*, 10-12; Balleine, *Dictionary of Jersey*, 378-379; *Dictionary of National Biography*, XXXIII; Philipart, *Military Calendar*, II: 23.

[24] Richard Glover, *Peninsular Preparation. The Reform of the British Army. 1795-1809* (Cambridge, 1963), 198-205; R.H. Thoumine, *Scientific Soldier. A Life of General Le Marchant. 1766-1812* (London, 1968), 61-79.

[25] Glover, *Peninsular Preparation*, 40; A.F. Mockler-Ferryman, *Annals of Sandhurst* (London, 1900), 10-13; and Hugh Thomas, *The Story of Sandhurst* (London, 1961), 37-40.

[26] Letter to author from Mr. A.A. Orgill, Senior Librarian, Royal Military College, Sandhurst, 27 November 1991.

[27] Journal, August 1810.

[28] Michael Glover, *Wellington's Army in the Peninsula, 1808-1814* (New York, 1977), 39.

[29] PRO, WO 31, vol. 311, Colonel John Le Couteur to Torrens, 4 September 1810.

[30] Journal, January 1811.

[31] "Light Bob" was period British military slang for light infantry. The term possibly originated during the American Revolutionary War when the men of the light infantry companies shortened ("bobbed") the long tails of their coats and cut back their awkward tricorn hats to enable them to move with greater ease in the woods.

[32] Glover, *Wellington's Army*, 84.

[33] Journal, 21 November 1811.

[34] Inspection return, 104th Foot, 11 June 1812, see PRO, WO 27, vol. 108.

[35] W. Austin Squires, *The 104th Regiment of Foot (The New Brunswick Regiment). 1803-1817* (Fredericton, 1962), 23-43; 81-82.

[36] Journal, 18 December 1813.

[37] Journal, 5 February 1813.

[38] Journal, 5 February 1813.

[39] Journal, 5 February 1813.

[40] Journal, October 1815.

[41] Charles James, *The Regimental Companion; Containing the Pay, Allowances and Relative Duties of Every Officer in the British Service* (2 vols., London, 1811), I: 272-273.

[42] J.B. Priestley, *The Prince of Pleasure and His Regency, 1811-1820* (London, 1969), 145.

[43] James, *Regimental Companion*, I: 272; *General Regulations and Orders for the Army*, Adjutant General's Office (London, 1816), 95.

[44] Glover, *Wellington's Army*, 76-80.

[45] *General Regulations*, 37.

[46] Michael Glover, *Wellington as Military Commander* (London, 1968), 25.

[47] Glover, *Wellington's Army*, 82-80.

[48] *General Regulations*, 29.

[49] Journal, June 1812.

[50] Journal, 31 December 1812.

[51] Journal, 13 July 1812.

[52] Journal, 9 January 1814.

[53] Journal, 26 June 1812.

[54] Journal, July 1812.

[55] Journal, 27 July 1812.

[56] Journal, April 1813.

[57] Journal, 28 May 1813.

[58] Journal, 28 May 1813.

[58] Journal, 28 May 1813.

[60] Journal, 23 June 1813. "Nitchie," period military slang for North American native warriors, derived from the expression "Sago Nitchie," a corruption of the Ojibway salutation "Shaygo Niigii!" meaning "Hello, friend" or "Hello, comrade."

[61] Le Couteur to Bouton, 24 October 1813.

[62] Journal, 7 March 1814.

[63] NAC, RG 8 I, vol. 1708, p. 34, Morning Sick Report, Centre Division, Four Mile Creek, 15 September 1813.

[64] Journal, 1 October 1813.

[65] Journal, 6 October 1813.

[66] Journal, October 1813.

[67] Journal, 25 July 1814.

[68] Journal, 25 July 1814.

[69] Journal, 2 August 1814.

[70] Journal, 2 August 1814.

[71] Journal, 14 August 1814.

[72] Journal, 8 August 1814.

[73] Journal, 15 August 1814.

[74] Journal, 15 August 1814.

[75] Journal, 15 August 1814.

[76] Journal, 15 August 1814.

[77] The heaviest British casualties of the war occurred at the battle of New Orleans on 8 January 1815.

[78] Journal, 15 August 1814. For recent accounts of this action, see Donald E. Graves, "William Drummond and the Battle of Fort Erie," *Canadian Military History,* I (1992) 25-54, and Joseph A. Whitehorne, *While Washington Burned: The Battle of Fort Erie, 1814* (Baltimore, 1992).

[79] Journal, 19 October 1814.

[80] Journal, 20 October 1814.

[81] Journal, Le Couteur to Bouton, 24 October 1813.

[82] Journal, 10 September 1813.

[83] Journal, 11 September 1813.

[84] Journal, 16 March 1815.

[85] Journal, 23 May 1812.

[86] Journal, 26 November 1815.

[87] Journal, 2 February 1816.

[88] Stevens, *Victorian Voices,* 61.

[89] Le Couteur resigned from active service, going on half-pay as a captain on 25 August 1817. See H.G. Hart, ed., *The New Annual Army List for 1847* (London, 1847) 340.

[90] Unless otherwise noted, all details of Le Couteur's later life are from Stevens, *Victorian Voices.*

[91] John Le Couteur, *On the varieties, properties and classification of wheat* (Jersey, 1836; reprinted Jersey, 1836 and London, 1842; second edition printed in London, 1872); *On the Use of the Great or Jersey Plough, etc.* (London, 1842); *On the rise, progress and present state of Agriculture in Jersey* (Jersey, 1852). Le Couteur also published a pamphlet on *The Rifle: its effect on the war; on national military organization; and preparation for defence* (London, 1855).

[92] Stevens, *Victorian Voices,* 218.

[93] Hart, *New Annual Army List for 1847,* 354.

[94] Le Couteur to Halkett Le Couteur, 29 July 1869, NAC, MG 24, F 96, Scott Papers.

# *Chapter One*

## "GENTLEMAN CADET"
## Childhood, Preparatory School and the Royal Military College
## *1794-1810*

*"What have I done?"* said a Gentleman Cadet? A question suggested by my journal while at the Royal Military College at Marlow which came under my eye while I was laid up, disabled from locomotion by a kick from a Trooper's horse on the 9th Sept[em]b[e]r 1851 while in command of the St. Helier and St. Lauren's[1] Battalions as [a] Brigade.

*Imprimis.*[2] I was first breeched by being laid out *al fresco*[3] on a piece of cloth while my Mother was at St. Helier[4] and I at St. Peter's,[5] when three merry young Aunts cut out my first dress on my shape. It was so tight that my Mother hardly knew her walking Sausage!

I quote from my dear Mother's notes:

> Jack (*c'etait moi*[6]) reads English tolerably at four years old. He began to write letters legibly at five but about this time he had sore eyes which prevented his reading and writing for nearly six months,which put Him very back. He began Arithmetic at Six, but it was discontinued for near two months whilst I was in childbed of Gordon.[7] He took to it again in the winter of 1801. He knew his multiplication table perfectly before he was Seven and a half year's old and before he was Eight he began the rule of three. I began Him in Grammar at Seven — without [a] book by making him understand the nature of the different parts of speech & before he was Eight he made very few mistakes in telling the part of speech of any word.
>
> He began to read Euclid at Seven & got through the first book before he was Eight. French and Geography he also learnt at Seven. At Eight

years old he began again the First Book of Euclid for the second time and went on with the second, third, fourth and fifth books which he finished in July, 1804 for which his Father gave him a Silver spoon with his name on it.[8] He was then nine years and nine months old. In April, 1802 he began vulgar fractions with his Father at Ten years old and could then translate French into English or English into French pretty correctly. Jack began Algebra with his Father as soon as he was eleven years old. He had then gone over the whole Arithmetic and could extract the Cube root. About this time he finished the fifth book of Euclid for the second time and I then sent for Dalby's *Mathematics*,[9] the book taught at Marlow. He again began Geometry in it.

In August, 1805, before he was eleven years old, he began to learn German with Mr. Pierpedron, a French emigrant who came to Him twice a week. In January, 1806, l'Abbé Cabri came three times a week to teach him the upper branches of Arithmetic and Mathematics. He continued his Latin, German, French, Algebra, Geometry and Arithmetic until he went to School at High Wycombe in July, 1807. He could then solve a quadratic equation in Algebra pretty correctly before he left.

My Father, who was Inspector of Militia, sent me to drill with the Boys of St. Helier in 1805. We lived in Sand Street then. Philip DeQuetteville, Philip DeCarteret & I strove for a Prize. De Quetteville, being a strong boy, conquered. [In] 1807, we commanded Divisions[10] as Officers....[11]

I was sent to a preparatory School for the Military College, the Rev[eren]d Mr. Sproston's at High Wycombe.[12] He was a worthy sincere Man with whom I was very happy. The French Usher thought me his best French scholar, thanks to the Abbé Bourge in Jersey.

One morning in 1807 I attended Mr. Sproston who was taking a number of Candidates for examination to the R[oyal] M[ilitary] C[ollege] at Marlow where I watched what was proceeding in the Board Room when Gen[era]l Le Marchant (Sir Gaspard), the Governor,[13] called me to him. "How do you do, Le Couteur, are you come up for examination?" "No Sir, I am not of age for it yet." "Do you think you could pass?" "Yes Sir." "Will you try?" "Certainly, sir."

Up I went to Old Black Swat, Professor Dalby.[14] Got through my Arithmetic perfectly and all the rest easily and took my papers to the Governor. "Very well, my boy. Many have not passed today. Write to your Father and Mother that, although you can not be admitted now, You have earned your admission. I wish you joy."

And it was great joy to my dear Parents to be in *à l'improviste*.[15] On the

21st Oct[obe]r., 1807, My dear Mother wrote me a warm letter of congratulations [on] my success.

The French usher [at Sproston' school] was a great brute, a savage. He was not satisfied, which was yet fair though severe, to give a boy a violent slap on the palm of the hand for idleness which sometimes incapacitated him for writing well the whole day but he would pull a boy's ear to that degree that he would make it bleed — this especially to the day boys, and it did not escape us that he never did so in the Master's presence.

One morning in the absence of the Master, the Usher, the wretch, absolutely pulled a day boy's ear which was already sore to that degree so as to tear the lower part to make it bleed freely. The boy screamed with agony & we shouted with rage & indignation: "Shame! Shame!!!" Watts, who was next Him, gave Him a good right and left on the muzzle and I jumped on His back like a monkey to throttle Him. In a second, the whole school, like a swarm of Hornets, were pummelling the fellow and each other indiscriminately, such was their rage.

The cry "the Master!" brought us back to our Senses, who came in, wondering at the astonishing disturbance, which Fire alone might have created.

The Frenchman's battered visage, disfigured by rage and defeat, his incoherent gestures & menaces, would have made a Horse laugh but our respectable Master, from our sullen and not altogether downcast countenances, perceived that there must have been some cause. He invited the Frenchman to retire, heard his story, returned to the school, mounted his chair and, in his most solemn sepulchral tone, [said]: "Young Gentlemen, this is a very serious and highly discreditable affair to my establishment. I should be unworthy to fill the important station I hold were this circumstance to pass unredressed. I must hear the exact truth, and nothing but the truth from you." I was heard with a plain, honest statement of fact and the boy's still bleeding ear was produced.

"Such an occurrence can never happen again in this establishment, you are highly to blame in taking the law into your own hands, the only palliation with me is that it was a sudden and instantaneous act of indignation and excited feelings. Return to your studies and shew by your diligence and attention that you will endeavour to wipe off the stain you have put on the respectability and order of my establishment. I shall provide myself with another French Master."

The tyrant never [again] made his appearance and, for some time, having passed for the College, and being the head boy in French, I acted as French usher and never were the classes so attentive or the whole school more orderly, from the feeling of satisfaction at our respected Master's just and impartial decision.

It was considered at the preparatory school a very fine thing to be a Cadet, and the moment of emancipation from school to enter the College, an eventful one.

### *2nd February, 1808*

I joined B Company, commanded by Captain Charles Wright, after the Vacation as B-100. It was considered to be the "Crack" company of the Royal Military College and being the Senior Captain's, took the right of the line.[16] My weekly allowance was a shilling — the rules of the College permitting an increase of pay as it was considered according to the advance in study of the Cadet.

The drilling which I had undergone in Jersey told wonderfully on Old Sergeant Major Willis and indeed on Captain Wright, the best drill[master] in military parlance I have ever met with! It must have been ludicrous to see a well-drilled lad fall in with the Johnny, Paddy and Sawney Thaws[17] that constantly joined the College. We fell in, a squad of a dozen maybe. The Position[s] having been systematically explained by the "Major", so the Sergeant was called for shortness, "with the clear comprehandshion" as he stated, "that when I says 'As you were', I means — As you were! B-100, very smart, you know something. Do you know your facings?" "Yes Major. R[ight] F[ace]. F[ron]t. The ab[ou]t face." "Oh well, well! Go to that squad."

I had been placed with Lance Corporal Crofton, B-99, in a double bedroom by Capt[ain]. Wright as He was a steady Cadet. A most excellent friend he proved. Crofton had charge of the drill Squad to which I was removed but on finding me so perfect in the use of the Carbine,[18] had me removed to the first Squad in Arms. In the course of six weeks, I was given charge of a Squad of recruits — this aroused the impulse to "Command." After four months I was allowed eighteen pence [more] weekly.

At this period, the Cadets had to clean their own shoes, gaiters, Coats, Buttons, Belts, plates, Arms and Accoutrements. We had Heelball,[19] Pipeclay,[20] Platepowder,[21] Buff sticks,[22] Brushes, all to buy — and the most clean and tidy Soldiers were sure of preferment under the sharp, clear and uncompromising eye of Charley Wright.

### Inspection of Troops

"To inspect your Squad, Mr. Le Couteur, Begin at the Right or Left hand man's tuft or feather.[23] Let your eye go down his person seeing whether every article is clean, accurately buttoned and placed according to order, down to his shoes, then up the next man's to his tuft. Correct or blame everything, quickly — punish if the individual repeats a fault. Continue so to the last man then examine the reverse in the same way and the rear rank afterwards. Never let your men have unnecessary fatigue. When the Front rank has been examined, Order Arms and Stand at Ease. Then see the rear rank."

### *10 June, 1809*

I had got into the Upper School and had been promoted to the rank of Lance Corporal — further command.

### *14 December [1809]*

I was promoted to the rank of Under Officer (or Sergeant) with three Stripes on my arm and a Sword instead of a Bayonet.[24] We did not draw the Swords but carried our arms at the Advance like Sergeants.[25] For this honour my Father gave me a beautiful single-barrelled gun by Richards[26] and my Mother gave me a watch.

Guards were a delightful lounge. The Sentries were regularly posted and relieved every hour by the Acting Corporal and the Guards mounted in due form. The too easy Sergeants and Corporals who commanded Guards, as soon as the Cadets were hushed in study, allowed Cards, refreshments and jollity of all sorts. [The] Sentry at the Guardroom door was to give due notice of any rounds, or by Serg[ean]t. Major, when all the cards or viands were instantly concealed in writing desks or secret deposits. Woe befall the Non Com[missione]d officer on Guard if discovery took place. Instant relief, close arrest, confinement to College for a Month or, if an old delinquent, reduction to the ranks.

The Hospital too, when it could be reached by a sham, offered an agreeable break in the dry and laborious course of studies. Many and clever were the dodges to deceive our Scotch Esculapius, a dry but timid old Galleypot.[27] When the fear of the Black hole, or darkroom, or a month's Confinement to College, was strongly before the eyes of a Cadet, the sick list was often had recourse to. There might be seen a Knocking of elbows against the wall, washing the eyes with a solution of Goulard[28] to redden the eyes, gargling the throat with Vinegar to fur the tongue, rubbing chalk powder on the cheeks to give a pallid hue to the laughing, but alarmed, visage, nevertheless. Well, some got in, others stayed out with a jolly black dose in their stomach[es].

In the hospital, low diet was, indeed, close upon starvation. Weak tea and gruel, nothing else. Woe to the half-starved shammer who had to fatten upon that fare! Middle diet afforded Broth & a bit of meat. Full diet was good and plentiful.[29] But money was the charm. Oh merry were the days of good King Cole! B-64 was an ingenious [illegible] a Youth of a fertile invention and ready resources. We were a demure half dozen, on the starving diet — plenty of money in the room and no servant was to be bribed — all thought to be too ill to be indulged with meats or confections! Even the gentle-hearted maids, when they were visible, and theirs were Angel visits. Cerberus John was the distributor of poisons; He was inflexibly imbribable! Two sick and four shammers, hungry as wolves in a Siberian winter.

B-100 [Le Couteur] had a smooth face something like a girl's. The reward was tempered by the danger. At nightfall one stormy evening, He was departed to the maids' room while they were sipping their tea where he borrowed for a time a Bonnet, Gown and Shawl. These were speedily put on and the Bonnet, Gown and Shawl walked [out] the front door which was readily opened by the Janitor.

Off ran the Maid Cadet to the Pastry cook, a trusty and tried friend. The astonished and alarm-struck pie woman was unwilling to supply the hospitallers. "I'll [illegible] you refuse then the vengeance of the Cadets when it is known that you refused Supplies amply paid for on such an awful emergency!" Tongues, Sausages, Shrub Rolls and Confections were deposited in a basket — off went the little Maid Cadet.

While the well-placed Sentinels watched her advance, [the] Janitor was called from the door by one, for a case of fainting, and dread alarm. Another opened the door while the little Cadet Maid skipped upstairs, deposited the supplies under a bed, replaced the Bonnet, Gown & Shawl in the Maids' room. Then, when all were sound [in] the arms of Morpheus,[30] came the repast. Blankets placed over the windows prevented the possibility of light being seen from the street, while meal [and] mirth were to be enjoyed in silence. Sweet indeed are such stolen joys!

I was again in the Hospital from an attack of pleurisy with George Fitz-Clarence,[31] afterwards the Earl of Munster, in the same room. We became great friends, sickness is a bond of sympathy! I was weakly dozing one Morning when, suddenly, a fair being with a sweet, compassionate, beaming countenance, beautifully dressed, with a voice like a seraph's, sat by me and gently took my hand. Was it a dream? No, I felt the soft and delicate touch. "My dear young friend, how are you? You are George's friend, I am his Mother, therefore you are my friend. How do you feel today?" "Better Madam, thank you." "Yes, you are better, you have been very poorly but the danger is over. My George is still dangerously ill and I have come to nurse him myself. When you are well enough, I shall ask you to grant me a favour." "Oh certainly, Madam, I shall, what is it?" "That you will have the kindness to allow me to have your bed and remove into another room, as I wish to stay by Him. I shall go and see you frequently and attend to your wants." Which the gentle lady did.[32]

This incident led no doubt partly to Henry FitzClarence, the Duke of Clarence's next eldest Son, being later placed under my charge at College.

### *December, 1809*

The promotion to the rank of Under Officer, allowed me have 2/6 a week, a great sum in those days, affording daily means for a really luxurious lunch. A friend, B-90, gave me a richly embroidered Jack[e]t. It was really a very handsome Uniform, thirteen rows of rich Vellum silver lace in Front, with handsome Cuffs & Collar of blue. This I took to Jersey to attract the eyes of the fair in the winter Vacation.

### *April, 1810*

In the Month of April, Captain Wright informed me that Henry Fitz-Clarence,[33] the second Son of the Duke of Clarence,[34] was coming to the College. He had been removed from the Navy because he was too unmanageable and that I had been selected by Colonel Butler[35] to have the charge of Him as the Duke of Clarence wished Him to be under the eye of a steady Cadet. I probably had been named by George FitzClarence or by Mrs. Jordan, or both, to the Duke.

I strenuously objected to such a responsibility as the Boy, if ill-conducted or bad-hearted, might lead to my disgrace with His Royal Highness. I begged for time to consult my Mother on the Subject who, on learning my fears, doubts and objections, as my ever best counsellor, to whom my Father left all the guidance of my mind, wrote to me:

Belle Vue,[36] 14 May 1810

My dear John,

I do not know if You are to rejoice or not, at having the son of a Prince under your care. From the earliest times it has always been a difficult task to educate Princes. You should represent to Him that Princes ought to show the example of steadiness and propriety of Conduct, recommend to Him good books, in particular *Telemachus*[37] and tell Him it is because He is the Son of a Prince that you take the liberty of naming such a book

> to Him, as it is that which is best calculated to form a great Prince. It is not with an air of superiority or in the form of a Sermon that you are to endeavour to correct your pupil, but there are means which if you can find out may have such an effect as will never be forgotten by Him, if He is at all clever, or worthy of your attention. If otherwise, still You must do your duty and acquit yourself of the trust reposed in You to the best of your abilities.

On receiving this letter I intimated my readiness to take charge of Young FitzClarence with the condition that He should be placed in my own room, which as Responsible Under Officer, was my privilege to occupy alone. The afternoon of his arrival, I showed Him his bed, explained to Him that I had required Him to be placed in my room because if He had gone among the Cadets in the larger rooms, He must have been fag[38] to some one, bullied, misled and played tricks with and, if He had borne this impatiently, beaten and misused.

Alone with me, He would merely have to take care of his own kit and fetch water in the morning for Himself and me. I would show Him how to clean his cloths, shoes, Arms and accoutrements, after which He must learn to do for Himself. As perfect steadiness in the ranks was indispensable in Captain Wright's Company, I would never punish him without a warning, a private signal — if I moved my hand to my face in speaking to the Company, he was unsteady, after that, He would be punished as would any other Cadet. Attention to these trifles would enable Him to lead a very happy life with me and I would also assist Him in his studies.

"Where is your kit, Brushes, Combs and dressing Case?" The Boy burst into a flood of tears: "I have nothing, they destroyed all my things, cut up my bedding, cut me down, beat me, made me drink. I have been cruelly used on board of His Majesty's Ship the __________ and never got a good word from any one. I never was so kindly spoken to in my life before. You may rely upon it, Sir. I shall do everything in my power to please you. I shall be perfectly happy with such a kind friend." The tears came into my own eyes, when I rejoined: "I am sure of it, my dear boy, all will go well, your heart is in the right place."

The Youth was, for his station, shamefully destitute of comforts owing to the ill-usage on board ship. He was untidy and rough-looking, from the Middys[39] having resolved to take all the polish out of Him, in which they had succeeded but too well. We got on admirably together — private drills, a fashionable outfit which I was authorized to procure for Him, constant care of His person & appointments, made Him one of the smarter Cadets in the College.

Some months later, the Duke of Clarence with his lovely daughter, afterwards Lady Delisle,[40] came to the College to see his Son. I was sent for and His Royal Highness, shaking hands with me after my salute (put forth with some trepidation at the Royal presence for the first time) [said]: "Mr. Le Couteur, what have you done to my son?" I coloured and felt droll, looked to the sweet and beaming eye of Miss FitzClarence — all must be right from that beautiful smile! I bowed.

"What have you done, I say, to my Son? He was reported to me as being too unsteady for the navy, quite intractable and discontented, slovenly [but] here I see a fine smart lad, contented, bearing an excellent character. How have you affected this transformation, I know not but this I will assure you — that, at any time, or under any circumstances that may happen, if ever I can be of service to you, You need only remind me of this circumstance to ensure it." The Duke then enquired very graciously into my history and I was dismissed with favor.[41]

## *August, 1810*

At the expiration of the first fortnight in August, I was the Second Senior Under Officer of B Company, when I was promoted to the position of Senior or Responsible U[nder]. O[fficer]. in command of 103 as fine lads from eight onto thirteen as were to be seen in His Majesty's far and wide spread Schools or Colleges, and frequently in command of the whole College, a battalion of three hundred Cadets. This I considered as the greatest event in my life — a captain of fifteen with the powers of a Colonel. Power to confine to the Black hole on bread and water for forty-eight hours, to the Dark room for two or three days, confinement to College for one, two, three days or even weeks, to extra drills and extra Guards.

What horrid petty tyrants some were. Yet Charley used to say to me sometimes: "Mr. Le Couteur, do not seek popularity by excusing faults — keep them in order!" "Is not the B Company in high order, Sir? Are the A and C Companies half so clean or near so steady? Persuasion and esprit de Corps do more than punishments, Sir." "Very well, Le Couteur", he would often frown, "only take care."

The Cadets and the Bargemen had frequent wars. Marlow was a sort of Port for Barges. The Cadets were in the habit of playing the Bargees, as they were called, all sorts of tricks — throwing dirt or missiles from the Bridge onto the Barges as they swept down or toiled up the river. Sometimes the

Bargemen would land, assemble, and thrash the first Cadet they laid hands on — which to Him at least, if unoffending, was a grievance.

Up came one of these maltreated, on half holiday, bruised and wailing: "the Bargees were in force and would not let a Cadet cross Marlow Bridge." A Cadet, who had the form of Mercury with a giant's strength and pluck for any row, was named the General. A hundred and fifty volunteers were soon armed, some with cudgels, the others with pockets full of stones — these, the slingers and throwers, were the light troops and advance guard. As they came to the Bridge end, they were to extend to each side, and commence a rapid and independent fire on the enemy who, having been reconnoitred were found in force three or four deep, armed with Oars, boat hooks, Bludgeons, holding the pass in stern and quiet defiance. The Forlorn hope[42] were the strong, big boys; the reserve, stout lads.

On taking up the points of attack, which the Bargees looked upon with [the same] calm determination which the Duke did at Waterloo, while Napoleon unfolded his army — the word was waited for. Once given, a shower of Missiles nearly blinded the enemy who were quite unprepared for such a Cannonade. An indication of retreat led to the charge when Bludgeons, Oars, boathooks and stones came into active and serious play. One Cadet, a Lord, who was in the hands of two Bargemen who were in the act of giving his Lordship a pitch into the river but the standard of Achilles was flashing to the rescue. Two strokes right and left, over the body of the Cadet, sent a broken jaw and a broken head to the ground. The skill of fence and cudgel of this Youth was marvellous. His form towered and flew everywhere and the Bridge was cleared in Ten Minutes of all but the wounded, several of whom lay stunned in the roadway.

The Officers and Sergeants soon appeared and all were confined to College for the day and the Victory led to a prolonged peace for several Cadets were severely hurt and stringent orders were issued against the recurrence of provocation.

The examination for Commissions took place — what an awful day. Four of us had worked pretty hard, by repeating our Mathematical problems in turn, in the dark at night. While one went through a problem, the others watched and corrected if necessary. It prepared us thoroughly as far as it went.

I was given the third case of Trigonometry with the attendant problems and theorems. The Room was full of Magnates and Ladies, some fair, beating bosoms, anxious for Brothers or friends. B-86 whispered in my ear while, rod in hand and bold in voice, [I was saying]: "the angle TH is equal to ..." "Johnny, look at that lovely girl eyeing you, wouldn't you like to kiss Her?" This to me in the midst of my examination! I gave a kick back and felt that I had lost my place, hesitated, and thought my Commission was in jeopardy. Sir Howard Douglas,[43] the accomplished, the learned, the kind Sir Howard, had overheard this mischief and saw my distress — whispered: "Very well, the Angle TH SF is equal to the Angle FGP" and therefore I went on "they are both of them equal to the third, etc." and saved my Commission.

I was appointed on the 15th November 1810 an Ensign in the 96th Regiment then quartered in Jersey but remained at the College till the close of the year.[44]

I must mention a case. My Grandfather used always to send me a half Guinea under the Seal[45] when He wrote to me. It was contrary to rule and, if known as a double letter, was always detained by the officials for examination and the money placed, when found, to the account of the Cadet.

On one occasion, the Battalion was in line: Colonel Butler, Major MacDermott,[46] Capt[ain]s Wright, Otto,[47] and Erskine,[48] and the Staff were all in front, waiting for Guard mounting. Two or three Cadets, who had double letters addressed to them, were called up. As they opened their letters, they successively had to hand over to Colonel Butler the Guinea or One pound note the letters contained. The moment I saw my Grandfather's handwriting, I guessed what might be under the Seal, so I quietly tore it off and dropped it near my foot, glancing where it lay.

"There's nothing here", said Old Blinkeye, looking close into the letter, "Cap[tai]n Wright, there's nothing here." "Nothing, sir, I see", gave me my letter, "he must recover half the postage — fall in, Sir!"

The instant the Parade was over and the coast clear, I ran and picked up my Seal and half Guinea. Now came Charley's joke. "Mr. LeC[outeur], here. Cole is come to repay thee the overcharge on postage." "Oh." "But you must first declare, Upon your honour, that it contained no money." "Oh, indeed, Sir, then it don't signify, Sir, it is not worth a declaration upon honour. Oh, but it is not fair, thank you, Sir. I really don't care about the half postage" and [I] burst out laughing. He laughed too, and turned off, saying: "it was very cleverly done!"

He [Captain Wright] did not forsake me in another case of real difficulty, the only serious row I ever got into at College. At the time I was the Responsible Under Officer [of the College] and an Ensign in the 96th Regiment.

Lord Bury, who had been a midshipman, Harry Burrard, Hawly, Tyndale and I used to hire a six-oared boat often and row up to Henley or down to Cookham and about. But one time we were all short of money. Three of us were officers [and] a lucky thought crossed my mind: "Supposing we ran over to Wycombe[49] and we draw lots who shall draw on Greenwood[50] for Ten pounds as Cornet or Ensign in the Regiment to which we belong. Old Greeny will think it is an officer in the Senior Department and we shall have a jollification — it is our money, isn't it?" "To be sure, it is a capital idea."

Off we started to High Wycombe. The toss fell to me, I wrote a check for Ten pounds payable to the order of our Respectable, kind friend, the Pastry cook, who received the Cash the following day and duly remitted it to the Drawer. Wasn't it a jolly go? Didn't the Cornets and Ensigns keep it up gaily and the greatest wonder was that everyone was told and did keep the secret about drawing, till the last was to leave the College.

But with the day of temptation came the day of trial and of judgement. We unfortunately felt bound in gratitude to give a boating party to the Pastry cook's daughter and one or two of her fair friends with a Pic Nic up the river. We had been suspected to be Rowers but as many Gentry pulled up and down the river in waterman's garb as well as ourselves, we had not yet been detected.

Our boat was taken some distance to a place of concealment, where we embarked and the Middy, who was steersman and had trained us perfectly, [ordered]: "Give way!" and off we pulled up stream to insure a very rapid pull down the Stream, so fast as to distance any Sergeant-Major on the banks, if such a troublesome Spy should be on the lookout.

The day was lovely. A bright sky and a cheering Sun smiled upon our happiness. The gay-painted barge flew through the silver stream while the ripple broke the transparent water. At the end of a seven-mile stretch, we received the word: "Show easy in Bow! Out with the landing Board! Hand out the Ladies! Get out the Baskets!"

No sooner said than done when just beyond us, from a sort of shrubbery, emerged a fair damsel with a Man. "Oh what a pretty boat, do let us go and see it." Murder and confusion — Jamotte Butler, the Colonel's daughter, and an opposition Pic Nic.

"Jump in, Girls, with the baskets! She won't know us, if she does, she won't peach, provided the Colonel does not see us!" Never was a more hasty retreat made but, retreat as we might, we had to face the foe at starting. Though we had backed out for some distance, then away, Jamotte twigged us — but did not peach, we fancied. Yet a worse fate awaited us.

We enjoyed our Pic Nic lower down then away to be in by time. Within a mile of Marlow, to our horror, were two Sergeants *en sentinelle*,[51] one on each side of the river. "Look down, Lads, and pull your best!" We quite distanced and fagged out the runners, got to a safe landing, left the boat in charge of the Ladies, and ran for our lives, got to the Pastry cook's in safety, on Uniforms, and in College by time.

After the evening parade, Sergeant-Major (tall, I forget his name) came. "Under Officer LeC[outeur], was that you in a boat with some Ladies today?" "My good friend, Do you think I would be such an Ass as to own it if it were me. If you know I was out of bounds, report me!" "I could not report you for being out of bounds because you were not so, when I knew you but it is for being in a Boat. Own it and I will not report you." I did not believe him but told him to do his duty — sillily enough as I was a favourite and might have begged myself off but Pride would have a fall. He reported me.

Col[onel]. Butler placed me in close arrest in my own room. Captain Wright [was] in a great rage, as much as having his Responsible U[nder]. Officer in arrest, as with me. "So, Sir, you wish to be broke — perhaps to lose your Commission." "What Sir, for learning to row a boat in order to be able to teach my Soldiers hereafter?" "It is disobedience of orders, Sir, because you misled others, as the Head of this Company." "Well, Sir, I am very sorry for it but I never saw an order not take a row in a boat, it ought to be allowed as a matter of instruction!" "You never saw an order to that effect?" "Never, Sir, look through the Orders since I am at College and you will see that I am right." Charley looked amazed and confounded too for He guessed I was right. "But you were out of bounds?" "No, Sir, the Sergeant-Major admitted He could not report me for being out of bounds!"

Charley left me to my griefs and went to report to the Colonel. I was forthwith sent for. "So, Mr. LeC[outeur], You who ought to set the best example to the Cadets, who have hitherto done so, have at the eleventh hour got into serious disgrace, and may lose your Commission." "Indeed, Colonel Butler, I am very sorry to have displeased you but I do not consider that I have done anything to disgrace myself — rowing a boat is what I have seen officers of the army do in Jersey, it is done by the Gentry of all ranks, and if I were to lose my Commission for such an offence, it would not have been worth holding!" "How dare you speak so, Sir — a Commission not worth holding — and disobedience of orders!" "Sir, I assure You I disobeyed no orders, there is no such order as not to row a Boat in our Orderly book." The old Veteran was thoroughly vexed that the order had not been renewed. "Well, Sir, if you will tell me who the four cadets are, who were with you, I will excuse you." "What, Sir, report or betray my fellow Companions, I would sooner lose my Commission and seek another profession!" "Go to your arrest, Sir!"

Captain Charley came soon, half scolding, half condoling. "So you slammed the door in the Colonel's face?" "No, Sir! Did I though? I might really. I was vexed He wanted me to betray my friends. If I do lose my Commission for this folly, not disgrace, My Father and Mother will forgive me and I have that within me to seek a better profession." "Come Young Gentleman, You take it too high. Your friends are all known and are all in the Blackholes. They are as honest as yourself and will not tell." "Captain Wright, I have been an Under Officer with you a good while and [you] have never had to find serious fault with me. I have had the honour of the Company as much at heart as yourself and have ever striven to please you. I am confident that you do not blame me much in your heart for the mere fact of boating. I hope that you will be my intercessor with Colonel Butler. I am ready to make Him every apology for apparent but unintentional rudeness. Pray do not let my Parents have to regret my constant good fortune till now."

Charley could not stand this appeal but went to the Colonel and begged me off — I making a due and sincere apology at the end of Eight and Forty hours of arrest, with my word of honour that I would not allow boating or engage in it — though it became a custom in consequence the following year at Sandhurst.

## Notes

[1] The town of St. Lauren's or St. Lawrence is located in the central part of Jersey.

[2] "Imprimis." In the first place.

[3] "Al fresco." In the open air.

[4] St. Helier, the largest town on the island, is the capital of Jersey.

[5] St. Peter's is a village in the western part of the island of Jersey and the residence of John Dumaresq, Le Couteur's grandfather.

[6] "C'etait moi." That was me.

[7] Gordon Le Couteur (1801-1817) was Le Couteur's younger brother. Thrown from a horse at an early age, he was an invalid most of his life.

[8] Le Couteur adds a note here: "which I still have 1851."

[9] Isaac Dalby, *A Course of Mathematics Designed for the Use of the Officers and Cadets at the Royal Military College* (2 vols., London, 1805).

[10] Le Couteur is using the word "division" here not in the modern sense as a military formation of all arms usually consisting of between ten thousand and twenty thousand men, but in the sense it was used in British infantry drill of the Napoleonic period as an *ad hoc* formation into which an infantry battalion was divided for the purpose of firing or manoeuvring.

[11] A small portion of the original Journal, an invented and laborious conversation with an old gentleman on a mail coach, has been omitted here.

[12] Known as the Royal Free Grammar School or simply as "Sproston's" after William Sproston who was master there for forty years, this institution specialized in preparing boys for the Royal Military College. See R.H. Thoumine, *Scientific Soldier. A Life of General Le Marchant. 1766-1812* (London, 1968), 98n.

[13] Major General Gaspard John Gaspard Le Marchant (1766-1812). A native of Guernsey, Le Marchant was one of the intellectual leading lights of the British army at the close of the eighteenth century and urged the creation of a professional training institution for officers. In 1801 he was appointed lieutenant governor of the Royal Military College and held this post until 1811 when he was appointed to command a cavalry brigade in Spain where, the following year, he was killed at the battle of Salamanca. See Thoumine, *Scientific Soldier.*

[14] Isaac Dalby (1744-1824), mathemetician and professor of Mathematics at the at Marlow and later Sandhurst. Dalby completed one of the earliest trigonometric surveys of England.

[15] "A l'improviste." Unexpectedly.

[16] In 1809 the companies of a British infantry battalion formed according to the seniority of their commanding captains, the company of the most senior captain taking the post of honour at the right of the line.

[17] "Sawney Thaws." Bumpkins, rubes, hayseeds.

[18] Carbines, shorter and lighter versions of the standard infantry musket, were issued to sergeants, cadets, gunners and mounted troops.

[19] A mixture of wax and lamp black used to polish shoes.

[20] A fine, white clay used to clean white breeches and belts.

[21] A scrubbing powder used to clean metal buttons, buckles and badges.

[22] Cleaning implements for buff leather belts and pouches.

[23] "Tuft or feather." Plumes fastened to the upper portion of the shako, the standard infantryman's headgear.

[24] In 1809 British infantry sergeants wore a short sword, known as a hangar, on parade.

[25] The rank and file of the infantry (privates and corporals) carried their muskets in the "shouldered" position with the butt resting in the left hand, trigger guard to the front and the barrel resting on the left shoulder. Sergeants and officers carried their longarms in the "advanced" position with the trigger outward and the barrel resting on the left shoulder but with the left hand holding the weapon around the trigger guard rather than under the butt.

[26] Probably Theophilus Richards, gunmaker, 33 High Street, London.

[27] "Galleypot." A small, glass medicine bottle. The medical practioner in question was either Surgeon Ninian Bruce or Assistant Surgeon Alexander Robson, both on the staff of the Royal Military College.

[28] A lotion composed of the sub-acetate of lead in a solution.

[29] Le Couteur's description of the paucity of the low diet is not exaggerated. According to the *Instructions to Regimental Surgeons, for regulating the concerns of the Sick and of the Hospital* (London, 1808) the "low diet" for military hospitals consisted of one pint of milk porridge (three parts gruel, one part milk) or rice gruel for breakfast and supper while lunch consisted of one pound of bread made into a pudding with milk, or sago.

[30] In classical mythology, Morpheus was one of the sons of Somnus, the god of sleep.

[31] George Augustus Frederick FitzClarence, lst Earl of Munster, (1794-1842), eldest child of the Duke of Clarence, later William IV, by Mrs. Jordan.

[32] This lady was Dorothy Jordan or Bland (1762-1816), one of most famous actresses of the English stage during the last decade of the eighteenth century and the first of the nineteenth. For twenty years she was the mistress of the Duke of Clarence, later William IV, and bore him ten children who took the name FitzClarence.

[33] Henry Edward FitzClarence (1795-1817), second son of the Duke of Clarence by Mrs. Jordan. After leaving the college, Henry was commissioned with his older brother George in the 10th Hussars, a regiment notable for its large number of

aristocratic officers. In 1815 the officers of the 10th petitioned to have their commander removed for cowardice. This act resulted in a court martial and the officers' forcible transfer to other regiments where they became known as the "elegant extracts." Henry and George were sent to the 24th Light Dragoons in India where Henry died from cholera in 1817.

[34] William Henry, Duke of Clarence, later William IV of England (1765-1837). The third son of George III, Clarence joined the Royal Navy in 1779 and was on active service until 1789, attaining the rank of rear admiral. Perpetually in disfavour with his father over his relationship with Mrs. Jordan and other matters, Clarence passed most of his life in relative obscurity. In 1818 he married Adelaide of Saxe-Coburg Meiningen and, in 1830, ascended the throne to become William IV on the death of his eldest brother, George IV.

[35] Colonel James Butler, Commandant of the Junior Department of the Royal Military College.

[36] Belle Vue at St. Brelade, Jersey, overlooking the little port of St. Aubin, was Le Couteur's parents' home in Jersey.

[37] Probably an English translation of Francois de Solignac de lat Mothe Fenelon's *Les Aventures de Telemaque, fils d'Ulysse* (Paris, 1699), perhaps *A New Translation of Telemachus* by Gibbons Bagnall (2 vols.; Hereford, 1790). Fenelon's book was a guide for the education of royalty.

[38] "Must have been fag." Forced to act as a servant to the other boys.

[39] "Middys." Midshipmen, junior naval officers.

[40] Sophia FitzClarence, afterward Lady De l'Isle and Dudley.

[41] A note on the manuscript at this point reads: "King William the IVth named [me] his A[ide] D[e] C[amp] in 1830 on this being recalled to his memory. LeC,. ADC, 1866."

[42] "Forlorn hope." A period military term denoting the advance guard of an assault, especially an assault through a breach in the wall of a fortress.

[43] Major General Sir Howard Douglas (1776-1861). An artillery officer, Douglas served in Canada, 1795-1798, before being appointed commandant of the Senior Department of the Royal Military College at High Wycombe, a position he held until 1820. In 1823 he was appointed Lieutenant Governor of New Brunswick and served in that capacity until 1831. Douglas was the author of several important military treatises.

[44] Le Couteur's appointment to a regiment in Jersey was no accident. On 4 September 1810 his father had written to the Horse Guards, the headquarters of the British army, requesting that his son be appointed an ensign in a "Regiment of the line" but, as he was "yet too young for immediate active service," asking that John be appointed to a unit stationed on Jersey. This wish was granted. See PRO, WO 31, vol.

311, Le Couteur to Torrens, 4 September 1810; Harcourt to Torrens, 12 September 1810.

[45] "Under the seal." Under the wax seal on the envelope.

[46] Major James McDermott, second-in-command, Junior Department, RMC

[47] Captain John Otto, cadet company commander.

[48] Captain David Erskine, cadet company commander.

[49] In 1810 the Senior Department of the Royal Military College was located at High Wycombe, five miles from Marlow.

[50] Greenwood was a firm of financial agents who handled monetary matters, both official and personal, for the British army.

[51] "En sentinelle." On sentinel or on guard.

# Chapter Two

## "A BRAT OF A BOY WHO HAD NEVER SEEN A SHOT FIRED"
The Young Officer,
*January 1811 to June 1812*

***[January, 1811]***
I was appointed by Colonel Lee[1] [of the 96th Foot], its Commanding Officer, to the Light Infantry Company.[2] They were all Welshmen, as active as Goats, very smart, nice fellows but quarrelsome.

I mounted perhaps the first guard in Fort Regent[3] for on that day Sir George Don,[4] the commander-in-chief, then General Don, came to visit the still unfinished works. After presenting arms and turning in my Guard, He asked what sort of a Guardroom I had?. "Indeed, Sir, a very uncomfortable one, for if Your Excellency were to alight, I could not offer you a Seat." "Oh, indeed, let me See!" Sure enough there was only a stretcher and a table in the guard room. "Well that is scanty indeed — regular campaigning accommodation. Now, open your desk, write an order for anything you like, and I will sign it." I instantly wrote: a table, six chairs, a Bedstead, one Cupboard, a wash stand. I looked up: "Is that too much, Sir?" The good General laughed: "What did I say?" "Very true, Your Excellency, but I do not wish to be unreasonable." A Fender and fire Irons and a few utensils. And he signed the order, which made our after Guards very snug.

One evening at our Rollicking Mess, after I had left, they got up a race, the Light Company officers against the Regiment — a Sweepstakes. The distance from the Sands below the Blue Barracks, where the 96th [Regiment] was quartered, to St. Aubin — up the Ships, through the street, down by La Haielle and back.

All began training — Colonel in Greatcoats and Jackboots, O'Halloran,[5]

Leahy,[6] Rickards,[7] Cusine.[8] All, including Myself, took long runs daily for about a month.

The eventful day arrived. We were clothed in flannels, Mine trimmed with Green. My Marlow training led them to back me freely. Off we started, I in no hurry at the steady slow trot was soon left behind but, by the time, I had held the same pace to St. Aubin, there were only O'Halloran, Colomb[9] and Rickards in company and I took the lead up the hill at a running pace. Well do I remember the cheers and the waving of handkerchiefs from the thronged windows, for half St. Helier was out to witness the great foot race as it was called.

Captain, now Sir George, Arthur[10] rode by me and urged me not to hurry. "All right" I said and off again on the sands, then only O'Halloran was up. I lengthened my pace in the last mile, and quickened it in the last hundred yards distancing all but the Welsh Corporal of the Light Company, who could have run past me like a Greyhound, but the honour of the Company was his also and He only cheered his Sub [on]. He & I ran five miles, two furlongs and a half, measured, in thirty-one minutes and a half and I won the Sweepstakes.

The moment I got to the winning post, to my utter astonishment I found myself whipped off my legs and muffled up in blankets, as if I had been a Baby in arms. Four of the Light Bobs ran up the Sand Hills with me, amidst the cheers of the Company, who relieved the Bearers by turns till I got a barrack room where I was unceremoniously stripped naked, popped into a warmed bed. Then the Doctor stood by and saw me rubbed down by a detachment who were laughing, full of joy and triumph at the victory and treatment of their Subaltern. After being rubbed dry, and drinking some weak negus,[11] I fell into a deep sleep and, some hours after, awoke quite fresh and ready for anything.

My dear Mother, however, made me promise that I would never run another foot race for *money*. She had been under uneasiness at a Boy having to run a race against grown men though I had lately ran from High Wycombe to Marlow College which is five miles, and Wycombe Hill one of the most steep in Buck[ingham]s[hire], in half an hour....[12]

### *21 November, 1811*

I was promoted to a Lieutenancy in the 104th Foot after a year and a Month at the age of Seventeen and one Month.[13] I regretted parting with my 96th friends but was delighted at the idea of going abroad. My father had objected to my exchanging into the 77th [Regiment], then quartered in

Jersey, but ordered to join Lord Wellington's army. However He was Himself soon to move, being appointed a Major General on the Staff in Ireland at Armagh. He applied for my appointment as His Aide de Camp which was refused as I had not been enough on regimental duty.

I well remember the break up of the Establishment in old Belle Vue — the sale of all the comfortable old furniture, the Old Horses on which I had learned to ride, Farm stock and Implements. On the 23rd of December [1811], two days before that happy day of Xmas which for so many Years had been my burthen of delight at My Grandfather's most happy Mansion at St. Peters, We all embarked in the Government Scout, Capt[ain]. Wooldridge[1],[4] with a Gun Brig as a Convoy sent by the Admiral, the Duke of Bouillon.[15]

My father paid his respects to the Duke of York[16] [in London] to whom He owed his appointment but did not take me to the levee,[17] fancying me, I suspect, too young looking for a Lieutenant. I had leave of absence to the 1st of March so started for Dublin with my Parents which We reached on the 9th of January and got my quarters in Dawson's Hotel.

The following packet brought news that my Father was appointed to the Staff in Jamaica, a more troublesome and dangerous command, but of far greater value. It made my heart rather sore to think of the climate to which all those I held most dear were to be exposed and I was the most distressed of the party at the change. However My Mother always concluded with: "whatever is, is right!"

I nevertheless passed three happy weeks in Dublin. The Magees,[18] Shaw the Banker, MP, the Needhams,[19] Prossers, Percivals,[20] Ponsonby Shaw,[21] were most hospitable. Their dinners (the Shaws and Needhams) rivalled Royalty. We met the great Plunkett[22] and choice company everywhere — the most lively and entertaining society I have ever met. Doctor Magee, the future Archbishop, was then in his zenith — polite, eloquent, handsome and a Courtier of exquisite polish.

### *4 February, 1812*

The rumours of a War between Great Britain and the United States of America affected small people as well as Rulers. I received orders to join my Regiment in New Brunswick. With a heavy heart, I took leave for the first time in my life of My beloved parents and my dear Brother, to be thrown into the wide world on My own resources. The alarm at the bad climate of Jamaica, which was generally felt throughout the service, tended not a little to disturb my equanimity. Should I ever again meet all those dear faces, they going to the hot and pestilential regions of the Yellow Fever,[23] I towards the frozen region of eternal snows. My Mother bade me put my constant trust in Providence and bravely follow my Career in the profession I had selected, wherever my duty called!

I embarked in the packet for Holyhead and buried my short-lived grief in my berth. Paid Ten pounds for my Fare to London inside the Mail on the 6th and only got to London late on the 8th and took up my quarters with My Kind friends, Mr. & Mrs. DeLisle.[24] One scene on the journey I relate for the benefit of any Youthful travellers who may read this and be similarly circumstanced.

At Owestry, My only inside fellow traveller, Plunkett, a Nephew of the celebrated Uncle whom I had met at Doctor Magee's in Dublin, and I alighted for dinner. In those days it was well understood that a mail dinner was, in vulgar parlance, to be bolted. We both ran to the kitchen, washed our hands and faces. We had not breakfasted, mind, when we rushed to the parlour, saw a nice Roasted fowl and a boiled Ham. Ready! I carved one, Plunkett the other, Cut bread, and just as a morsel approached our Mouths, in came the waiter with the Bill, "three and sixpence each, Gentlemen", with the Guard behind Him: "Gents, the coach is ready. Time is up. The Mail can't wait."

"Ye Villins!", said Plunkett in good Irish brogue, "Plunder us of our money fur nothing — I'll be quits with ye Mister Waither!" "Le Couteur, give me yer pocket Handkerchief, waither, give me the Mug of beer. Le Couteur, cut off Six Inches of Ham", placing the Fowl in the Handkerchief, "hand me the Ham, that y'll do, give me the bread and the Salt cellar." I thought he would take the Knives and Forks, but he didn't. "Mr. Waither, I am a lawyer and I'll have justice — there's yer Money, 3/6 each." Waiter: "I'll expect you will remember the waiter, Sir." "Never shall I forget ye in all me life and I'm sure ye'll recollect me when I come again." The astonishment of Waiter and Guard was beyond telling but the latter, when clear of his fellow thief, curried favor by saying what a clever go that was.

### *28 February, 1812*

On the 28th, I left London for Newport, Isle of Wight, the Depot where I was ordered to proceed. I joined the mess of the Depot, which was made up of officers from a variety of corps — some of the worst looking scamps I had ever seen wearing the King's Uniform. In those days of raging wars, all sorts of men obtained Commissions, some without education, some without means, some without either, and many of low birth. It was a Society so vulgar, so drunken, so vicious and so disorderly that, on meeting [it], One absolutely dreaded who to sit by or who to converse with.[25]

I was ordered to sit on a Court Martial. We were all Officers from different Regiments. At this period of our military era, Corporal punishments were ferocious. From three hundred lashes to a thousand, or Nine hundred and ninety nine, might be awarded. I have known the latter figure sentenced.

The Prisoner was on trial for being drunk when on waiting for Guard. I was the junior Subaltern and wrote the proceedings. It was proven that the Prisoner was drunk when on waiting for Guard but He proved in mitigation that He had not had due warning because it was not his turn for duty and the call upon him was unexpected and sudden. He admitted it to be a case of intoxication but certainly not when for duty. He would have disdained being drunk when for duty. He was a manly fellow and I considered He had justified his plea.

On being asked My opinion first as the Junior Member,[26] I stated my opinion why I only found Him Guilty of Simple drunkenness and awarded Him the least punishment of those bloodthirsty days — One hundred lashes. The two next junior Subalterns awarded the same punishment on like grounds. The Captain and the Senior thought the case quite made out against them, that no distinction as to warning should be made, intoxication ought to be punished severely — He should have had three hundred [lashes] at least. That was the award of the Court and we should report the case to General Taylor.[27]

The next day the Court was made to re-assemble. The President said the Major General was highly dissatisfied with the award.[28] He took the view which the President of the Court had done and the Case must be reconsidered. On being asked my opinion, feeling that the President had insinuated I was the Person to be blamed, I said that my Father who was an old Soldier, a General Officer on the Staff in Ireland, had taken much pains to make me comprehend the nature of a Court Martial, always to watch when there were flaws in the evidence and, if there were any mitigating circumstances, to lean to the side of mercy, and to judge according to my conscience and the best of my judgement. However I would ask leave to read over the whole case, which all agreed to hear aloud.

I read the whole trial over, then again gave my reasons for adhering firmly to my judgement. I confess I felt a little nervous for fear my brother Subs. should desert me but they were as sincere as myself and the judgement was not reversed. The President was indiscrete in his reproofs to us, but we none of us made answer, He belonged to neither of our Regiments.

Charley Wright's "No reply, Sir!" had its weight with me already.[29] Happy would it been for me and for many if we could most frequently adhere to the rule when provoked. General Taylor issued a severe censure on three members of a Court Martial for an ill-judged Sentence which the whole garrison nearly thought very ill-timed and uncalled for. I was complimented by many old officers.[30]

### *Spithead, March, 1812*

The General thought to punish me after a fashion of his own by sending me, then a youth of seventeen only, to take charge of a detachment of wounded Soldiers, two hundred Peninsular heroes who were on board of a transport then lying at Spithead, on passage to Deal to the military hospital. I found the *Harford*, Capt[ain]. Landels, a fine Ship of 600 tons, among the fleet.

What a glorious sight it was. Some Forty or Fifty Line of Battle Ships and a bevy of Frigates and sloops of war besides three hundred Sail of Vessels — never did I behold such a sight. My Uncle Philip Dumaresq[31] was then Captain of Lord Nelson's famous ship, the *Victory*.[32] She was at anchor, with the Flag of Sir James Saumarez[33] flying, as Commanding the Baltic Fleet. Well was it that my excellent Uncle happened to be at Portsmouth.

I took a shore boat which cost one and six shillings to the Transport where I found an Assistant Surgeon on the Staff, Doctor Bradley,[34] in charge of the wounded invalids. I found him a well-educated, amiable Companion — we became great friends.

As soon as I got on board, I mustered my Detachment. Never was [there] such a disorderly set of Veterans, old and young, all of them having received some sort of wound. I was resolved to treat them with great indulgence. Some of the Squads had a Sergeant in charge of them, others no non-commissioned Officer whatever. There were some fine old Sergeants of the Fusiliers[35] and others, the Senior of whom I named acting Sergeant Major, after Myself in command. Some of the Sergeants had no legs, another one arm. One man no legs, another no arms. I went below [decks] to visit the sick — when the heat and stench were so great from a number of women and children[36] being among the men, that it was quite unbearable. However, all was smooth as yet.

When the dinner hour[37] arrived, the Grog[38] was served out as to the Seamen — the consequence was that some of the men having sold their Grog to others and to the women, many got very drunk, and by the evening parade or roll call, were insolent in the last degree. The Doctor wrote to me officially to say that the grog issued at that strength would endanger the health of the men, many of whom should have none whatever.

So the following day I ordered Six waters to be mixed with the Grog explaining to the Men that it was the Doctor's desire. There was a regular mutiny. They threatened to pitch me overboard, a brat of a boy who had never seen a shot fired, to ill use veterans in that way. One of them tripped up my one-legged Sergeant, on which I knocked the fellow down and called on the Captain and his crew to assist in quelling the Mutiny. Many flung away their weak Grog to my great satisfaction.

About 3 o'clock all being quiet, I went ashore for sea stock for the Doctor and myself. I hastened to get all we required, after running to my Uncle to say good bye. When I got to the hard with the Provisions, to my horror, the Waterman told me that my ship had sailed. What was I ever to do — to overtake Her was impossible. Reported absent! Ruin! A Court Martial and my Commission gone!

I ran back to my Uncle who, by the merest chance I met coming down to the hard, told Him of my misfortune. "Never Mind, you must go by Mail to Deal, get on board your ship the instant she arrives, and land your men. No one will report you as you are Commanding officer. Even you would not be to blame as you were without provisions."

While he was endeavouring to console Me, My good fortune had not yet deserted me. "There! there!", I exclaimed, "is the Captain of the *Thracian*,[39] Sloop of War on Convoy. He is going on board perhaps." My Uncle made me run after Him, when I apologized and said that Capt[ain]. Dumaresq of the *Victory*, begged to say a few words to Him. He walked back at once, took off his hat very respectfully to his Superior.

"My Nephew has come ashore for Provisions, his ship is under Your Convoy but has got under weigh and He may miss Her in a shoreboat. I shall thank you to give Him a cast on board when you near Her." "With the greatest pleasure" [he replied], put my arm under his own, walked to my shoreboat, sent a man for my stock, and off.

Jolly luck this! Moreover He[40] took me on board of the *Thracian* to dine with Him when I took occasion to tell Him of my Mutinous troop which amused him greatly. "If that should happen again, hoist a Yellow Burgee[41] at the Peak and I will send a boat's crew for the offenders & I'll give them a dose that will keep them all in order."

In the evening we ran close to the Transport and I was sent on board of Her quite happy. My friend Bradley was greatly rejoiced to see me, fearing I had been left behind. My arrival in a Man of War's boat aided my Authority and I cautioned the men that any attempt at disobedience or insubordination while on parades or duty would meet with punishment.

The next day when the Grog was to be mixed, a most riotous Scene occurred. I drew my Sword and declared I would cut down the rascal who again knocked the Sergeant over. I instantly hoisted my Signal for aid. The Boat, with a Crew manned and armed, came off and I had the most violent offenders seized — one to be well flogged, the other to look on. I promised to send off any woman who misbehaved, to remain on board of the Man of War, till the voyage was over.

This brought them into some order but, in about Five hours, our delinquent returned — the most fierce, as tame as a lamb. He had no notion of a Man of War's flogging. Made Him strip before the whole who could parade and marched Him along the ranks while the Midshipman and some of the Sailors stood by, declaring to them if there was not perfect discipline and silence I would send them to be punished. I reminded them that I had been educated at the Military College, I had risen from the ranks to be a Corporal and Sergeant Major and to command a Company of one hundred Lads, and a Battalion of three hundred, and if they dared to disobey me, I would carry out the articles of war with full rigour. There was no more trouble — My troops were in hand.

### *Monday, 11th March, 1812*

A Heavy gale from the NE obliged us to anchor in Dungeness Bay. The following morning a lull enabled us to weigh [anchor] and beat up[42] the Downs but on the 16th, it came on to blow great Guns.

I was sound asleep in My berth about 7 A.M. when, all at once, I heard an immense crash and perceived a great beam poking through the stern windows, tearing and breaking all it met with, then a violent jar which shook the ship to her Keel. I flew on deck where I saw we were driving on, and riding down, a sloop of war. We had carried away her sprit sail yard, knocked some of her guns over, stove in her bow, and the Jacks were striving to shove us off and swearing at us Manfully. We had parted our Cable. We soon got clear of Her with little damage to ourselves — being the larger vessel and much higher out of the water. It was some time before we could get a storm sail up, so as to enable us to bring to,[43] when we let go another anchor which fortunately brought us up.

### *17 March [1812]*

The hurricane continued all day but moderated in the night. The next morning the Deal boats, splendid Pilot boats, came about in a heavy sea, offering to land for a Guinea a head, and to fish up the missing anchor for Twenty Pounds. After some delay, Bradley and I offered half a Guinea each to be landed and embarked ourselves and Portmanteaux.

We were about three miles from Deal beach, a fearful looking spot to land on in a storm — the breakers seemed over Twelve feet high. As we got within a Yard or so below the Cutter's draft of water, she was run up in the Wind's eye[44] and she then laid on her Beam[45] and a mighty wave took us fifty yards up the Beach and, as it returned, left the boat high on the Beach. "Run, Gents, as hard as You can, You will be safe before the next wave comes!" So we were — the Boat was brought up some thirty yards more or less with our Luggage in perfect safety.

I went to report my arrival to L[ieutenan]t. Colonel Williamson,[46] the Commandant, who was aware of my duty. The weather was too boisterous all that day to land my invalids but the next day being calm, they were all landed in safety. One incident amused me greatly, and defied the fable of the Body and Members refusing to assist each other for here, Legs without arms agreed to carry arms without legs, which raised much admiration and many laughs and encomiums on the two hardy bodies that thus aided each other!

Captain Dennis,[47] a Gentleman of fine manners and high fashion, who had been Major of Brigade at Norman Cross, joined the Depot. He met me in High Street and recognizing the Uniform, he introduced himself to me, when I invited Him to my lodgings and offered Him a bed. He took me at my word and, the next Day, asked to share my sitting room — a handsome apartment at W[illia]m Baston's near the Bridge. I showed Him what a vile mixture the Depot Mess was composed of, when he agreed to get up a 104th [Regiment Officer's] Mess in our Room if our brother officers liked the idea. It was greatly approved and, with Dennis and I as President and Vice, we raised the character of the 104th Mess as a model of good breeding. Very happy we were — Nine in number after a time.

On the 29th of April I was on the Main Guard and, at night about Two o'clock, I went round the Sentries attended only by the Corporal of the Guard. All at once I heard a cry of "Murder! Help!" The Corporal and I ran towards the cry where I could perceive a Man running from several Men in pursuit of Him. I shouted: "Here is the Patrol!" and the person came to us.

The men stopped, swearing loudly at Him, and retired. I begged the officer, for he was in Uniform I perceived, to come away at once but no, He ran after the men who turned on him again, while I followed to bring him away. They then attacked us, My Corporal ran for the Guard, and the [[officer][48] ran away, leaving me to be beaten and my skull fractured of which I carry the mark to my grave. The Guard came and picked me up fainting and deluged in blood. It would have cost me my life, so said the Doctor if the wound in the front of my Temple had been a quarter of an Inch forwarder. The wound on the Crown of my head was some weeks in healing.

### *9 May, 1812*

We received orders for embarkation and, on the 13th, three months advance of pay with directions to provide our passage as we might. This was secured in the *Anns*,[49] a clumsy brig of three hundred tons.[50] One officer was arrested for debt. I lent him Ten pounds to aid towards his liberation and, although he afterward inherited a fortune from an Uncle, He has not repaid the debt.

A scurvy but clever trick was paid to an imposing Jew by a young officer a few days before this. He had contrived to get on board before being arrested but the Jew discovering the vessel, He took an Officer and the warrant for his arrest, and pulled alongside of Her. The instant the Young Delinquent saw the Jew, He grasped the rail, told his brother officers: "Now save me, mind you are civil to the Jew and everyone drink wine with Him."

He went to the ship's side. "Ah! How d'ye do, Mr., I'm so glad to see your, where's your bill, I can settle it now, come into the Cabin, and refresh Yourself after your long pull." The kind, offhand, friendly attention of his Young friend who had spent his money freely with Him, put Him off his work. He walked into the Cabin, sat down "Bon gré, Mal gré",[51] to dinner. Every attention was paid Him — how very condescending and attentive — all the Young fellows took wine with Him. Our Hero slipped out, told the Officer all was right, his old friend would sleep on Board, He might return, paid Him his fee and boat hire, and sent Him ashore. In the meanwhile, Isaac got very happy, very drunk, and very drowsy, turned in.

The vessel weighed anchor, sailed and was off for the Cape of Good Hope. About Six in the morning, Isaac awoke wondering where He might be, ran on deck. "Where am I, where's am I going?" "Only to the Cape of Good Hope!" "Oh Murdersh! Murdersh! Letsh me go ashore! Letsh me go ashore!" So they did — somewhere along the coast.[52]

We sailed on the 18th, dropped down to Yarmouth on the 19th, sailed once more and had to put into Torbay where Colonel Ross[53] of the 28th, formerly of the 18th, invited me to dinner. Here we saw what's called a wrestling match between the men of Cornwall and Devon. Fine athletic models of humanity, stripped to the waist, armed with tremendous thick shoes, loaded with nails. The Kicks over the shins which they dealt each other showed the true Bulldog endurance of the Briton — it was painfully disgusting even to us young Soldiers to see such valuable limbs maimed. Yet when a clean heave or throw took place, it was beautiful. Fair wrestling should take place in slippers!

### *23 May, 1812*

We left under convoy of the *Comet*,[54] Captain Blamey,[55] and passing the Lands End on the 27[th], bade Adieu to Old England with heavy hearts, three of us destined never to revisit its blessed shore.

It was scarcely possible to be more exposed to discomforts than we Ten passengers crowded in a small Cabin fit for four persons. Our Captain was aware of his want of room, for he stipulated that we should not complain of want of accommodation before starting but, as we were anxious to join our Regiment by the first vessel to be had, we embarked in the dark as it were, but were soon awakened to our miseries. Three of us had to sling our hammocks every night.

The first gale of wind we had, conveyed an important lesson. We were at dinner, Mrs. P. as well as every male passenger, holding on by one hand, while the other was employed in steadying the Soup, Leg of Mutton, or dumplings — and occasionally snatching a mouthful during a level.

The old brig was rolling, gunwale under[56] — there's a lurch for you — the swinging lamp touched the ceiling planks. Away went seats, Soup, Mutton, dumplings, crockery, knives, forks, Mustard, Pepper, Sauces and such like. The Lady screamed, as well she might, the Gentlemen shouted. I grappled a berth, and laughed heartily, snatched hold of the Lady when, again at the next roll, away went the others, with all the implements of industry, in an alarming confusion and mess. All our chairs were broken, our table cloths cut, the Cook ill or sulky — obliged to cook for ourselves and to prepare our own Meals. Nor was this the worst, the rascal Sailors stole a considerable portion of our stock as we discovered. However, Merry hearts make light days!

### *[June 1812]*

The month of June is beautiful, even at Sea. Our poultry had been under the charge of an excellent fellow who had been brought up on a large farm. He had charge of the poultry but He had never seen them cooped up in a ship's deck, exposed, wet and cold. Feed them as he would, they got sick, lost their plumage, [got] thin, and died. If we did not pick them, as our Irish sub. said, to save their lives! But they were not eatable — bones and whipthongs, roast or boiled.

I happened to go down into the hold one morning to get some linen from my trunk when I perceived that I was walking, as it were, on a nice sandy, gravelled, beach rolled by the old brig into gentle undulations and all the small stuff at the surface. It was clean, sweet, warm and with scarcely any motion down there.[57] "Oh, Ho," thought I, "I should like to be here myself, but at all events, this is a splendid spot for poultry."

The Captain consented, I ran to the mess. "I say, old fellow, You're no farmer, You're starving and killing all our poultry, with your West country kindness." "Well, why don't you try your hand at it, Johnny? Let's see what your Jersey farmers will do." Done! Jersey forever, against the world.

The Sailors brought down the Coops — Geese, turkies, and fowls — turned them loose on the fine, large, beach, gave them lots of water. The Cocks sang out a Merry tune, the fowls flew about the hold, rolled in the sand. The Turkies strutted and the Geese and Ducks paddled in the water. Never was such joy. Every morning they were regularly fed by me and in a week I had beautiful poultry in fine feather, and what remained alive on the Sunday, 21 June, were as fat and fleshy as a *Poulard grassé*.[58] It is an admirable mode of keeping poultry on board ship. Space, gravel, and the want of light, induces them to sleep and feed much.

*View of Halifax, 1817, by George Parkyns. On "a balmy, soft evening" in June 1812, the seventeen-year-old Lieutenant, John Le Couteur, arrived in Halifax harbour to begin his service in North America.* G. Parkyns/National Archives of Canada/C-981

## Notes

[1] Lieutenant Colonel Michael W. Lee, 96th Foot.

[2] "Light infantry company." In 1812 each British battalion of foot (infantry) consisted of ten companies; eight were known as the centre, or battalion, companies, the remaining two were the flank, or elite, companies. The flank companies were the grenadier, which formed on the right of the battalion when it was in line, and the light infantry company which formed on the left. The grenadier company was the shock or assault company and was, in theory, composed of the strongest and steadiest soldiers in the battalion. The light infantry company was composed of skirmishers who fought in open order and formed the advance and rear guards of the battalion. Theoretically, the light company was recruited from the most intelligent and agile soldiers.

[3] Fort Regent in St. Helier was the major fortification on Jersey. Construction commenced in 1802 and was completed in 1815.

[4] Lieutenant General Sir George Don (1754-1832), Lieutenant-Governor of Jersey as well as colonel of the 96th Foot.

[5] Ensign Maurice O'Halloran, 96th Foot.

[6] Captain Henry Leahy, 96th Foot.

[7] Lieutenant Harry Rickards, 96th Foot.

[8] Ensign John Cusine, 96th Foot.

[9] Lieutenant George T. Colomb, 96th Foot.

[10] Sir George Arthur (1784-1854), see *DCB*, VIII, 26-30. At this time (1811) a captain and military secretary and aide de camp to General Don, Arthur later served as Superintendent of Honduras (1814-1822) and Lieutenant-Governor of Van Diemen's Land (Tasmania) (1824-1837) before becoming the last lieutenant-governor of Upper Canada (1838-1841).

[11] A mixture of sweet mulled wine and water.

[12] In the original manuscript, an anecdote concerning Le Couteur's days at military college was placed here. It has been moved to Chapter 1.

[13] Le Couteur was promoted much faster than average as a recent study has shown that, during this period, infantry ensigns were not promoted to lieutenants until they had served an average of 2.1 years in the lower rank. See Michael Glover, *Wellington's Army in the Peninsula, 1808-1814* (New York, 1977), 84.

[14] Captain James Wooldridge, RN (d. 1814).

[15] Admiral Phillipe d'Auvergne, RN, the Duke of Bouillon (1754-1816). Bouillon was charged with maintaining communications with the French Royalist movement on the western coast of France. See H.W. Kirke, *From the Gun Room to the Throne; being the life of Philip d'Auvergne, Duke of Bouillon* (London, 1904).

[16] Frederick Augustus, Duke of York (1763-1827). The second son of George III, York was commander-in-chief of the British army in 1811. Although largely remembered for the nursery rhyme: "The grand old Duke of York, he had ten thousand men, he marched them up a hill, and marched them down again," York was a competent and industrious administrator who brought much-needed reforms to the army. For balanced accounts of his life and work, see Alfred Burne, *The Noble Duke of York* (London, 1949) and Richard Glover, *Peninsular Preparation. The Reform of the British Army, 1793-1809* (Cambridge, 1963).

[17] A levee was an official reception regular held by the Duke of York for officers stationed near and visiting London.

[18] Reverend William Magee (1766-1831). At this time Dean of Cork and professor of mathematics at Trinity College, Dublin, Magee was later (1822) appointed Archbishop of Dublin of the Church of Ireland. He was famous for the eloquence of his sermons.

[19] Possibly the household of General Francis Jack Needham (1748-1832), MP for Newry in Ireland and later 1st Earl of Kilmorey.

[20] Either Robert Perceval (1756-1839), first professor of chemistry at the University of Dublin and later founder of the Royal Irish Academy, or Alexander Perceval (1789-1858), politician and Sergeant-at-Arms of the House of Lords.

[21] Possibly George Ponsonby (1755-1817), Lord Chancellor of Ireland in the Fox-Grenville cabinet of 1806-1807.

[22] William Conyngham Plunkett (1764-1854). A member of the Irish parliament and fervent champion of Catholic emancipation who opposed the Union of Ireland and Britain, Plunkett held a number of public positions including Solicitor General and Attorney General of the United Kingdom and was later Lord Chancellor of Ireland.

[23] Le Couteur is not exaggerating the health hazards his family was facing in the tropics. In the four years from 1793 to 1796, the British army lost forty thousand men in the West Indies from yellow fever. See John W. Fortescue, *History of the British Army* (13 vols., London, 1899-1930), IV: 496.

[24] Mr. and Mrs. Frederick DeLisle. Mrs. DeLisle was the aunt of Le Couteur's future wife, Harriet Janvrin.

[24] Le Couteur's opinion of the quality of the officers at the Depot on the Isle of Wight was shared by Surgeon William Dunlop of the 89th Foot. Arriving in April 1813, Dunlop "went once, and only once, to the Garrison Mess, in company with two or three officers of my acquaintance, and saw among other novelties of a mess table, one officer shy a leg of mutton at another's head, from one end of the table to the other. This we took as notice to quit ... and never again returned, or associated with a set of gentlemen who had such a vivacious mode of expressing a difference of opinion." See William Dunlop, *Tiger Dunlop's Upper Canada* (Toronto, 1967), 4.

[26] "As the Junior Member." It was the procedure at military courts martial for the most

junior officer of the court to give his opinion first lest he be swayed by the opinions of officers of higher rank.

[27] Lieutenant General James Taylor, Commanding Officer, Isle of Wight.

[28] A garrison court martial's findings were subject to review by the garrison commander, in this case General Taylor.

[29] "No reply, Sir!" This expression must have had a special significance for Le Couteur but he provides us with no further information concerning it.

[30] It is not clear from Le Couteur's text whether this "severe censure" was issued to him and his two fellow subalterns or to the members of another court martial, but it is inferred, since Le Couteur "was complimented by many old [senior] Officers," that the censure was aimed at his court martial.

[31] Captain Philip Dumaresq, RN (d. 1819) was the brother of Le Couteur's mother: lieutenant, 1799; commander, 1801; captain, 1806.

[32] HMS *Victory*, Ist Rate ship of the line, 100 guns. Launched in 1765, *Victory* was Nelson's flagship at the battle of Trafalgar, 1805, and is still in commission today as a museum ship at Portsmouth, United Kingdom.

[33] Vice Admiral Sir James Saumarez (1757-1836). A Guernseyman and contemporary of Nelson, Saumarez had a long and distinguished naval career. By 1812, he was commanding the Baltic fleet and returned each winter to refit his ships.

[34] Probably Assistant Surgeon Nicholas Bradley, RA.

[35] In 1812, the British army included three regiments of fusiliers (the 7th, 21st and 23rd Foot). These regiments had originally been raised in the late seventeenth century to escort the artillery of the army. For this reason, they were armed with "fusils" (from the French *fusil*, or flintlock musket) rather than the common matchlock weapon as the latter firearm posed a danger around the large amounts of powder present in artillery positions. By connection, the three units became "fusiliers" and by 1812 were regarded as elite units.

[36] According to the *Regulations and Orders for the Army, 1811*, 250-251, 370-371, twelve enlisted soldiers' wives per company were allowed to accompany regiments of the army sent to garrison overseas possessions and six wives per company were allowed if a regiment was sent on active service. Thus, an infantry battalion overseas might be accompanied by as many as 120 women (and their children) who drew army rations at a reduced scale. The lot of these military dependants who shared all the travails of campaign and garrison life was miserable.

Instead of alleviating their problems, however, the military authorities tried their best to prevent enlisted men from marrying. According to the *Rules and Regulations for Cavalry, 1795* (London, 1795), 74, "Marriage is to be discouraged as much as possible. Officers must explain to the men the many miseries that women are exposed to, and by every sort of persuasion they must prevent their marrying if possible."

[37] Throughout his Journal, Le Couteur uses "dinner" to mean a meal served at midday.

[38] The daily rations of the British army and navy in 1812 included alcohol. For sailors and soldiers on board warships, this consisted of 1/8 pint of raw Demerara rum which, by regulation, had to be diluted one part rum to four parts water and drunk immediately. The alcoholic content of this rum was much higher than its modern Canadian equivalent.

The word "grog" derives from the name of the officer who instituted this rum ration in the 1740s, Rear Admiral Sir Edward Vernon, who wore a waistcoat made of grogram, a mixture of silk, mohair and wool and was thus known by his men as "Old Grog".

[39] HMS *Thracian*, brig/sloop of war, built 1809, broken up 1829.

[40] The officer in question was Lieutenant and Commander John Carter, RN.

[41] A burgee is a swallow-tailed pennant.

[42] "Beat up." Sail with an unfavourable wind direction by constant tacking or changes of course.

[43] "Bring to." Stop the transport, which had lost her anchor, from drifting.

[44] "Run up in the wind's eye." With the wind blowing from dead ahead.

[45] "Laid on her beam." The boat was lying broadside to the waves and, if the water had been deeper, would have foundered.

[46] Lieutenant Colonel George Williamson, Commandant, Royal Military Asylum (hospital) at Deal.

[47] Captain Peter, or Petit, Dennis or Dennis (b. 1774), 104th Foot.

[48] The original text describes the "doctor" running away. This is probably a typographical error and Le Couteur meant to write "officer."

[49] The *Anns*, brig, Captain Saunders, out of London, see *Royal Gazette and New Brunswick Advertizer*, Saint John, 30 June 1812.

[50] Such obedience to sailing orders does not seem to have been general among the officers at the Isle of Wight Depot. According to Surgeon William Dunlop, "all the worst characters in the army were congregated at the Isle of Wight; men who were afraid to join their regiments from the indifferent estimation they were held in by their brother officers. These stuck to the depot, and the arrival of a fleet of transports at Spithead or the Mother-bank, was a signal for a general sickness among these worthies. And this was particularly the case with those who were bound for Canada, for they knew full well if they could shirk past the month of August, there was no chance of a call on their services until the month of April following." See *Tiger Dunlop*, 4.

[51] "Bon gré, Mal gré." "Willy nilly," whether one likes it or not.

[52] As Le Couteur's ship was bound for Canada not the Cape of Good Hope, it is clear that he was not present when this cruel trick was played.

[53] Lieutenant Colonel John Ross, 28th Foot.

[54] HMS *Comet*, sloop of war, 20 guns, built 1807, sold 1815.

[55] Captain George W. Blamey, RN: lieutenant, 1794; commander, 1802; captain, 1810.

[56] "Gunwale under." The vessel was rolling so hard that the waves were coming over the sides of the ship.

[57] Le Couteur is describing the rocks, gravel and sand being used as ballast in the hold of the ship.

[58] "Poulard grassé." Grass-fed poultry, a delicacy.

# Chapter Three

## "I HAD SEEN WOUNDS AND DEATH IN REAL WAR!"
Nova Scotia and New Brunswick,
*June 1812 to March 1813*

*[21 June 1812]*
It was about half past nine o'clock on a balmy, soft evening, the 21st of June, that we glided gently into Halifax harbour. As the breeze wafted a rich odour of the Spruce Pine, I remarked it to my brother officers. "Oh Yes, Johnny — and see your Dido[1] pointing the Partridges in the Spruce Pines." It was true, nevertheless, the flavour was quite perceptible.

The next morning early We landed, to our great joy, and buried all our troubles in a capital breakfast at Smith's snug Hotel.[2] We called on the Governor, Sir John Coape Sherbrooke[3] — a fine old Martinet. He used to attend the Guard Mounting parades on horseback. One day there was some broken pieces of glass on the parade — when the Quarter Muster of the day was sent for. "D__n You, Sir! How dare you allow broken glass to remain on parade?" "Sir John Sherbrooke, I am not used to be d__ned. I can discharge my duty without such language. I was here this morning to examine the parade, it was not there at that time." Sir John is said never to have sworn at any one since!

The officers of the 98th, 99th [Regiments] and Artillery were very civil, inviting us to all their messes. I found my old friend and Countryman, George Lemprière,[4] the Second Lieutenant on board of the flag ship, the *Africa.*[5] He was most kind, took me to parties at the Cochranes,[6] Heads,[7] Hartshornes,[8] W[illia]m Tucker's, etc. M[ajor] General James Saumarez[9] arrived on the 24th and applied for me to become his Aide de Camp but the fated regimental duty still stood in my way.

### *[26] June, 1812*

On the 26th, I was dining in the Gun room of the *Africa* with Lemprière when it was announced that the *Belvidera*,[10] Frigate, coming in, had made her private Signal. A moment after, an Officer hurried down: "She has no boats, no anchors, and shot holes through her sails!" Up flew all. She soon came alongside, when indeed we saw signs of battle. She had been chased by Commodore Rodgers[11] in the *President*[12] and by an American squadron. They would not run along side of Her, or She must have been taken, but yawed and raked Her but She cut away everything weighty, fired her stern chasers, and got off. It had a fatal effect, however, for it inspired our Jacks with a sad confidence that our small Eight and Thirty gun frigates might cope with their small, disguised line of battle ships, Frigates of 60 Guns, and full of our reckless deserters.[13]

Lieutenant Rainsford[14] of the Grenadier Company of our Regiment came express from Saint John on that, or the following day, with official news of the American declaration of war. On the 30th, we were therefore placed under convoy of the *Indian*,[15] Sloop of War, Captain Jane,[16] and sailed for St. John's in the Bay of Fundy — the wind being fair we hoped to reach it in two days.

### *July, 1812*

On the 3rd of July, a Friday, the *Indian* having spoken the *Juniper*,[17] was informed that there was not an enemy in the Bay of Fundy but, she having caught sight before us of two suspicious rakish looking craft, she hailed us speedily and desired Captain Dennis to prepare all his officers and their luggage to come on board the *Indian*. He also wished our Skipper to give up the clothing for the 104th [Regiment] which He had on freight. This he would not consent to, and it was taken the next day by the *Rover* of Salem, a Privateer of mischievous renown to our trade.[18]

On Saturday, the 4th of July, we were under a press of sail in delightful weather with a gentle breeze just ruffling the water when we made out the two rakish vessels very distinctly to be anything but Merchant vessels.[19] The *Indian* bore down upon them and, when within range, gave them a shot to bring them to, and to show colours, which We had done. Just then it fell calm.

Captain Jane then lowered his Long boat and despatched her under Lieut[enant] Delafons[20] and sixteen men, well-manned and armed with a twelve pounder Carronade[21] in her bow, to bring the nearest to, a fine, low schooner. The Captain in the meanwhile got sweeps out, turned us all to work which we jollily did and we, all hands a long pull together, the forcing pump wetting the Sails to help them draw, swept the Sloop of war Three knots an hour. But Brother Jonathan[22] was sweeping four in his long, low craft.

Nevertheless, Delafons got within pistol shot and gave her a Shot across the bow to bring Her to, which she would not do but hauled closer to what little wind there might be. When he fired into Her — instantly up went the Stars & Stripes and [she] fired Her broadside, three great guns and about Sixty fine small arms, at the boat.

We had volunteered to go with the boat but Capt[ain]. Jane said boarding from a boat was no Soldier's work — if we came to close action, there were plenty of small arms for our amusement. Never shall I forget the beating heart and anxious desire I felt to be aiding our gallant handful engaged with such a fierce disproportion. We were scarcely within Carronade range and had no long guns.[23]

Delafons had got within pistol shot astern of the Schooner. His gun was loaded with round & grape[24] and, at his first discharge, we saw the crowd of men run from the Stern, while our brave fellows kept up a rapid fire of small arms. This lasted for half an hour when the breeze springing up, away went the Clipper, when we soon picked up our boat & Crew with three men wounded, one mortally.[25]

Captain Jane hoisted Sky scrapers and Moon Rakers,[26] studding sails, etc., but both the Yankees, a Sloop and Schooner, had the legs of us in smooth water and were out of sight by night. The Schooner lost several men killed and wounded we afterwards learnt.

On the 8th [of July 1812], we retook a large Mast ship[27] from St. Andrew's and Capt[ain]. Jane being resolved this time not to discover Himself as a Man of War, dirtied one side of the vessel and painted the other black, placed his boats like a Merchantman's with some straw and stuff in them to look business like, struck his lofty masts, unsquared his yards, and contrived most cleverly to disguise his Majesty's ship so as to look most Mercantile.

The ruse told quickly. A splendid brig[28] made us out, hauled up to reconnoitre us. After a while moved in a little more, hauled up again. We kept lolling on our course apparently, we then hauled up Yankee Colours. She did the same, and immediately ran down to know where we were from, [and] ask questions *à la* brother Jonathan, when within hail. The Captain was invited to come on board and take a Mouthful. He did so, a fine, rough spun Sailor. When He placed his foot on our deck and saw the Guns, and Man of

War's men concealed in all directions. "Is this an American Man of War — the *Hornet*[29] I s'pose?" It was a provokingly ill-suited name and we all burst into a laugh! "Britishers, I swear!" As the awful truth broke upon his mind, He danced with rage and tore his hair.

We really felt for the poor fellow for He was owner as well as Captain and pretended He was ruined. However, our kind words and good cheer in the Gun room made Him declare He had known friends not half so kind as his enemies. "Ah Captain", He said once, "If you would let me have a fair start neck and neck, I do not think His Majesty's ship would catch me, barring the Guns." It was quite true — Delafons, who was sent in Her as Prize Master, ran away from us. She had a good cargo and Two thousand five hundred dollars in cash on board which gave me Two pounds, Ten shillings in prize Money,[30] some thirty years afterward, *with which I bought a ring for my wife.*

What strange and new thoughts had then crossed my mind. I had read of battles and of the thrill of actual contest but now I had seen the reality. A brave handful under a dear friend seeking the bubble in the Cannon's mouth.[31] I had seen wounds and death in real war!

### *13 July [1812]*

We made Saint John on the 13th and landed on the Monday afternoon. We all turned out in the new uniform of that day and were looked upon as Dandies of the finest make and the first fashion. The old Uniform had been a long Coatee, with cocked hats worn very low on parades. For Guards: Knee breeches and black gaiters with some fifty little round buttons up their sides; a Sword belt, Gorget and Sash. The Light Companies wore Jackets, wings, with a Cap like a sugar loaf, the peaked Square turned up, a Bugle in front, with long cords and tassels of Gold or Silver, and a Green plume.[32]

The new uniform was a perfect Contrast. A Cap like a straight quart mug only the size of the noddle it was meant to fit — a sort of Screen rising above the front half of it — a very rich Gilt Cap Plate, a Small feather, and very rich cords and Tassels of Gold, intended to secure the Cap from being lost while skirmishing. A short Jacket with pockets so small that a pocket handkerchief in them disfigured one's line while loosish grey overalls with six buttons in two figures like a brace, ornamented the front over pockets in pretence, and six more at bottom, on each side, enabled those appendages to be buttoned over the boots. A vile dress it was for Service, too tight for a run, so that we soon got to grey trowzers. The neat Hessian boot and tight pantaloons, the most dressy of all uniforms, was the evening or Full dress.[33]

There were some of us who prided ourselves on being well got up

*Saint John, New Brunswick, 1835, by Mary G. Hall. Le Couteur served two periods of garrison duty here during the summer of 1812, and thought it a "large town pretty well built."* M.G. Hall/National Archives of Canada/C-30959

merely for the honor of the 104th [Regiment], the double of the Crack Corps,[34] and formed by two of its officers! Well, lounging and reconnoitring, We saw two very pretty women laugh very heartily at our droll caps and clipped tails. "I won't be laughed at in that style", I exclaimed to my Comrade, "I'll kiss my hand to that sweet one." No sooner said than done, tho' my friend said wisely "[don't] do it, Johnny". The deed was done — a heart to be won thought I — the Ladies retired.

I had delivered my letter of introduction at Government House where we were soon marshalled by Major Drummond,[35] our new Commanding officer. General George Stracey Smyth,[36] an *eleve*[37] of the Duke of Kent,[38] and his Equerry received us very politely, with much stately dignity however. After all the information we had to convey had been duly delivered and we made our bows, the General said: "Mr. Le Couteur, Be so good as to stay a moment. You are entrusted to Mrs. Smyth's care, and she desires to see You." I bowed and expressed my gratification at being in such custody in a far distant Country.

He rang the Bell and I was shown into the drawing room. Well thought I, *en passant*,[39] if the dear Lady is only half a dozen years younger than her Lord, I shall have plenty of good stiff advice, and be well kept in order. However a Lady's patronage is always something and that Lady a Governess. I went to the door's threshold, prepared to make my best, my practised bow for, best known to you Gentle reader, I had not only been drilled to march at Marlow but I had been drilled to dance and to bow by that renowned Master of dance and bow, even D'Egville Himself! I had prepared my first, my second, and a repetition of two steps, even a third bow if necessary, with the gentle bend of the Head and the soft "let fall" of the arms. It was meant to be striking, my first appearance in high life abroad.

The Footman announced Lieutenant "Le Cutter". Confusion! The Footman could scarcely close the door for my elbow I felt somewhat rooted to the ground, a rapid retreat was out of the question. I felt my face redder than my new coatee. My sin was before me - I had kissed my hand to the Governor's own wife.

"Mr. Le C. pray to be seated." "Ye'es Ma'am, thank you Madam." I felt like a *chien fouetté*[40] though I perceived the most gentle, the most lovely being before me, my eyes had ever beheld. The Governor's wife might be about Six and Thirty, but her looks gave Her only Thirty. Such glowing auburn hair, in wavy profusion, over soft full, grey eyes — a nose of Grecian purity, a faultless mouth disclosing with bewitching smiles, teeth like pearls, an oval face with a delicate ruddiness, a matchless complexion, a light airy figure, rather below the standard of perfection, but elastic and graceful in gesture. A voice so musical, it was a seraph's when singing. Such was the fair Judge before whom I sat dismayed.

Her dear little girl, an only child, then came in. The new uniform and new young face fortunately attracted her notice. She would see my smart cap and tassels and, as I was ever so fond of and free with children, we were friends in a minute and my chagrin disappeared.

I dined at Government House and was told that, although I was to leave Saint John for Head Quarters at Fredericton tomorrow, I should be held in recollection and should find a home at Gov[ermen]t House.

Saint John is a large town pretty well built, with two or three good streets, and some few good houses in it, but not one of Stone. The barracks are very bad ones. Major Drummond of the 104th commanded the Garrison. He was a splendid looking man, the personification of Rhoderic Dhu,[41] a kind-hearted, noble sort of *liberal* Scotchman!

We left Saint John for Head Quarters on the 15th [of July 1812] in a Sloop, a sort of Government trader between Fredericton and Saint John. It was delightful beyond expression to sail on a beautiful River after the misery we had endured in the Brig, which we had not yet forgotten, even through the comforts of the Man of War.

The Saint John River was the most beautiful I ever saw, the first Twenty Miles you sail up a broad rapid stream, with high bold rocks jutting out on both sides, well covered with Pines, and Brushwood. Above Long Island is the Village of Gagetown when You skirt the Grand Lake, the largest piece of fresh water I had ever seen — indeed it was so to most of us. The land, after leaving the rocky Scenery, is low and well-cultivated and the river is variously interspersed with lovely little Islands, entirely clothed with verdant grass and Noble trees — some more elevated than others and of many diverse forms. On landing on one of them we found quantities of wild Strawberries and raspberries and ate as we pleased without being troubled by any one to drive us away. The further you advance, the more Cultivated is the Country, the land low, but well supplied with Timber, and fine long grass, seemingly much more fertile than about Saint John. It is much more level, more like what we call Meadowland at home. Near Fredericton, which is about eighty miles from Saint John, the views are soft and beautiful, more entirely cultivated than below.

### *July [1812]*

On our arrival we reported ourselves to Colonel Halkett[42] and were most kindly received by a nice corps of brother officers. I was doubled up with a

Brother Lieutenant for Ten days during which time I was introduced to all the Families in Society: Judges Saunders[43] and Bliss,[44] the O'Dells,[45] Robinsons,[46] Phairs,[47] Millers,[48] among whom the most cordial intercourse existed — dinners, Balls and Suppers. However My fate was to be attached to No. 2 Company at Saint John. I had taken the precaution to put in my claim as an old Light Company Officer with Captain Shore,[49] to be appointed to his company on the first Vacancy, which He most kindly promised.

### *27 July [1812]*

On the 27th I again set on my travels in a new fashion — in an Indian Birch Canoe, which I had taken some previous lessons to paddle. Lieutenant Basserer[50] & I with Woodward,[51] a New Brunswick Canoeman, as expert as an Indian, for our helmsman & Pilot — our Portmanteaus and Provisions for lunches, the only ballast.

We paddled off merrily, cheered by our brother officers who promised two Vacancies to the Ensigns[52] — however, "Hee'aiee Hi, Hi", the Indian cheer, "Hi, Hi, Hi" — away sprang the Light Canoe like a thing of life, over the clear stream, at the rate of Ten miles an hour.

We paddled all day and all night also, till we got to the *Grand Bay* when the most terrible Thunderstorm I ever witnessed overtook us. The wind was happily fair and we had placed a low blanket for a sail, on a tree cut for a Mast *en route* which made the Canoe scud like a Nautilus before the gale. Basserer was in the bow, a little in front of the sail. He could not turn to assist and I was between the Mast and the stern where the Helmsman was steering by a paddle for our lives — and a broach to — we were lost, in the now stormy waters. It came on to rain like a deluge, the Blanket got heavy and held the wind like a bag. "Mr. Le C.", said Woodward, "You must lower the blanket or we shall be swamped before we cross the lake. You must place your hands on each gunwale of the canoe, balance your body, and slide close to the Mast then let go the sail steadily and draw it in as you lower." I did as directed, got the Sail down, and even lowered the Mast. "Very well done, Sir! Now you must both bail out the Canoe, as fast as you can, She is getting too deep in the water." This we also did with a bowl and my foraging Cap.

Woodward at length ran us into a little inlet where a woodman's hut afforded us protection, while we wrung our clothes, not dry, but from dripping, got hot spirits and water, emptied our Canoe. The storm having abated we started afresh — not to get chilled, paddled vigorously and arrived at Saint John on the Wednesday evening about 7, more like drowned rats, than two gay Subs.

Major Drummond received me very cordially so did my worthy Captain Maule[53] — the most easy officer on earth. I confess so much so, that my Marlow discipline was sadly hurt when I inspected the Company in the Morning. It was the most slovenly Company in our clean regiment. I took a sly occasion to hint to my Captain that I had been the Senior Under Officer of a Company of one hundred smart lads at Marlow and in the Light Company of the 96th [Regiment], a very smart one. If He would permit me to do so, I would make our Company the smartest in the Corps without any punishments. "Indeed, I don't interfere much with the Men, but if you can do so, without punishments, I shall like it vastly!" "Very well, Sir."

The next day I took four very dirty Soldiers and placed them by the side of the cleanest four. I made the whole laugh at my remarks. "Now give me some pipeclay!" I cleaned their belts, explained how their pouches must be heel balled, and examined their arms, and told them how to burnish them. This took effect — step by step, ours was the cleanest Company. I had risen from *the ranks* at College so nothing was taken amiss!

General and Mrs. Smyth, Major Drummond [and] Major Phillott[54] of the Artillery made our Society very gay although it was now war time and we had drills, Guards and Picquets[55] at night, and the duty was pretty hard, we had none of its horrors. Couper[56] of the Artillery, who had been at Marlow with me, was a delightful acquisition to my personal comfort. He was a most amiable, high-minded, cultivated and religious young man. Time sped happily.

I must relate a shooting anecdote. The Doctor[57] and I got leave for a few days' sport. Dido was of no use because a Pointer is soon lost in the woods where we were to sport. I was to keep close to my Mentor — no, Dennis was called my Mentor and I the young Telemachus — my Apollo, how like one! We shot a few Snipe *en passant* but Partridges or the Wood Spruce Grouse were to be our game. By and by, I saw the old Doctor raise his hand and creep stealthily like an Indian towards his prey. I crept on too. The Doctor had taken off his hat and thrown it aside, to see into the Tree more closely I suppose, or fancying his looks more engaging to the bird than his hat. I crept on closer and closer. "Hush! Hush!" whispered the Medico when — lo! — a wonder! His bald head, which should have been as white as snow seemed a nice brown head of hair. Surely he didn't put on a wig, thought I, not a bit, I saw Him with his bald pate a while ago! Well, I crept nearer to examine his wig, forgetting in my amusement the Covey in the tree. He made a sort of kick or motion back, and put up his hand to me and to his head, away frisked his wig in a cloud of Mosquitoes! I screamed with laughter — off flew the Partridges, and the Doctor screamed with rage at my folly in frightening the Birds.

It is a curious fact, that if you shoot the lower bird in the tree, and shoot *upwards* you may kill the whole Covey, but if you shoot an intermediate Bird, the falling or fluttering bird sets them all on the wing.

I had settled myself very snugly in Lodgings for the winter, when on the sudden, I found myself removed to the Light Company, the object of my ambition, commanded by a smart, intelligent officer.

### *3 September [1812]*

I left Saint John on the 3rd of September very grateful for much kind hospitality. The Gun boat, under the command of a provincial officer, was the slowest conveyance that could be imagined. We were four whole days getting up, against the Stream it is true, where our Canoe had been paddled down by ourselves in Two!

On our passage up we paid a visit to General Coffin,[58] a fine old Veteran who owns a large estate on the Lake shore. He was noble in his hospitality and as the wind was foul, or we fancied it so, we staid to dinner and slept at his house. He would have detained us for a week if we had yielded.

His daughter Sophy is a splendid girl. She and her Father were crossing the Lake one morning when a great Bear attacked them, and would have swamped the boat if Sophy had not stood by the General with discretion and courage. For, while the General was battering Bruin with the Butt end of an oar, Sophy pushed the point of the boat hook into his Eye which made Bruin scratch it and retreat. If I had been a rich Captain I should certainly have tried to captivate, if not capture, such a brave girl![59]

### *4 October [1812]*

Coyne[60] came into my room and announced the heartrending intelligence that my dear friend Couper had been upset in a Birch Canoe and was drowned.[61] What a sad loss to his family. He was possessed of many virtues which few can boast of, with almost too much diffidence in his great talents. A sweet amiable youth. How thankful I was a the escape which Bass and I had in our Canoe in the Storm.!

### *11 October [1812]*

First snow this season. [Visited?] Colonel Gubbins and his wife,[62] old acquaintances at BelleVue.

*Fredericton, New Brunswick, 1853, by William S. Wolfe. Le Couteur was stationed in Fredericton during the winter of 1812-13 and particularly liked the barracks there, which were "as warm and comfortable as possible."* W.S. Wolfe/National Archives of Canada/C-122463

### *23 October [1812]*

The River froze over. General and Mrs. Smyth were constant in their kind attentions. Mrs. Smyth used to send me books to read whenever I was on Guard. The Balls and Grigreys [gregorys], a local name for routs or cards and Ladies' parties, were incessant.

Guard readings: Emma[63] — how suitable; Scott's ballads;[64] the Erle King;[65] Lewellyn;[66] the Eve of St. John;[67] Shakespeare; Sir Charles Grandison,[68] meant to be my model, [and] Scottish border.[69]

### *Xmas Day*

I dined at Gov[ermen]t. house. The General was in high Spirits, full of fun and entertaining anecdotes.[70]

### *31 December [1812]*

Some idea may be entertained of the Society at Fredericton when I relate that I was at Thirty five dinners, evening parties, or balls since I came up here on the 4th of September.

### *13 January [1813]*

The Light Company ordered to march to St. Andrew's tomorrow morning. Packing up smartly. L[ieutenan]ts. Phair[71] and Graves[72] marched with part of the company, L[ieutenan]t. Jobling[73] with Twenty more men the 15th. Captain Shore and I to march the next day. Countermanded after being in Suspense to the 18th when the General held a Levee and gave a General Ball in the evening when He told Shore we should not move, to our Joy!

### *28 January [1813]*

The Batchelor officers gave a grand ball in our Mess room, which cost us only Five pounds each. It was very handsome, the Ladies, our friends, however made all our Jellies and ornaments, we sending them the materials.

### *5 February [1813]*

Both good and bad news we all thought. The 104th Regiment got orders from Quebec to march for Canada without delay — the Light Company to form the Advance Guard and to march on Thursday the 11th.[74]

Mrs. Smyth most kindly made me a present of various furs, a Cap, leather Jacket, thick flannels, and a variety of Comforts, portable soups, sufficient for our long march of four hundred miles, through Snow and endless forest. We had all become so intimate with the various families — the

Robinsons, Bliss[es], O'Dells, Saunders, Millers, Coffins, Hailes,[75] that it was high time we should quit a place in which we were thoroughly domesticated.

The General and Mrs. Smyth had an only daughter who was about Ten Years of age — a very clever child extremely forward and womanly in all her motions from being the spoiled child of two fond parents. The dear child had taken a strong fancy to me, and through our barracks were above a mile from Govern[men]t house, she once, on a quarrel with her Governess, ran away to my quarters, to my great consternation and horror. Moreover she would insist upon having a lesson of drawings in Colors,[76] before I could induce Her to return. I was on thorns for fear some of my playful brother officers should have caught me at my task, but fortunately Missy got back without being discovered and Governess and Mama, very delighted to have the child safe, did not inform the Governor of the escapade.

One night it was freezing very hard, the Thermometer somewhere like 30 degrees below zero. I had the Main Guard and visited my Sentries about two in the Morning. I had a Corporal and a file[77] of men with me. The most distant sentry was placed near a wood which was our most vulnerable point from the United States — if a moose could have travelled in such intolerable cold. When I got near the Sentry, He never challenged us. I went close to Him and saw He was staggering and I might have snatched his Arms from Him. I fancied He was in liquor, had Him relieved, and ordered Him to go thro' the facings in the Guard room but he appeared quite tipsy though He denied having drank any Spirits. However the Sergeant as well as Myself and the visiting Corporal fancied Him to be intoxicated. I desired him to lie down and in the morning took him in as a Prisoner.

Drunkenness on a main guard, and on Sentry, was a most heinous offence — however the man being of fair character was ordered to be tried by a regimental, not a garrison Court Martial, which would have placed his life in danger, to which I should have been highly adverse.[78] I gave my evidence as Prosecutor, the Sergeant corroborated my evidence, but when the Corporal who went round the Sentries with me came to depose, He swore that the man never staggered, was not drunk, indeed was quite sober. The Court looked at me with astonishment. I felt quite odd, indeed could scarcely believe the evidence of my own senses.

I reflected a little, then said to the President: "I believe, Sir, that the Corporal being French Canadian, may be a Roman Catholic. Be so good as to ask Him whether He considers the Oath which has been administered to Him as binding on his conscience?" "No." "Now be so good as to have Him sworn on a Catholic Missal and on the Holy Cross according [to] his worship." He was thus sworn, and then confirmed every word I had said. The Corporal was sent to the Guard house by the Colonel — tried and broke for perjury.

Now upon reflection after many years, and much military reading, I suspect two great, and one of them very unfortunate, mistakes were made. I now believe from what I have felt and read about cold that the poor Sentry was chilled to a stand still and benumbed, not intoxicated, and that not a soul, Canadians[79] or New Brunswickers, should suggest the possibility of it, is to me a wonder to this day. As a youth of Seventeen, I could have no idea of it.

Next I question whether the man should have been tried for perjury — because in his Conscience, He only told a lie. When sworn on his own volume of faith, had he spoken falsely, it would have been perjury.

I confess that I had a sort of instinctive horror of corporal punishment. The tyranny and brutality of our Usher at High Wycombe had implanted a rooted objection to it in my mind which led me always to punish men myself lightly rather than report them and bring them to Court Martial. My plan worked admirably for never were more kind or more devoted Soldiers. They understood my meaning perfectly, and appreciated it — their honor was mine!

The punishments at this period, throughout the British army, were tremendous in the extreme. Our worthy Colonel was rather averse to them, his brave Scotch heart held for his men when He thought duty required the lash. Not so, others. In a corps in Garrison with us in Jersey, in which My Old Butler and my Father before me, was a Private — a dirty Button or a foul belt, would lead men to a Court Martial and to Two or three hundred lashes.

On one occasion at Fredericton, a private of the Light Company had offended deeply. He was condemned to receive three hundred lashes. He was paraded and placed on the Triangle close in Front of the Light Company. He was a stout, active fellow, *on bon point*.[80] The lash lacerated his back speedily and the blood flowed freely. He stood close in front of me, the inward groan, at each lash, from being stifled, went sufficiently to my heart but, soon after, the Drummer, in swinging his Cat of Nine Tails, switched a quantity of his blood over my Face and Belts. I fainted away like a Sick girl to my own great horror and Confusion but it was not unnatural after all. The Officers laughed at me but the men did not.

Once I saw a Grenadier receive nine hundred and some lashes, put on his shirt, shake himself like a Hero and walk away apparently unconcerned. What a pity to ruin such a bold Spirit and fine Constitution.

One of the punished men deserted from Fredericton and fancied, poor fellow, that He could make his way through eighty or ninety miles of the aboriginal forest to the United States. At the end of four days He was found in a dying state by some of the MicMac Indians who dressed his sores in their clever way, saved his life, and brought Him to the barracks. He was a fine young Man when in health but in Him the human form divine was marred, completely marred. Every, I verily believe, every part of his poor Body, had been preyed upon by myriads of Insects small and large — Sand flies, Mosquitoes, Bugs, Worms and Beetles. His face was a mass of inflamed sores, no eyes distinguishable — it made one Sick and weep to see Him. His crime was lost sight of in his misfortune.

In a day or two, He could walk perfectly and the Colonel most wisely and judiciously, to the great joy of every Officer, gave up all ideas of a Court Martial but he paraded the Regiment in great form, made an appropriate speech on the heinousness of desertion, said He would on this occasion spare further punishment because that which the Deserter had brought upon Himself, was far greater than even the law would administer. He would shew them their unfortunate Comrade. The ranks were opened to double distance and the Front rank faced about. When the Prisoner was marched slowly through the ranks, there was an unrepressed groan moving along the line, as the hideous object strode along in his filthy overdress, which was put over his clean underclothes for the occasion. There were no more desertions through the woods.

I had suggested a system of Prizes to my Captain in the 96th Regiment who liked the idea. He would have carried it out had I remained with Him, because he saw the effect of them on the Jersey boys. But though I was anxious to do the same in the 104th [Regiment], I could find no one to comprehend me. Promotion was fancied to be sufficient encouragement.[81]

At length the day arrived for leaving dear Fredericton where the Regiment had been at home literally. Our noble barracks, for though they were wooden, I had never seen any so good, were as warm and comfortable as possible, close to a fine River, with a fine parade ground, good stables — in short, comforts of all sorts which a prolonged Head Quarter establishment had created.[82] The mess was the best I had ever seen, wines old as in a private Cellar. The messing was very cheap, from 1st to 21st September, 1812, My account[s] show £3-11-0. A Partridge, Sixpence. To an Indian dressing an Otter skin, 1/3. A Hearth Rug, 5/. A Pair of Snow shoes, 14/6. A pair of moccasins, 5/.[83]

## Jobling under the Ice

Lieutenant Jobling of our Light Company had left after a ball at Government house, Fredericton, while in an overheated state from dancing, to return to the Barracks by skating down the River. The ice was very good, fresh made, on which many had been in the morning. It sometimes happened that the ice broke into a long fissure all across the river on a change of wind. Jobling never gave the occurrence a thought, but skated off at top speed.

Presently He found Himself plunged deep in the water, quite under the ice on the opposite side of the fissure. It was an awful position, but feeling confidence in his good powers of swimming He paused an instant to feel which way the stream was taking Him, struck out *against it* with his head rubbing below the ice when, in a moment, He felt himself rise above it. He then struck towards the shore, got on the ice and skated at speed safely to the barracks where some hot brandy and water set Him right. The fissure or break was some Eight or Ten yards wide.

One evening after a party, being Subaltern of the day, I went visiting rounds, about 2 o'clock after midnight.[84] It seemed a fine, clear night in December, cold below zero but calm. I took no patrol with me but after visiting all the Guards and Sentries about the Town, started for the Government house Guard. It then began to snow pretty sharply. By the time I had crossed the common when I got into the closed road near the Governor's, [it] was not traceable, however, with [two] or three falls off the road into the deep Snow, I visited the Guard, turned and hasted back.

It was now snowing so heavily that I could see nothing but the large glare of the moon's beams. The road was knee deep in snow. When I reached the common I knew my chance of finding the opposite opening leading into Fredericton would be small indeed if I wandered off the road so on I pushed through the snow, it was too deep for walking. Presently I got off the road and fell into the depth on the side of it. I crept onto it, walked on straight, then plunged into the deep snow on the other side. This I repeated a dozen times or more, till at length I could not find the road, but kept pushing through nearly four feet of snow for an hour when, just as I was going to lie down from exhaustion and cold, to sleep the sleep of death, I caught a glimmering of light as I was recommending my Soul to my Creator. This gave me a new strength and I found the opening leading to the Town.

## Notes

[1] Dido was the daughter of the King of Tyre who fled from that city and founded Carthage about 850 B.C. Figuratively, "Dido" might mean "fugitive" but as Le Couteur, uses the name frequently to indicate a hunting dog, possibly his own animal was named "Dido".

[2] "Smith's snug Hotel." This was actually the Prince Edward Hotel on Hollis Street, Halifax. Founded in 1794, it was run by a man named Smith and his wife, Rachel, who being of "athletic proportions" sometimes intimidated travellers. The Prince Edward was in business until the 1820s, see George Mullane, "Old inns and coffee houses of Halifax, Nova Scotia," Nova Scotia Historical Society, *Collections*, XXII (1933), 1-24.

[3] Lieutenant General Sir John Coape Sherbrooke (1764-1830), see *DCB*, VI, 712-716. General Sherbrooke was appointed Lieutenant Governor of Nova Scotia and commander of the forces in the Atlantic provinces in 1811. He served in this capacity until 1816 when he became Governor General of British North America which post he held until 1818.

[4] Lieutenant George Ourry Lemprière, RN: lieutenant, 1807; commander, 1813; captain, 1825.

[5] HMS *Africa*, ship of the line, 64 guns. Launched in 1761, she served in 1812 as the flagship of Vice Admiral Herbert Sawyer, Commander in Chief, America and West Indies Station, RN. She was broken up in 1814.

[6] Possibly William Cochran or Cochrane (1757-1833) and his wife, Rebecca, see *DCB*, VI, 156-158. Cochran was a professor and sometime President of King's College, Windsor, Nova Scotia. Le Couteur may have met their son, Andrew Cochran (1792-1849), later secretary to Sir George Prevost, Governor General of British North America.

[7] Possibly either Captain Michael Head, RN (d. 1844), a captain on the Halifax station or his brother Samuel Head (1776-1837), a physician and pharmacist, see *DCB*, VII, 390-392.

[8] Either Lawrence Harteshorne (1755-1822), a prominent Halifax merchant, see *DCB* VI, 312-314, or his son Lawrence (1786-1865), also in business in the city.

[9] Major General Sir Thomas Daniel Saumarez (1760-1845). Brother of Admiral James Saumarez, Thomas commanded the garrison at Halifax from 1812 to 1813. In 1813-1814, he also served as Commander in Chief of New Brunswick.

[10] HMS *Belvidera*, frigate, 36 guns, Captain Richard Byron, RN. Launched in 1809, she was sailing off New York when chased by an American squadron. *Belvidera* had a long career; entering harbour service in 1846, she was still in commission in 1906 when she was sold out of the navy.

[11] Commodore John Rodgers, USN (1771-1838). One hour after he received news of the declaration of war against Britain by his government on 21 June 1812, Rodgers sailed for New York with a squadron of six warships hoping to intercept a large British convoy from the West Indies. Instead, he fell in with Byron's *Belvidera* which escaped after a day-long chase. Rodgers personally aimed and fired what was probably the first shot of the War of 1812 from a bow gun on his flagship, the *President,* at 4.30 A.M., 23 June 1812. See Theodore Roosevelt, *The Naval War of 1812* (New York, 1882; reprinted Annapolis, 1987), 87-91.

[12] USS *President*, frigate, 44 guns. Built in 1800, the *President* was one of the large American frigates that proved superior to British vessels of the same type. She was captured by the Royal Navy in 1815 and sold in 1817.

[13] The Royal Navy's confident attitude evaporated after a disastrous series of single-ship engagements against the U.S. Navy. Some British officers attributed the Americans' success to the fact that British deserters were serving on board their ships but their success actually resulted from superior warships, better gunnery and good leadership. In early 1813 a desperate Admiralty forbade British frigates, most of which were armed with 18-pdr. guns, to engage single-handed the larger American vessels of the same type armed with 24-pdr. guns. See William Clowes, *A Naval History from the Earliest Times to the Present*, vol. VI (London, 1901), 58-62.

The Royal Navy's luck changed on 1 June 1813 when HMS *Shannon*, Captain Philip Broke, captured the USS *Chesapeake* after a short but bloody action. For a study of single-ship actions of the War of 1812, see H.F. Pullen, *The Shannon and the Chesapeake* (Toronto, 1970).

[14] Probably Lieutenant Andrew Rainsford, 104th Foot (1784-1868). Both Andrew and his brother Charles (1788-1822) were officers in the regiment and the sons of a prominent New Brunswick Loyalist. See Charles Rainsford's account of the winter march of the 104th Foot in the *Saint John Daily Sun* 23 August 1889.

[15] HMS *Indian*, sloop of war, 18 guns, launched Bermuda, 1805, sold in 1817.

[16] Lieutenant and Commander Henry Jane, RN: lieutenant, 1800; commander, 1810; captain, 1825.

[17] HMS *Juniper*, schooner, 10 guns, Lieutenant Vassal, RN, launched in Bermuda in 1809, sold in November 1814.

[18] Le Couteur is mistaken here, it was not the *Rover* but the privateer *Madison* of Salem, Mass., that captured Transport No. 50 carrying the 104th Foot's uniforms across the Bay of Fundy. On examination, the crew of the *Madison* found the transport's cargo to consist of "one hundred casks of gunpowder, eight hundred and eighty suits of uniforms for the 104th British Regiment ... some bales of superfine cloths for officer's uniforms, ten casks of wine, drums, trumpets, and other camp equipage." See George Coggeshall, *History of the American Privateers and Letters-of-Marque, During Our War with England in the years 1812, 13 and 14* (New York, 1861), 39.

Ironically, these uniforms ended up being worn by American soldiers. At this time, the musicians of the U.S. Army wore red coats trimmed with blue rather than the more usual blue coats trimmed with red. There was a shortage of red cloth in the United States and, on 22 January 1813, Callendar Irvine, the official in charge of uniform procurement for the U.S. government, informed the Secretary of War that "I have purchased a short time since Eleven hundred Coats taken in a vessel captured by a Salem Privateer which coats were intended for the 104th Regt. at Quebeck [*sic*]. They are red coats, white or buff collars, cuffs & Tips handsomely decorated .... might they not be issued without alteration except for the buttons, for the musicians." See U.S. National Archives, Record Group 92, Commissary General of Purchases, Letter Book A, p. 293, Irvine to Monroe, 22 January 1814. The Secretary of War approved the suggestion and the 104th's coats were issued to Americans.

[19] These "rakish looking vessels" were the privateers, *Polly* and *Dolphin* out of Salem. See Coggeshall, *American Privateers*, 39-40.

[20] Lieutenant William Delafons, RN.

[21] A carronade was a type of naval ordnance designed to fire a large projectile a short distance. First cast by the Caron Company of Scotland in 1779, carronades were short and squat in appearance and were ideal close-range weapons in naval battles. They were designated, as was all smoothbore ordnance, by the weight of the shot they fired — thus a 12-pdr. carronade fired a roundshot weighing twelve pounds.

[22] "Brother" or "Cousin Jonathan" were British terms of derision for Americans that dated from the Revolutionary War and implied a backward, clumsy, bumbling oaf.

[23] "Long guns." Guns were the main type of naval ordnance and were designed to throw a projectile the farthest distance with the maximum impact velocity. Long in form compared to carronades, they were also designated by the weight of the roundshot they fired. When Le Couteur states that the *Indian* "had no long guns", he means she was armed entirely with carronades.

[24] "Round and grape." Roundshot was the proverbial "cannon ball." Grape shot consisted of several small lead shot placed in tiers around a wooden spindle and covered with a canvas bag. It resembled nothing so much as a bunch of grapes, hence its name. When fired, the bag disintegrated producing a lethal spray of small shot that wreaked havoc on human beings and ships' rigging.

[25] Naturally, the American account of this action is somewhat different. According to Coggeshall,

> ... the Polly and Dolphin privateers discovered a ship and brig in company, both of which they took to be merchantmen, and their determination was in the first place to board the ship, but having proceeded nearly within gunshot of her, discovered she was an English sloop-of-war of twenty-two guns [the *Indian*], when she immediately crowded all sail and stood for the Polly,

firing several shots, which, however, did not reach her. It afterwards became calm, when the sloop of war manned out her launch, and several boats with about forty men; coming within musket shot, she gave three cheers, and commenced a brisk fire of musketry and one four-pound cannon, which the Polly immediately returned with such a tremendous fire of musketry and langrage, that in a few minutes the launch was silenced and struck her colors, and the other boats were glad to return to their ships; the sloop-of-war being nearly within gun-shot, the privateer took to her sweeps and succeeded in making her escape. (*American Privateers,* 39-40)

[26] "Sky scrapers and Moon rakers." Sailors' names for light, studding or extra sails that were set above the main sails in calm weather.

[27] This was the British bark *William*, which was sent into Halifax. See the *Royal Gazette and New Brunswick Advertizer*, Saint John, 13 July 1812.

[28] This was the American brig *Mars* from Portugal bound for Portland. See the *Royal Gazette and New Brunswick Advertizer*, Saint John. 13 July 1812.

[29] USS *Hornet*, sloop of war, 18 guns, built in 1805. She foundered with all hands in the Gulf of Mexico in September 1829.

[30] During this period, merchant ships or enemy military equipment captured by the forces of the Crown were evaluated and, whether purchased by the Crown or private individuals, a portion of the profits were distributed among the sailors or soldiers who participated in the capture according to a complex system of shares. The use of the prize money system persisted in the British (and Commonwealth) armed forces until the end of the Second World War. During the twentieth century, however, prize money was deposited in a general fund which was used to succour the families of servicemen who lost their lives.

[31] "Seeking the bubble in the Cannon's mouth." This is a quote from Shakespeare, *As You Like It*, Act II, Scene vii, line 139: "Seeking the bubble reputation even in the cannon's mouth."

[32] Le Couteur is describing the uniform of the British infantry prior to 1811. As a light company officer, Le Couteur wore wings on both shoulders, not the single epaulette on his left shoulder that his rank would normally have dictated.

[33] Here Le Couteur describes the new uniform for British infantry prescribed by the General Orders of December 1811. He is wearing this uniform, with his light company officer's wings, in the portrait which illustrates this book.

[34] "Double of the Crack Corps." A reference to the regimental number of the 104th, which was double that of the 52nd (Oxfordshire) Regiment of Light Infantry, an elite unit. Their number being the exact double, the 104th regarded itself as being twice as good as the 52nd.

[35] Major William Drummond, 104th Foot (d. 1814). William Drummond plays a major part in Le Couteur's memories of the war and is worthy of a longer than

usual introduction. He was the fifth son of John Drummond of Keltie, Perthshire. He began his military career with the Bredalbane Fencibles but transferred to the regular army, obtaining a commission in the 2nd West India Regiment and later the 60th Foot. Drummond survived fourteen years of service in the West Indies and was awarded a one hundred guinea sword from Lloyds of London for animating the crew of a merchantman on which he was a passenger to successfully repel the attacks of two French privateers. He exchanged into the New Brunswick Fencibles in 1809 as a major. For an account of his life, see Donald E. Graves, "William Drummond and the battle of Fort Erie," *Canadian Military History* I (1992), 25-44.

Drummond impressed everyone who met him. Dunlop described him as "everything that could be required in a soldier; brave, generous, open-hearted and good natured, he added to all these the talents of a first-rate tactician." See William Dunlop, *Tiger Dunlop's Upper Canada* (Toronto, 1967), 40.

Captain Jacques Viger of the Canadian Voltiguers, who served with Drummond in the spring of 1813, was eloquent about this "brave and excellent officer" and described him as "above the medium in height, had a dignified appearance, regular and clear-cut features and a charming expression .... He is easy of access and not at all repellent in manner as is so often the case with officers of his rank and even junior rank .... So many estimable qualities, together with his reputation for courage .... caused him to be idolized." See *Reminiscences of the War of 1812-1814. Being Portions of the Diary of a Captain of the "Voltiguers Canadiens" While in Garrison at Kingston, etc. Translated from the French by J.L. Hubert Neilson, M.D.* (Kingston, 1895), 10-11.

[36] Major General George Stracey Smyth (1767-1823), see DCB, VI, 723-728. Smyth was an officer of the 7th Foot, commanded by the Duke of Kent. He became a royal protégé and followed Kent to Canada where he served on the duke's staff. In 1812 Smyth was appointed lieutenant governor and, except for brief periods, served in that capacity from 1812 until his death at Fredericton in 1823.

[37] "Elève." A student or protégé.

[38] Edward Augustus, Duke of Kent and Strathearn (1767-1820), see DCB, V, 296-298. The fourth son of George III, Edward entered the army at an early age and became colonel of the 7th Foot in 1789. He was a thorough martinet; problems with his subordinates clouded his military career and ultimately curtailed it. From 1791 to 1799 Kent was in Canada and served as commander of forces in the maritime colonies from 1794 to 1799. The standard biography is David Duff, *Edward of Kent* (London, 1938, reprinted 1973).

[39] "En passant." In passing.

[40] "Chien fouetté." Whipped dog.

[41] "Roderick Dhu." A character in Walter Scott's epic poem, *The Lady of the Lake* published in 1810. An adventurous outlaw and bandit chief, Dhu was nonetheless a man of strict honour.

[42] Colonel Alexander Halkett (1775-1851), commanding officer of the 104th Foot. Halkett joined the regiment in 1810 and in 1813 marched six of its companies to Kingston where he had a series of disagreements with Lieutenant General Sir George Prevost, the commander in chief, and Major General Francis De Rottenburg that caused him to apply for an extended leave of absence. See NAC, RG 8 I, vol. 165, p. 171, Halkett to Torrens, 30 May 1813. Although he later received a brevet promotion to brigadier general, Halkett never returned to the 104th.

A member of the upper stratum of New Brunswick society who met Halkett at this time described him as a man "very much given to drink and appears to want common understanding, but is of a good family." See W.O. Raymond, ed., *Winslow Papers, A.D. 1776-1828* (Boston, 1972), 668, Penelope Winslow to Edward Winslow, 6 June 1811.

[43] Judge John Saunders (1754-1834), see *DCB*, VI, 683-687. Saunders, a Loyalist, was one of the largest landowners in New Brunswick and judge of the Supreme Court of the province as well as a member of the appointed Executive Council that advised the governor. Saunders became chief justice of New Brunswick in 1822.

[44] Judge Jonathan Bliss (1742-1822), see *DCB*, VI. A prominent Loyalist and Attorney General of New Brunswick, Bliss served as Chief Justice of the province from 1808 to 1822 and was President of the Executive Council.

[45] Reverend Jonathan Odell (1733-1818) and his wife Anne (see *DCB*, V, 628-631) and probably their son William Franklin Odell (1774-1848) see *DCB*, VII, 657-659, and his wife Elizabeth. Jonathan Odell was the Provincial Secretary, Registrar of Deeds and Clerk of the Executive Council.

[46] John Robinson (1761-1828), see *DCB*, VI, 654-655, and his wife Elizabeth. Robinson was Speaker of the House of Assembly of New Brunswick.

[47] Probably Andrew Phair, a Loyalist of Fredericton and Postmaster of New Brunswick and his son, Lieutenant William Barry Phair (1783-1853) of the 104th Foot, who later succeeded his father as Postmaster of the province.

[48] Possibly Stephen Miller of Fredericton, a prominent Loyalist or his son, Edward Winslow Miller (1773-1847), a magistrate for York County, New Brunswick.

[49] Captain George Shore, 104th Foot (1787-1851), see *DCB*, VIII, 801-803. Shore joined the 104th when it was still the New Brunswick Fencibles and obtained a captaincy in 1810. In 1815 he married Ariana, the eldest daughter of Judge John Saunders of the provincial Supreme Court. Shore was a protégé of Smyth and had a long and distinguished career in provincial politics and militia matters.

[50] Lieutenant Rene-Leonard Besserer, 104th Foot (1783-1823). He spelled his name Besserer but Le Couteur usually calls him Bass or Basserer. On the Besserer family in Canada, see P.-G. Roy, "Les Besserer de la province de Québec," *Bulletin des recherches historiques* (Lévis), vol. xxiii (1917), 30-31.

[51] According to the roll of enlisted men of the 104th Foot contained in W.A. Squires,

*The 104th Regiment of Foot* (Fredericton, 1962), there were no less than six soldiers named Woodward serving in the ranks of the regiment.

[52] Under the complex promotion system of the British army at this time, the Duke of York, as commander in chief, had the right to fill vacancies caused by the deaths of officers on active service, other than deaths in combat. In practice, however, these vacancies were usually filled by regimental seniority, thus, the most senior ensigns of the regiment would be promoted to any positions become vacant by the drowning of either Le Couteur or Besserer, both lieutenants.

[53] Captain John Maule, 104th Foot (1779-1837). Although Le Couteur is somewhat critical of him, Maule may not have had much time for his company because he was also brigade major at Saint John.

[54] Major Henry Phillott, RA (1784-1839). Phillott had served in Flanders in 1793, Holland in 1799 and Martinique in 1808. He later reached the rank of major general.

[55] A picquet or picket was small detachment of troops stationed outside a garrison or camp for security.

[56] Second Lieutenant Alexander Couper, RA. Some sources spell his name Cooper.

[57] Probably Surgeon Thomas Emerson, 104th Foot, see *DCB*, VII, 274-278.

[58] Lieutenant General John Coffin (1751-1838), see *DCB*, VII, 197-199. A Loyalist from Boston, Coffin fought in the Revolutionary War and attained the rank of major. He settled in New Brunswick and became one of the largest landowners in the province and a powerful political figure. Coffin served twenty-five years in the Legislative Assembly before being appointed to the Executive Council of the province. Although on half pay most of his life, Coffin continued to obtain promotion through seniority and ended his life as a lieutenant general although he saw no active service after 1783. During the War of 1812, he raised the New Brunswick Regiment of Fencible Infantry.

At this point in his text, Le Couteur adds the note: "His Son Vice Admiral Coffin with his daughters dined at BelleVue with us on the __ August, 1860."

[59] Here Le Couteur adds a note: "Sophy Coffin is now a widow, Mrs. Barrett."

[60] Ensign James Coyne, 104th Foot (1789-1816).

[61] The *Royal Gazette and New Brunswick Advertizer* of Saint John informed its readers on 14 October 1812 that "It is with regret we have also to record the death of Lieut. A. Cooper of the Royal Artillery, on Sunday the 4th inst.... Captain McLauchlan, R.E., Lieut. Cooper, and a Soldier, were proceeding to Fredericton in an Indian canoe, and on which they had set a sail; when at the upper end of Long Island, a flaw of wind unfortunately upset the canoe and Lt. C. was drowned. The other two with some difficulty reached the shore."

[62] Lieutenant Colonel Joseph Gubbins (1777-1832), Inspecting Field Officer of Militia in New Brunswick and his wife Charlotte. Gubbins kept a journal of his travels

through the province in 1811-1813, see Howard Temperley, ed., *Lieutenant Colonel Joseph Gubbins. New Brunswick Journals of 1811 & 1813* (Fredericton, 1980).

[63] Emma Plantagenet or the "Saxon" was a character in Robert Southey's epic poem *Madoc*, published in 1805.

[64] Probably a reference to Walter Scott's *Minstrelsy of the Scottish Border* (3 vols., London, 1802-1803).

[65] The Erle King was the malevolent spirit of mischief in the Black Forest area of Germany. Le Couteur is possibly reading an English translation of the German *Sir Olaf and the Erl-King's Daughter.*

[66] Lewellyn was the protagonist in Southey's *Madoc.*

[67] This probably a reference to Walter Scott's epic poem, *The Bride of Triemain; or the Vale of St. John.*

[68] Sir Charles Grandison was the protagonist of Samuel Richardson's early novel, *The History of Sir Charles Grandison*, published in 1754. Grandison was meant to be the perfect hero, a union of good Christian and English gentleman. The book was not everybody's cup of tea — Robert Burns complained that Richardson's characters were "beings of some other world, & however they may captivate the unexperienced, romantic fancy of a boy or girl, they will ever, in proportion as we have made human nature our study, disgust our riper minds." See Burns to John Moore, 28 February 1791, in J.D. Ferguson, ed., *The Letters of Robert Burns: 1790-1806* (Oxford, 1931), 57.

[69] Probably a reference to Scott's *Minstrelsy of the Scottish Border.*

[70] Not everyone shared Le Couteur's warm opinion of the Smyths. Penlope Winslow, member of a prominent New Brunswick Loyalist family, wrote that Smyth "is not very popular. He is a stiff, pedantic old thing — his wife, young, handsome, gay and thoughtless — quite unfit to be at the head of such a society as this." See Penelope Winslow to Edward Winslow, 20 November 1812, in Raymond, ed., *The Winslow Papers*, 676.

[71] Lieutenant William B. Phair, 104th Foot.

[72] Lieutenant Sharpland Graves, 104th Foot (d. 1813).

[73] Lieutenant George Jobling, 104th Foot (b. 1790).

[74] As it turned out, the light company did not leave Fredericton until 21 February 1813, see Chapter IV.

[75] Probably the family of Captain Harris W. Hailes, 104th Foot (1752-1819) and his wife Isabella (Cooke) Hailes. Hailes was a brevet lieutenant colonel and brigade major of the troops at Fredericton in 1812-1813.

[76] At this time, topographical sketching was an essential talent for all officers because of the lack of accurate maps. For this reason, drawing was taught as a subject at

both the Junior and Senior Departments of the Royal Military College and many British officers became accomplished artists.

[77] A file is a group of soldiers ranged one behind each other. It can also mean a sub-unit of two or three men.

[78] This is a reference to the fact that a regimental court martial could impose a maximum penalty of only three hundred lashes while a garrison court martial could order up to 999 lashes, with sometimes fatal results.

[79] Le Couteur is using the term "Canadians" here, as he does throughout his journal, in its original sense of French Canadians or francophones. Possibly he also used the term to mean Acadians from New Brunswick.

[80] "On bon point." In good form or in good style.

[81] This proposal requires some explanation. The Jersey militia used a system of awards rather than punishments to encourage its soldiers. Le Couteur wanted to introduce such a system into his former regiment, the 96th Foot, because his company commander saw its positive effect on the militia. The reaction in the 104th was much cooler.

[82] Unfortunately these barracks were burned to the ground on 1 May 1815.

[83] As discussed in the introduction, Le Couteur had a disposable income of about six shillings a day, about £110 per year. In contrast, a private received a shilling a day from which so many deductions were made for uniforms, equipment, etc., that he often received but a few pence for each day he spent in the army.

Typical annual civilian income at this time was as follows: shopkeeper, £150; farmer and clergyman, £120; skilled artisan, £55; miner, £40, and farm labourer, £30. See J.B. Priestley, *The Prince of Pleasure and his Regency, 1811-1820* (London, 1969), 145.

[84] Le Couteur adds a note at this point: "lost in the Snow the last night. Ord[erly]. Off[ice]r." This implies that the incident he is describing took place on the last night before the regiment left Fredericton for Upper Canada.

# *Chapter Four*

## "WE MUST MARCH FORTY YEARS BEFORE WE HALT!"
## Overland to Upper Canada, *February to April 1813*[1]

It cannot be denied, that at the breaking out of war with the United States, in the month of June 1812, Sir George Prevost[2] found himself very inadequately provided with troops to defend the extensive line of frontier under his command, being upwards of eleven hundred miles from Quebec to Michilimackinac, and assailable at many points, particularly all along the river St. Lawrence from Cornwall up to Kingston and along the Niagara Frontier from Fort George to Fort Erie. His disposable force of regular troops did not exceed three thousand men to guard all the important points of this very prolonged base.[3] Indeed, it was currently reported at the commencement of the war that the highest authorities of the country were of opinion that Upper Canada would not be maintained with this inadequate force. However, the judicious and firm measures of the gallant General Brock,[4] assisted by the then formidable Indian force, which the General well knew how to humour and to wield, saved the Upper Province from being occupied by the enemy in 1812.

The imposing preparation made by the United States for the campaign of 1813 induced Sir George Prevost to run the chance of weakening his force in New Brunswick, which was considered less assailable than Upper Canada. Sir George Prevost therefore determined that the 104th Regiment should perform a winter march from New Brunswick to Canada, which was effected as follows. Major-General Smyth, who commanded in New Brunswick, had received private information that the regiment was to march for Canada, which he kept secret, though the frequent drills and marches it performed by companies or as a corps in snow-shoes, it was evidently being prepared for some movement. On the 5th of February a garrison order announced the intended march. It was hailed by men and officers with enthusiasm as an effort yet unknown in British warfare and therefore well worthy of British soldiers to accomplish.[5]

It must here be observed that the regiment was admirably composed for the service, having been raised in Nova Scotia and New Brunswick, principally in the latter province, from the descendants of the veterans who had served in the former war, a class of loyal settlers, equally attached to the soil and to Old England. There were also a considerable number of Canadians in it, so that these, as well as the New Brunswickers being, as it were, indigenous to the country were thoroughly fitted to endure cold and hardships; good axemen, able to build a log hut with an axe alone; good boatmen, good marksmen, many of them as expert as Indians in a canoe, and as alert as hunters on snow-shoes. The *morale* of the corps was not at all inferior to its *physique*, — there is a characteristic cheerfulness in the Canadian soldier, inherited from his French ancestry, which being lively and good tempered, tended much towards lightening the labours of a heavy march, or the hardships of a campaign, and accorded perfectly with the dogged and varied characters of the English, Irish and Scotch, which completed the regiment.[6]

There had already fallen a greater quantity of snow than had been known during the nine preceding years and the weather was remarkably cold. On the 4th or 5th of February [1813], the thermometer had been as low as 17 degrees below zero. It had been understood that the Indians or natives were to have been sent on to construct wigwams or huts to shelter the men in at every fifteen miles distance, in order to relieve them from the fatigue of hutting themselves at the close of a long day's march but, by some misunderstanding, this was not carried into effect.

Every arrangement being completed, and the regiment in good marching order, some detachments having already come a hundred miles up to Fredericton, Colonel Halkett, with the head-quarters and the grenadier company, marched on the 16th February, 1813[7]; a battalion company following on each succeeding day and the light company, forming the rearguard, on Sunday the 21st [of February, 1813].

It may not be deemed altogether irrelevant to state, that on quitting Fredericton, the whole of the officers felt the deepest regret at parting from a circle of society that had treated them with the greatest kindness and cordiality; where a British uniform, worn with credit and conduct, was a sure passport, without a further introduction, to the friendly hospitality of the worthy inhabitants of New Brunswick.

I shall never forget the morning parade of that Sunday for, although we marched with the best intentions, it was impossible not to feel, in a certain degree, low spirited as our bugles[8] struck up the merry air, "The Girls we leave behind us",[9] most of our gallant fellows being, as it proved, destined never to revisit their sisters or sweethearts.

The company presented a most unmilitary appearance as it marched without arms arms or knapsacks, in Indian file, divided into squads, so many to each Toboggan, the rear of it being nearly half a mile from the front.[10] It would be needless here to detail our day's marches, as a general outline of them is sufficient.

The first seven days marches being through a tolerably well settled country, we found them comparatively easy, though sometimes the snow might be eight inches or a foot in depth, from the circumstances of the foundation of it being a beaten road, and, at the close of each day's march, houses or barns to lodge the men in.

On the 26th, while marching in rear of the company, a person of the name of Wilson overtook me in his sleigh. He had conducted the unfortunate Lord Edward Fitzgerald in the winter of 1789, who walked on snow-shoes through the then altogether untracked wilderness from Fredericton to Quebec. He said that Lord Edward had supported the fatigues and hardships of the journey with the greatest cheerfulness and aptitude and described him as a most amiable young man.[11]

On the 29th [of February, 1813[12]] we hutted. This operation was most fatiguing and disheartening after a heavy day's march, as it had snowed incessantly, and so heavily that we frequently lost our narrow snow-shoe track, and, if careless, were precipitated into deep snow. One man getting a fall of this kind caused a halt to all those in his rear for ten minutes or a quarter of an hour, until he had scrambled out from his cold bath. The inconvenience of keeping all the rear at a halt was found so great that it was soon agreed to march on and leave the straggler to regain his place when he could, which was by no means an easy matter, and made officers and men very careful not to fall if they could avoid it, from the fear of having to march some distance in the deep snow.

In order to relieve the men, each officer and man took his turn to brea the road, as it was called, by marching as leader for ten or fifteen minute then stepping one pace aside and letting the whole company pass him, whe he threw off his snow-shoes and marched on a firm, hard path in the rear.

must be seen by this arrangement the first pair of snow-shoes had to break a path in front, the second pair improved the track of the first, the third and every succeeding rendered it firmer and harder, till the Toboggans came which travelled on a pretty solid path.

We generally marched close along the edge of the river, whenever no rapids intervened to prevent it, and always constructed our huts on the windward side of it in the woods, in order to gain a little shelter. The mens' hands were frequently so cold that they could scarcely work; however, as they were divided into squads, the best axemen immediately set to felling young pine trees to form the rafters for the hut. These being trimmed of all their lateral branches, were cut to about fifteen feet in height. Others trimmed branches of pine for thatching it and others felled hard woods and cut into logs for burning.

While these were at work, some were clearing away spaces for the areas of the hut, which was done by taking off their snow-shoes and using them as shovels to throw back the snow till they got to the soil destined for the floor, four or five feet deep. The snow that was thrown back formed a high wall round it, which served to shelter us somewhat from the chilling wind. Within this area, the trimmed branches were placed in a conical or lengthened form and tied at top; they were then covered with pine boughs thickly laid over each, the points of the branches being downwards made it an excellent thatch, quite impervious to the snow, with the exception of the hole at the top which was left for a chimney. A blazing fire was then lit in the centre of the hut, and all around it was strewed a thick layer of small pine branches which formed a delicious and fragrant bed — here were no feather bed soldiers.[13]

The next precaution was to close the only aperture in the hut, which was intended for a doorway, made just large enough for a man to creep through edgewise, and a blanket, which everyone in turn grumbled to give up, served as an inner door to shut out the cold if possible. But I may well say if possible, as those who have not experienced it, cannot figure to themselves the extreme frigidity of a temperature from 18 to 27 degrees below zero, that is, from 50 to 59 degrees below freezing. While our feet were burning, which was sometimes literally the case whilst asleep, our heads were in a freezing temperature, as water immediately froze if placed near the outer circumfrence of the hut. It generally happened that we were as completely enveloped in smoke as an Esquimaux family but, like them, we found it much more agreeable than having no smoke at all, as it warmed the hut. Moreover, I imagined that sleep without fire in such cold would have proved the sleep of death.

### *[March 1813]*

On the lst of March [1813], we reached the grand falls of the river St. John, one hundred and fifty miles from Fredericton, where there is a small settlement.[14] We could not judge of its state of forwardness, every spot being covered with a mantle of snow but the inhabitants appeared to be quite happy and contented. They said they went down to Fredericton once or twice a year, to sell or barter their furs for what commodities they required, and added that their wants were few and simple.

After dinner most of the officers went to see the fall[s]; it presented a magnificent spectacle. In summer it was eighty-four feet high and nine hundred feet in width but it was greatly reduced by the quantity of ice which environed it. The spray, having frozen as it rose, had gradually so condensed itself that it had joined and formed a splendid, irregular, fantastical arch of surprising brilliancy and lightness, in all the rugged and mixed varieties of form which frost gives to falling water, suddenly arrested by congelation. The banks on each side from the same cause were like solid, irregular, glassy buttresses supporting the arch; and the surrounding trees being beautifully fringed with frost. When the sun rose on the ice and displayed the prismatic colors playing on it, the scene called to mind the idea of an enchanted palace of glass, fitter, indeed, for a person to gaze on than inhabit, which was strictly true, for desolation reigned around. No beast, bird nor even insect cheered the sight or enlivened the ear, the only sound that disturbed the icy death-like stillness around was the resistless, roaring river, rushing impatiently through its restricted and fringed bed of ice into the gulf beneath, whence surging on it hurried to a considerable distance before the frost had the power to conceal it under a bed of ice.

It may be proper to remark here that, as the grand falls was the last military post in the province of New Brunswick and although I am unable to give a correct description of it from the circumstance of the country being so completely covered with snow, it was neveretheless represented as being from its precipitous situation convertible into a very strong point of defence, the more important as it is the nearest point to the American boundary all along our line of march, and that by which the mail must pass in the winter season into Canada; besides being the only good line of march for troops similarly situated with ourselves, the St. John's and Madawaska rivers, and the Temisquata lake forming a level road of march on for two hundred miles, a circumstance of vast importance to the moving troops in winter, as they would otherwise have to march entirely through the brushwoods and forests, which would increase their hardships and retard their progress.

*View of Quebec City, 1834, by Russell Alexander. Le Couteur reached the capital of British North America after an arduous overland winter march from Fredericton through February and March 1813, and was stationed there briefly in 1817.* R. Alexander/National Archives of Canada/C-46907

On Wednesday, the 2nd of March [1813], we arrived at Laronciers at the head of the Madawaska settlement.[15] Here I began to find the French language of great service to me, as I did all through Lower Canada. The worthy cure, Monsieur Raby,[16] was delighted to meet a British officer who could converse with him freely and, accordingly, not only invited me to take my billet at his house but also insisted that one of my brother subs should accompany me, where he treated us with the greatest hospitality.

This insulated settlement is entirely separated from the busy world; a few hundred French are here settled in peaceful retirement. Their kind and worthy Pastor assured me that crimes were quite unknown in this peaceful spot, he was their confessor, their adviser, and their judge, and if a difference ever did exist amongst them, it was speedily referred to him, and his decision was final. Their habits and manners were simple and kind, altogether French. Like the ant in Lafontaine's fable, they told me, they grew enough in summer to supply their wants for the winter, which they passed in mirth and friendly intercourse. From the worthy Curé's description, and the lively and contented air of the people, I should take this to be the only Arcadia now existing in the world.

I am not aware that these good people considered us as great intruders, but they certainly did not give us much time to corrupt them as they mounted the whole of us, officers and men, in sleighs, and drove us through their settlement, twenty-one miles in a day, which by the way was a great treat, and the men vowed it was the pleasantest day's *march* that they had had.

On the 4th of March the cold was gradually increasing and an incessant snow-storm filling the track up rapidly made the dragging of the Toboggans exceedingly laborious, especially as we occasionally had to quit the Madawaska river owing to rapids in it which had not frozen, and the thickness of the brush-wood and the forest along the edge of it. When we got to the end of our day's march the cold was so intense that the men could scarcely use their fingers to hew down the fire-wood, or to build huts, and it was dark before we could commence cooking; if sticking a bit of salt pork on the end of a twig and holding it in a fire could be so termed.

On the morning of the 5th [of March 1813] the cold had greatly augmented and the thermometer once more fell to 27 degrees below zero, together with a gale, a north-wester in our teeth, which scarcely left us power to breathe; indeed, the intensity of the cold is indescribable, the captain of the company anticipated the effects of it, and went on with an officer and a few men to arrange the huts, and prepare fires for our reception.

About mid-day, on turning an angle or corner along the river, I was surprised to find that the head of the company had stopped, which caused the centre and the rear to halt as they came up. Knowing the dangerous consequences that might ensue from a prolonged halt in such excessive cold, I hastened in the deep snow to the head of the company and, going along, I observed that almost every man was already more or less frost-bitten and was occupied in rubbing his cheeks or nose, or both, with snow. In my progress I also was caught by the nose and, when I turned the corner in the river, I really thought I should not have been able to proceed, the cold wind appeared to penetrate through my body in defiance of flannels or furs.

I however urged the men on, as soon as we had taken time to lay one poor fellow upon a Toboggan whose whole body was frost-bitten, and covered him with blankets. By changing the leading file every four or five minutes we at length got to the huts, having about 90 men out of 105 more or less frost-bitten on that occasion.

On arriving at the huts, we found that the company which should have been a day's march ahead of us were still hutted.[17] They had attempted to cross the Temisquata lake in the morning but the cold wind blowing over it was so exquisitely keen as to freeze many of his men, the captain of it faced about and returned to the huts. It was impossible to get warm that night, one officer literally scorched his mocassins on his feet in his sleep, by being anxious to keep them warm.

The next morning, the wind having abated, both companies crossed the lake. The marching this day was very different from any thing we had yet experienced in our journeys. The sun having begun to have some power on the snow had thawed the surface of it, which froze again in the night, and formed a sheet of thin ice sufficiently strong to bear a light person but a heavy man would frequently break through, and sink into the substratum of snow, till he was arrested by the firm ice on the lake. This was very troublesome and laborious work but those who chose to keep their snow-shoes on, avoided it, and marched at a great pace over the ice. It was an eighteen-mile march and we were delighted to get to an habitation on the edge of the portage.

We had to leave poor Rogers, who was so severely frost-bitten on the 5th, in charge of a corporal, with the woodsman at the portage, who promised to recover him speedily by means of simples and herb, though to us his life appeared in danger. He was quite a hideous spectacle, altogether one ulcerated mass, as if scalded all over from boiling water. However, he rejoined us at Kingston in six weeks perfectly recovered.[18]

The next day's march was through a mountainous country which was called the "Grand Portage". Some parts of the pine forest through which we passed had been burned for clearing and presented a curious picture. The black and tall grim pine trees, rearing their scathed heads to the sky, seemed like the ghosts, or rather skeletons, of the noble forms they once possessed, and contrasted strangely with the virgin snow on which they appeared to stand. It was altogether a most dreary and laborious day's march as the snow drift in some places was ten or twelve feet deep, and the constant ascent and descent made it extremely fatiguing for the Toboggan men.

The descent of the hills was even more dangerous than the ascent, for if a Toboggan once got a fair start down hill, it shot to the foot of the hill like a car down a *montagne russe* with amazing velocity, excepting where the rider was awkward, and in this way there were several upsets, to the great amusement of those who escaped an accident.[19] It was necessary, speedily, to put an end to this, as some of the Toboggans got injured by it, and on this occasion delayed the rear of the company so much, that the head of it had finished its march by ten or eleven o'clock in the morning, whereas the rear-guard did not arrive till half-past five. After our frugal meal of biscuit and pork, we turned not in but, as usual, round the fire on our green bed of pine. But our refreshing sleep was doomed to be broken this night by a novel accident.

The wind being high had so completely dried the top of our pine thatch that it caught fire and, on waking from a sound slumber, I found myself in a blaze, in a complete *auto da fe*,[20] for there was no appearance of a door or outlet, so instantaneous was the blaze. However, a yell of despair from an officer of the regiment who dashed into the hut through the flames exclaiming: "Holy J___s, my money box!" which he snatched up with the fondness of a father saving his only child from peril, enabled me to dash out after him, dragging my *all* — a change of suit — in a hysterical fit of laughter at the strange lamentation of our brother-officer.

We were some little time occupied in snow-balling the fire to extinguish the flames, for fear the men's huts should also have caught fire; but it was a most ludicrous sight as we were floundering in the deep snow, up to our middles or shoulders, not having time to put on our snow-shoes. Several of the men and officers got frost-bitten in this adventure.

The next morning we started with joyful countenance under the impression that it was our last day's march through an uninhabited country and that the morrow should enable us to march in a region where the axe had mastered the forest, and cultivation, however rude and in its infancy, announced at least that the hand of man was there. It was so solemn a reflection that we had been completely left to ourselves for many days, with nothing but the snow, the sky or the interminable silent forest to look upon, that both men and officers were heartily rejoiced when they beheld a worthy gentleman of the commissariat with a *horse* in a sleigh who had been sent from Quebec to receive us and, in addition to the Government rum and rations provided for us, he kindly and considerately brought with him an ample supply of fowls, hams, veal and wines three miles into the portage, which afforded us the best meal we had ever tasted, and gratitude proclaimed our worthy friend ever after, a standing toast among us.[21]

After our repast, we moved on in the parish of St. Andrew's,[22] to a village from whence we saw spread before us the magnificent St. Lawrence, eighteen miles wide. We obtained comfortable billets for men and officers, and where for the first time in seventeen days we regularly washed and dressed ourselves, in addition, to which a well-cooked dinner, which more vitiated appetites would have probably called execrable, and good bed, made us forget our fatigues.

Our march from hence to Quebec was along a good beaten snow road and marches of eighteen to twenty miles, mere exercise for us, so that our last seven days passed away merrily, under the cheering smiles of the worthy Canadians, who welcomed us as nondescript race that had never been seen in those quiet parts before, being the first regiment that had ever been there, and our merry bugles were quite a novel treat to the Canadian lasses. The country along the river St. Lawrence up to Quebec was cleared in a belt ranging from half a mile to three miles in depth. We passed through several villages almost entirely built of wood, with neat looking churches roofed with tin, so that when the sun shone on them, they presented a brilliant and elegant appearance.

On the 15th[23] of March [1813], our 24th day's march, we entered Quebec [City], greeted by an immense concourse of people who appeared to consider us quite the lions of the army after our our unexampled march. The Quebec papers called us in the words of the poet:

> Fine young fellows, fit to pluck
> Bright honour from the pale-faced moon.[24]

Sir George Prevost, on inspecting our six companies,[25] 550 rank and file, paid us the highest compliments,[26] and to show us that he really thought us in good wind, he ordered the grenadiers and light company to march on the

25th [of March 1813], two hundred miles, for Chambly, to join the light brigade there.

But it appeared that every general officer who saw or heard of us considered that we were in thorough training for, on getting near Montreal, Major Drummond sent me on to General De Rottenburg[27] to report our speedy arrival when, on my honestly avowing we were in excellent wind, the General said: "Then he should send us on 200 miles further to Kingston!"

### *[April 1813]*

When I reported the circumstances to Major Drummond, who was marching at the head of the companies, one of the men exclaimed: "It's no wonder; they think we are like the children of Israel, we must march forty years before we halt!" Other hoped that, as it was the lst of April, the General merely meant to make April fools of us, and let us off with a fright. But the 2nd of April undeceived us; we were off for Kingston.

I do not describe this part of our march from Quebec to Kingston, as many other regiments have performed it, none however in so short a space of time; it was nevertheless very severe, as the sun now had the power to thaw the snow and the ice over the small streams, some of which we were obliged to ford up to our middles, when the water was so intolerably cold, that the sudden shock to our pores, open from perspiration, was not a little trying to the best constitutions, and caused excessive pain in the loins.

On the 12th of April we were marching up a gentle ascent, and just as the head files were rising it, there was a general exclamation of "The sea, the sea — the ships, the ships![28]" The whole of us spontaneously broke and ran to witness the novel and interesting sight. Some of us had been marching between eight hundred and a thousand miles in six weeks, with only ten days' halt, during which time we had never lost sight of a forest, when suddenly there lay before our astonished and delighted view the town of Kingston, the magnificent Lake Ontario, and what was far more surprising still, a squadron of ships-of-war frozen on its bosom. It produced a striking and indescribable sensation, as none of us Europeans appeared to have reflected on the circumstance of being sure to find a fleet of men of war on a fresh water lake....[29]

As my purpose was merely to describe a winter march in Canada, I shall avoid other descriptions but, as a few general observations may be useful, I may be pardoned for making them.

The comparative repose which necessarily followed our long march together with good feeling occasioned disorders amongst the men and, although we had not lost a single man during the march, many were ill and a few died from the effects of it. It was observed that these were all the hardest drinkers, indeed, there is no doubt whatever that dram-drinking is highly injurious in a very cold country as the heat that is momentarily conveyed to the body is followed by a reaction which the cold turns quickly into a numbness and retarded circulation.

Under the circumstances of a regiment having to perform a similar march, it would appear advisable to use snow-shoes for eight or ten miles daily, for at least a month previous to its march, in order to accustom the men not only to tie on their snow-shoes, and to wear them with ease to themselves, but also to enable them to know how to dress their moccasins properly, and to pack and drag their toboggans.

Indians or natives should be sent on a day's march ahead of the regiment to prepare huts for the officers and men, to cut wood and to boil water in readiness for their arrival, as I should consider warm tea or warm broth made from portable soup far more refreshing and restoring than the piece of pork that was allowed to the 104th Regiment.

The men were so fatigued and chilled by the cold on some occasions that they would scarcely exert themselves to cut wood for firing and I feel confident that, under similar circumstances, a corps differently composed might have been placed in a very uncomfortable situation but the advantage of having a great number of natives of the country in the corps was manifest.

Brother soldiers will pardon the *esprit de corps* which leads me to say that, during this long march, under considerable privations and hardships, not one single robbery was committed by the men, nor was there a single report made against them by the inhabitants to the commanding officer.

## Notes

[1] This chapter is taken from Le Couteur's account of the winter march in February and March 1813. Le Couteur submitted the original text to the New York newspaper, *The Albion,* where it saw publication 26 November 1831. Almost a century later, Major M.A. Pope of the Canadian Army reprinted the *Albion* article with annotations in the *Canadian Defence Quarterly,* VII, no. 4 (July 1930), 490-501. There are some minor differences between the two texts which were noted by Joan Stevens, *Victorian Voices* (St. Helier, 1969), 43-51.

The text that appears here is taken from the 1930 publication and is reprinted with permission of the *Canadian Defence Quarterly.* It is reproduced in its entirety with the exception of an introductory paragraph addressed to the readers of the *Albion* and a paragraph of material that is repeated in Chapter 5 (marked by ellipses). The original draft can be found in Le Couteur's papers in the Société Jersiaise, St. Helier.

Other accounts of the winter march of the 104th are those of Charles Rainsford published in the *Saint John Daily Sun,* 23 August 1889 and Lieutenant A.W. Playfair published in the *British Standard,* January 1862.

[2] Lieutenant General Sir George Prevost (1767-1816), see *DCB,* V, 693-698. After a lengthy military career that began in 1779, Prevost served in turn as the Governor of St. Lucia and Dominica before becoming Lieutenant Governor of Nova Scotia in 1808. A pragmatic and conciliatory personality, Prevost proved popular and effective and, in 1811, was appointed Governor General of British North America and commander of the forces. As his war record would demonstrate, Prevost was a better administrator than a soldier.

[3] Le Couteur's figures are incorrect. The strength of the British regular army in the Canadian colonies in 1811 was 8,600 men, see PRO, WO 17, vols. 1515, 2358. A trickle of reinforcements was received during 1812.

[4] Major General Sir Isaac Brock (1769-1812), see *DCB,* V, 109-115. A Guernseyman, Brock was serving as commander in Upper Canada in 1812 when the war began. His victories at Detroit and Queenston Heights saved the province from occupation. He is buried today in a magnificent memorial atop Queenston Heights.

[5] The overland route to Quebec was well known to the 104th as several recruiting parties had used it before during the summer months. It was also the established mail route between Lower Canada and New Brunswick. See Austin Squires, *The 104th Regiment of Foot* (Fredericton, 1962), 32-33, 118-119.

[6] According to the Inspection Return of the 104th Foot, dated 11 June 1812 and found in the PRO, WO 27, vol. 108, the ethnic composition of the unit was as follows: British Americans, 516; English, 116; Scots, 97; Irish, 91; foreigners, 44 — total, 864 men. The return does not differentiate between anglophone and francophone "British Americans." As the 104th recruited in both Lower Canada and New Brunswick, it contained French-speaking soldiers from both colonies.

[7] Charles Rainsford of the grenadier company states that it left Fredericton on the 14th of February. See his account in the *Saint John Daily Sun*, 23 August 1889.

[8] The 104th differed from most infantry regiments of the line in having no drummers attached to its companies, only buglers, see PRO, WO 27, vol. 108, Inspection Return of the 104th Foot, 11 June 1812. The regimental band did have drummers.

[9] "The Girl I Left Behind Me" is the traditional loth-to-depart march of the British army and is usually played when a regiment leaves a garrison after a long period of service. The song dates from 1758, see Lewis Winstock, *Songs and Music of the Redcoats, 1642-1902* (London, 1970), 67. The words of the first verse are as follows:

> I'm lonesome since I crossed the hill,
> And o'er the moor and valley,
> Such grievous thoughts my heart do fill,
> Since parting with my Sally.
> I seek no more the fine or gay,
> For each does but remind me,
> How swift the hours did pass away,
> With the girl I left behind me.

[10] Rainsford recorded details of the loads carried. The men "were provided with a pair of snowshoes, moccasins and one blanket each, and one toboggan to every two men. The train of each company consisted of upwards of 50 toboggans, containing each two firelocks and accoutrements, two knapsacks, two blankets and, at one period of the March, 14 days provisions for the men (each ration, one pound, two ounces), and two pairs of snowshoes ... each toboggan being drawn by one man in front and pushed or held back, as necessity required, by one man in the rear by a stick made fast ... to the stern of the toboggan. The officers were limited to a knapsack carried by themselves ..." See the *Saint John Daily Sun*, 23 August 1889.

[11] Lord Edward Fitzgerald (1763-1798), son of the 1st Duke of Leinster. Fitzgerald travelled in Canada in the 1780s. He was executed for his role as a leader in the abortive Irish uprising of 1798. His son, Edward Fox Fitzgerald (1795-1863), was a fellow cadet of Le Couteur's at the Royal Military College in 1808-1809.

[12] This is an error as 1813 not being a leap year, there was no 29 February.

[13] Rainsford's company camped somewhat differently, building shelters of snow walls overlaid by boughs but with no roof. See the *Saint John Daily Sun*, 23 August 1889.

[14] The present-day town of Grand Falls, New Brunswick.

[15] Present-day Madawaska-Edmunston area of New Brunswick.

[16] Monsieur Louis Raby (1787-1843), priest of Saint-Basile-de-Madawaska from 1810 to 1813, see J.-B.-A. Allaire, *Dictionnaire biographique du clergé canadien-français* (Montréal, 1910).

[17] This was Captain Edward Holland's company, see *Saint John Daily Sun*, 23 August 1889.

[18] Unfortunately, Rogers died the following year, see Squires, *The 104th Regiment of Foot*, 127.

[19] Squires, *The 104th Regiment*, 127-128, quotes Lieutenant A.W. Playfair of the 104th Regiment who wrote to the *British Standard* in January 1862 to say that "Some of the men would run the toboggans down the hills sitting on them, and would frequently capsize. Our big black drummer straddled the big drum, which was lashed to a tobagan, to try the experiment, but it got off the track, shooting him off at high velocity, and the sable African came up some distance from where he disappeared, a white man exciting roars of laughter."

[20] "Auto da fe." Literally, "act of faith", a sentence of execution by burning imposed by the Inquisition.

[21] Actually, this man, an army contractor named William Anderson, met the two companies after having been alerted by Rainsford of the grenadier company. Rainsford had gone on ahead two days before, with two volunteers, to procure provisions for the two flank companies. See *Saint John Daily Sun*, 23 August 1889.

[22] Present-day St. André, Quebec.

[23] In his original text, Le Couteur stated that the 104th arrived at Quebec City on the 25th of March 1813. This is an error; they arrived on the 15th and on the 25th, were ordered to march westward to Upper Canada, see NAC, RG 8 I, vol. 1203 1/2 G, p. 123, General Orders [March 1813].

[24] I have been unable to find this compliment in the Quebec newspapers of March 1813. However, in the *Kingston Gazette*, 6 April 1813, the following appeared:

> Quebec, March 16
>
> The greater part of the 104th Regiment are arrived, the remainder are at no great distance. The regiment is 600 strong and formed of fine young spirited fellows fit to "pluck honour from the pale-faced moon."

The quote is from Shakespeare, *Henry IV*, Part I, Scene iii, 201, and the full wording is: "By Heavens methinks it were an easy leap/ To pluck bright honour from the pale-fac'd moon."

[25] Of the 104th Foot's ten companies, six marched to Quebec in the winter of 1812-1813 while two followed by sea in May 1813. The last two companies, stationed on Prince Edward Island and Cape Breton, remained there until the autumn of 1814 when they joined the regiment at Kingston.

[26] Prevost wrote to the Duke of York that the regiment's "Officers & men have arrived generally in good health, a few only have suffered from the Frost" and reported that

their numbers consisted of "29 Officers, 32 Sergeants, 31 Corporals, 11 Buglers, 469 Privates and 1 Boy learning the Bugle." See NAC, RG 8 I, vol. 1220, p. 215, Prevost to Torrens, 18 March 1813.

[27] Major General Francis De Rottenburg (1757-1832), see *DCB* VI, 660-662. A veteran officer who had seen service in the Polish and French armies, De Rottenburg joined the British army in 1795 and raised and trained the first rifle-equipped battalion in that service. In 1810 he was sent to the staff in North America and served in Lower Canada until 1813 when he replaced Major General Roger Sheaffe as commander in Upper Canada. In December 1813 he returned to a command in Lower Canada.

[28] "The sea, the sea — the ships, the ships!" Intentionally or not, Le Couteur is quoting here from Xenophon's *Anabasis*, IV, vii, 24.

[29] A single sentence, which was repeated in chapter 5 of the main part of the Journal, has been here omitted.

# Chapter Five

## "A SCANDALOUSLY MANAGED AFFAIR"

Garrison Duty at Kingston and Action at Sackets Harbor,
*April and May 1813*

### Kingston, Upper Canada, 1813

*12 April*
Monday. At length our toilsome march of a thousand miles[1] nearly came to an end. We started at 5 o'clock in the morning from Gananoque, after driving the Voltigeurs[2] before us, and reached Kingston about twelve, a march of twenty-four miles through the woods. The Men, who wished to go in clean, being then bespattered with mud up to their knees, walked into a stream, and washed Pantaloons & Boots, at a Splash — so indeed did the Officers. Then our merry Bugles played us into the Town.

Colonel Pearson,[3] the Inspecting Field Officer of Militia, who we heard was a regular Tartar, saw to our billeting in as wretched quarters as the poor men had never been used to — however, any shelter was acceptable to them. Shore and I had none — not a bed, nor a shakedown to be had in any Inn or House.[4] We walked twice through the Town, sulky as well as weary.

At length we noticed a very neat house with a garden and porch to it — superior to most of them in the Street.[5] We were told it belonged to the Commodore's Widow, that no billets were ever given there but we might get beds there for a night or two. I knocked at the door. Out came a tall Venerable looking Old Lady, majestic as Mrs. Siddons,[6] as benevolent in appearance as Mrs. Fry.[7] I apologized, mumbling that it was a mistake, I begged pardon for the intrusion. "But what is it, young Gentleman? You knocked for some purpose?" "Why Madam, it was to ask whether we might obtain beds for a night

*View north along King Street, Kingston, Upper Canada, 1833 by Harriet Cartwright. During the winters of 1813-14 and 1814-15, Le Couteur boarded with Mrs. Elizabeth Robison in the "very neat house with a garden and a porch to it" pictured in the foreground here, surrounded by a picket fence. The house stands today.* H. Cartwright/National Archives of Canada/C-2751 or two, till some of the troops march out of Kingston." "Have you been to the Hotels?" "Madam we have tried every inn and every decent house in the town. We have marched twenty-four miles since five this morning; we have been twice round the town, it is now 3 o'clock, and we know not where to lay our heads — but I repeat it is a mistake our having called here, I wish you good morning."

The good old lady caught me by the collar: "For shame stay! Do you think that after hearing your story I would send two English officers from my door — Myself the Widow of an English Commodore. Come in, Gentlemen!" We were so dirty & wet, we feared to soil her carpet and well-furnished drawing room but in a short time — Bedrooms, Hot water, dry linen, a sumptuous breakfast, were all provided in the true Samaritan spirit. Dear kind Mrs. Robison,[8] she gave us hospitable shelter till the 14th, when Moore[9] and I took a Barrack room together.

We were subjected to great discomfort from not having our luggage, which was coming up the St. Lawrence in bateaux and was frozen in a little below Point Frederick. Captain Leonard[10] and I crossed over to Point Frederick with a view to get it forwarded but the convoy was frozen in so completely that it was only on the 17th the boat[s] could be disengaged when we got all the Baggage into the barrack Yard, and were heartily welcomed by our brother officers for our Zealous devotion, as they called it, to our own and their comfort. We had all been sneaking to our duty quite ashamed to be seen with dirty linen and foul Jackets in a smart garrison.

Sunday the 18th made it nine weeks since we left Fredericton. The Regiment marched to Church[11] for the first time since we left Quebec and the Second since quitting Fredericton. The Reverend Mr. Stewart,[12] the Rector, gave us a Capital discourse, but many of us were considerably discomposed by two Solos from a Jolly old Clerk who discharged his duty sonorously. It was distressing to listen to one voice after the fine singing of our band people at Fredericton.

Moore and I began our Menage. Bought Saucepans, a Gridiron, a frying pan, those indispensable, for a proper military breakfast turn out. Stock dearer than at dear Fredericton. Butter 2/6 per pound, Honey 5/, Blacking 5/, two quires of paper 8/6, a knife & fork 7/6, Porter 2/6 the bottle, eggs 3/ the dozen. Subs, the pride and safeguards of the army, are jolly housekeepers. While the heavy rains lasted, Moore & I used to turn in at Ten. The lads would often come and sit with us, drink our Brandy and water and sing us to sleep. These were when uninvited — when we saw Company, we did not turn in ourselves and themselves out, Mind you!

### *25th [April]*

Visited the Fortifications round Point Frederick, which is about half a mile across an arm of Lake Ontario. They are not very strong, but there is a Capital blockhouse which commands them as well as the Dock Yard. Captain Grey,[13] the D.[eputy] Q[uarte]r M[aster] Gen[era]l, a Half-horse, half-Alligator sort of soldier, sailor, carpenter etc. launched a small frigate, the *Sir George Prevost* of 24 Guns.[14] She went off prettily but the cradle broke to our terror, and there she stuck. It was a serious check because it was a war of Carpenters as to getting the command of the Lake — the Yankees being building at Sackets Harbor with that view also.

### *29 [April]*

Very disastrous news received from York, the Capital of Upper Canada, which was assaulted and taken by the Americans and that our army was in full retreat. Our Grenadiers were marched off to its support under the command of Major Drummond though the place could ill afford to spare men as it was expected to be menaced — the enemy being anxious to destroy the ships of war that we are building here.

### *1 May [1813]*

May day. Rumours afloat that we would be attacked forthwith, the American fleet being off the Nine Mile point. At nine at night a message came to the mess to say that the alarm Guns were to be fired immediately and get our men ready for action. At ten I was marched off with thirty of my company and a detachment of embodied Militia under Captain Viger[15] to the Centre Bridge five miles off through an abominable road knee deep in mud. We soon heard a shotted gun fired, which made us hurry to our Post. The river was about eighty Yards in width and, as our orders were to defend the Post to the last, I reconnoitred the Bridge and asked the Captain what he proposed to do. He declared that He knew nothing of service, [but] that He would fight to the last, and entreated me to take the command and act as I thought best. I instantly got our Pick axes and Hatchets to work. It was a wooden Bridge with a heavy planking over it — there was some difficulty in taking up the first plank, but making that a lever for the rest, the whole of the planks, over thirty yards up the Bridge, were lifted and brought to our side. They were laid in order in a sort of Parapet, across the head of the Bridge, and formed a capital defence, sufficiently thick to resist a Six-pound shot.

As our work was completed we were reinforced by forty militia and thirty Illinois Indians — these I detached on either flank in the woods. Our post was now impregnable — our line of sentries, front, flanks & rear being posted, the Officers visited them every hour, while our men laid down to rest, *al fresco.*

In the grey of the morning we had an alarm. We heard a tremendous noise, as of Artillery and Cavalry, coming down the road. "Stand to your arms, fall in!" Listened, concealed all our sentries, watched — not the American Army but an Army of market carts. They had to wait in great wrath, till 5 o'clock when Major Coore[16] ADC came to inform us that it had been a false alarm — admired our defences greatly. We laid down the planking and marched home, well pleased to be relieved.[17]

Colonel Pearson, the Inspector of Militia, they told me, was much feared by the militiamen and officers.[18] He was singularly intemperate, though a first rate Soldier. I heard Him abuse old Colonel Cartwright[19] at the Head of his Reg[imen]t one day for not performing some movement which a Militia officers could not be expected to know. Col[onel]. Cartwright told me some time afterwards: "He little knew what a zealous and anxious man He was reproving, and that He offended my Regiment much more than He did me."

Pearson being applied to personally by a Militiaman for leave of absence, the Colonel who was in a moody humour answered: "*Go to Hell!*" The man quietly said: *"Has your honour any orders for the Devil?"* Pearson looked at Him, smiled: "What leave do you want? Six days!!!" He doubled his leave and gave Him a Pound to take home!

### *5 May*

The remnant of the King's Regiment marched in from their defeat at York — their splendid Grenadier Company which left this last month 112 Rank & File, returned here 25 in number. Poor McNeale[20] their Captain was killed in a rash charge which He made, at the head of his Grenadiers, on a body of riflemen who were posted in a wood. Nearly all fell as they crossed a meadow.[21] Our Flankers,[22] with the Detachments from York, [the] Newfoundland[23] and Glengarry Regts,[24] were sent across to Point Frederick, in miserable quarters. Mounting two 68-pounders [carronades] and an 18 [pdr. gun] on the Lake battery.

### *Sunday, May 9*

Sent on detachment to McPherson's Bay to relieve L[ieutenan]t. Moorsom[25] with orders to complete a breastwork[26] and Abbatis,[27] cut a road through the wood, and protect my flanks. I had thirty-four men with me, Twelve of them axemen. With the assistance of these wonderful hewers of wood I completed my breastwork on Monday, and made it shot proof — then placed a very heavy and well-sharpened Abbatis thirty paces in its front, at the foot of a slope about fifty feet below the level of my battery breast work. In the days following I covered my flanks for half a mile on either side with an impenetrable mass of fallen trees.

The mode, was to commence with what the Axemen called a key tree, a Monarch of the wood, two men opposite each other, sometimes four, cut an enormous wedge as if done with the plane, from the two sides of the tree in the direction it was meant to fall. One great cut, the outer, being about Six inches below the other, the inner cut thus — the tree was then left, and the two next to it were cut partly through, then the three next, then four, five, six, to a hundred in one lengthened wedge to any desired extent. Then the forest was ready for the fall, and grand was the fall thereof. All the party went back to the Key tree, the four axemen, gave a few finishing rapid strokes with their ponderous axes, down went the Monarch, sweeping the two next and so on through the forest with the rushing sound of the fall of many waters — a forest Niagara! — a sound more rushing and crushing. Thrilling to hear, and wondrous to witness, the enormous gap in the time-honoured Wilderness. Nought save fire can penetrate to that ponderous matting.

Next, I had to construct a field battery to defend the main approach to Kingston. It was formed of very heavy butts of trees on each side and filled in with earth. The flanks were protected to a considerable distance by felled timber, as above described, and the front by a strong abbatis well pinioned to the ground. As I had orders to defend my post to the last extremity, and that I was three or four miles in advance — with an army of Eleven thousand Americans on the opposite side of the river, it was a wide awake post.

### *17 May*

I got word that the Yankee fleet was seen off Kingston, my own Sentry along the Shore got a view of one of them, a large ship. I completed a second, or Le Couteur's battery, on the 19th. They were both highly approved by Sir George Prevost and the Big wigs: Colonels Drummond, Moodie,[28] Heriot,[29] Viger, Johnstone[30] [and] Moorsom, Ass[istan]t A[djutant] Gen[era]l.

### *24 May*

Relieved from my alarm post and very well pleased to return to Camp which was after all worse than my hut in the woods. The rain was so heavy and constant that it drizzled quite through the tents — our chat was not even lively under such a chill.

### *27 May*

We were suddenly ordered to march from Point Frederick to Kingston — to our great relief. The Captain left me behind to see the baggage forwarded and I never thought of hurrying and meant to take my pleasure when to cross when a light bob came running to me: "Oh Sir, the troops and our men are parading in Kingston, the Bugles are sounding and Drums rolling — there is some great move, for the Men of War's boats are pulling to Kingston." I ran down with Him to the edge of the Lake — not a boat or Canoe to be seen but one with its stern stove in. He was a thorough Canoeman, a New Brunswicker, and offered to paddle me over with a bit of plank taken from the dock yard.

We both sat on the sound end of the wooden Canoe, cocked her broken bow over the water and launched our bark for fame and glory. It was, in vulgar parlance, a funky[31] affair but we got over safe. I got over in time to run for my haversack and to parade the company in Haversacks and light marching order with Sixty rounds of Ball Cartridge.[32] At twelve we began to embark in Boats — detachments of the 8th, 100th, 104th, Glengarry Light Infantry, Can[a]d[ia]n Voltigeurs, and Newfoundland Regiments — when it leaked out that we were destined for Sackets Harbor, as a set-off for the damage they had done us at York.

### *28 May*

On Tuesday morning the 28th, a beautiful morning, we were about Seven miles from the harbour. The fleet stood in close to reconnoitre the batteries — it was supposed they were thought too strong, for we stood off again. About 8 A.M., our fire eater, Major Drummond, had got us into the bateaux to practice pulling, as He said, and was pulling toward the landing place when Sir George Prevost sent an ADC to order Him to re-embark his Men instantly. Drummond said He would engage to take the place with his own Regiment if allowed because it was evidently a surprise — the enemy were quite unprepared for an attack. In standing off, however, we cut off a brigade of bateaux, with a reinforcement of three hundred men that was en route to Sackets.[33] It had come on to rain hard, and we were all thoroughly soaked, cold and shivering — having no great coats.[34] Sir George gave the Americans all that day and the next night ample time for a fair stand up fight, like the old French Guards, who never fired first, however.[35]

### *29 May*

On the 29th May, the fleet was pretty close in at day break. At 4 A.M., we got into bateaux, formed in line, and pulled steadily for the Shore. The American troops were formed in Line, about a hundred yards from the beach. As we neared, they plied us with round shot from a Battery on our left. Just before we touched the shore, a round shot passed close over our boat, and plumped into the Grenadier boat on our right — Killed and wounded a couple of men — cut the boat nearly in two, and down she went. The Grenadiers behaved admirably, raised their firelocks high, and could just touch the bottom, we little fellows would half of us been drowned.[36] We cheered lustily, so did they, soon Old Dick their Veteran Captain[37] formed them, so did we form. The whole line was soon landed & formed under a roll of musquetry, when we charged and the Americans ran. We drove them at a skirmishing run a mile and a half.

Sir James Yeo,[38] was running in front of and with our men, in a round Jacket and waving his cap, cheering the men on, without sword or pistol. His cockswain was hit by a musket bullet in the head — the Commodore desired him to go to the rear, to the Doctors. Not a bit, He swore He would not leave his Captain in a fight.

Our gallant Drummond was also running on Sword in hand, like Roderick Dhu in a foray. An American Soldier, who was skirmishing very gallantly, saw the effect of his presence. He quietly waited until Drummond was about twenty yards from Him, amidst shot and Yells of fury, levelled his piece and knocked the Major over, apparently stone dead. Our men bayoneted the gallant fellow in an instant. Drummond was lifted, said "tis not mortal, I can move my legs." No blood appeared. "Charge on Men!" He shouted. We had induced Him to remove his Epaulettes. He had deposited them in the front pockets of his overalls, which saved his life. The ball had struck the pad and steel plate — it was a dreadful bruise that He received.

Jobling, my Senior Sub., made a dash with half the Light Company at a Battery but lost half his men. We had then reached the Town. We saw the *Pike*,[39] a ship of war, on the Stocks in flames or rather smoke. We had turned the battery, and got up to the Stockade round the barracks I believe. It was ticklish work, for as I had nothing but a sword, there was nothing to do. The Yankees were poking the muzzles of their guns, on each side of me while I made myself as flat as I could edgewise behind one of the posts of the stockade. It was a really uncomfortable position there was neither glory nor pleasure in being riddled, or rather fringed, with balls. This did not last long, our men got round the flank and soon cleared the space.

Major Moodie & I with my Servant Mills[40] then tried to turn a small howitzer on the blockhouse in which a handful of men were keeping us at bay. My servant was slightly hit in five places, and Moodie was wounded in this operation. Moodie told me "it won't do." I said: "What is that Sir?" "The retreat is sounding, See our Men are forming, are you much hurt?" "No. It must be a mistake, there are the Americans running away en Masse to the left", which we both distinctly saw.

The Bugles continued to sound the recall so we formed in good Line, just out of range of the block house. Major Drummond immediately offered, wounded as He was, to proceed to summon the Americans to surrender which Sir George[41] permitted. But brother Jonathan was too grass sharp. "Why do you retreat, if you wish us to surrender?" "Only to form a fresh attack and to save a further effusion of blood." "Then tell Sir George Prevost, we will await the issue of his attack." Poor Sir George, if no worse, mistook the body of three thousand Americans Moodie & I saw in retreat for a fresh reinforcement. We continued our own retreat and embarked unmolested, save by a few straggling shot.[42]

Our young[43] troops went into action admirably, formed and advanced as on field day. It is a strange, an awful sense that first feeling of deadly encounter — it is not fear We feel, but a glorious sense of awe, the spirit desiring to urge the flesh to aid its fellow man. Strange to witness death and wounds on every side — still to rush into the very Jaws of danger.

As we charged, a fine young American Soldier fell and was caught by our light bobs, two or three bayonets were flourishing over his handsome imploring face, with hands uplifted. "For Gods sake spare me!" "For shame men, never kill an unarmed man who begs for quarter!" I struck their Bayonets aside, and sent the poor fellow to the rear.

A sad scene disturbed us much as were embarking. The D[eputy] Q[uarter] M[aster] G[eneral][44] had been killed in the action, and his Son a Youth of eighteen, an Ensign in our Regiment,[45] was in the saddest state of grief — desiring to remain by his Father's body. There was no *step*[46] in our Regiment but Maj[or]. Drummond, Major Moodie, Captains Leonard & Shore, Lieutenants Rainsford, Moore, and De Lancey[47] were wounded[48] — 25 men killed & 75 wounded of our Reg[imen]t.[49] Our force in all amounted to [870] men, and our loss was [48] killed & [195] wounded.[50]

It was a scandalously managed affair. We gained a surprise and threw it away to allow the enemy to gain time. The murmurs against Sir George were deep, not loud. Our sweet little Band was sadly cut up, three of them being killed in this affair. It was a folly to take them.

Dear W[illia]m[51] and Miss Robison[52] told me that their anxiety and alarm was indescribable. All the Ladies, who had relatives in the attacking force, with those who had only friends, were listening in breathless trepidation to the distant roar of Guns & musquetry while the action lasted.

My friend Moore was shot in the left Jaw, the ball had passed through the Cheek and horribly disfigured Him. I fed Him with a spoon for several days & nights and took his hand to mine in order to prevent his touching his bandages.[53]

## Notes

[1] Le Couteur is exaggerating here. According to Major M.A. Pope, "The March of the 104th Foot from Fredericton to Quebec, 1813", *Canadian Defence Quarterly* VII (1930), 491, the distance covered by the regiment was seven hundred miles.

[2] The Canadian Voltiguers were a militia unit recruited in Lower Canada to serve for the duration of the war and were commanded by Lieutenant Colonel Charles De Salaberry, formerly of the 60th Foot and a protégé of the Duke of Kent. In March 1813 four companies of the Voltiguers were ordered to Kingston under the command of Major Frederick G. Heriot. For a brief history of this unit, see E. A. Cruikshank, "Record of the Service of Canadian Regiments in the War of 1812. Part VI: The Canadian Voltiguers", *Canadian Military Institute, Selected Papers* X (1899-1910), 9-21.

[3] Lieutenant Colonel Thomas Pearson, 23rd Foot (d. 1847), Inspecting Field Officer of Militia, Upper Canada.

[4] Another traveller who arrived in Kingston at this time confirms the crowded condition of the town. Patrick Finan remembered Kingston being so "full of troops that all the merchants' stores were converted into barracks; the R[oman] C[atholic] church into a hospital, in addition to the regular barracks and hospital; ships of war were building, and various public works carrying on with the greatest activity." See Patrick Finan, *Journal of a Voyage to Quebec, in the Year 1825, with Recollections of Canada, during the late American War, in the Years 1812-1813* (Newry, 1828), 309. Finan was the son of Bryan Finan, quartermaster of the 8th Foot.

[5] This house, 57/59 Gore Street, Kingston, is still standing. It is said to have originally been one of the buildings brought to the town from Carleton Island and was certainly in place by 1796 as it is shown on a map dated that year. At that time it was the property of William Coffin. When he died in 1804, it passed into the possession of his brother, Thomas Aston Coffin, who sold it in 1807 to Elizabeth Robison. In 1816 she in turn sold the house to the Reverend George Okill Stuart who had married her daughter, Anne Ellice Robison, that same year. The Stuarts resided in the house, which was known as the Stuart Cottage or Rectory. It was described during this time as a "modest place — one story with four fireplaces". See Margaret Angus, "The Old Stones of Queen's, 1842-1900," *Historic Kingston*, 20 (1971), 7.

[6] The actress Sarah Siddons (1755-1831). Siddons specialized in tragic characters and was famous for her portrayal of Lady MacBeth. She retired from the stage in 1812.

[7] Le Couteur possibly means Peggy Fryer, a British actress of the late seventeenth and early eighteenth centuries.

[8] This was Elizabeth Robison (1750-1840). Born Elizabeth Cartwright, she was the sister of Richard Cartwright, a prominent Loyalist and Kingston merchant. In 1767 she married Captain Thomas Robison, RN (1741-1806) and had seven children: Thomas, Richard, Martha, James, Eliza, Ann and William.

[9] Lieutenant Fowk Moore, 104th Foot (b. 1792). Moore had joined the regiment in November 1812.

[10] Captain Richard Leonard, "Old Dick" (1776-1833). Leonard had joined the 54th Foot as an ensign in 1796, fought in Ireland in 1798 and in Egypt in 1801, where he had served as an assistant engineer at the siege of Alexandria. He joined the New Brunswick Fencibles in 1805. Leonard remained in Canada after the war, settling near Niagara Falls and served as sheriff of Lincoln County.

[11] St. George's Anglican church, Kingston. This was the first St. George's, located in the present market square behind the old city hall.

[12] Reverend George Okill Stuart (1776-1862), Rector of St. George's Anglican Church, Kingston, see *DCB*, IX, 770-771.

[13] Captain Andrew Gray, Nova Scotia Fencibles, Deputy Assistant Quartermaster General, involved with warship construction at Kingston in the winter of 1812-1813.

[14] HMS *Sir George Prevost.* Le Couteur states she had 24 guns, the *Kingston Gazette,* 4 May 1813, states she had 30 guns. She was later renamed the *Wolfe* and, later still, the *Montreal.*

[15] Captain Jacques Viger, Canadian Voltiguers (1757-1858), see *DCB*, VIII, 909-913. Viger became the first mayor of the modern city of Montreal in 1834. He was an enthusiastic amateur historian who published a number of books and articles, and amassed a large collection of documents. Excerpts from his account of garrison duty in Kingston in the spring of 1813 were translated and published by J.L.H. Neilson as *Reminiscences of the War of 1812-14. Being Portions of the Diary of a Captain of the "Voltiguers Canadiens" While in Garrison at Kingston, etc. Translated from the French by J.L. Hubert Neilson, M.D. (Kingston, 1895).*

[16] Brevet Major Foster Lechmere Coore, 3rd West India Regiment (1781-1837), Prevost's ADC and Deputy Quartermaster General.

[17] Viger's account of this incident is quite different. According to Viger, he was ordered to the bridge with thirty Voltiguers and a subaltern (Le Couteur) and ten men of the 104th. His

> ... first care was to render the bridge impassable. I had been authorized to destroy it with axes. I contented myself with loosening the planks. In the stillness of the night the distant sounds of chopping informed us that the other two bridges were being destroyed. I deferred the destruction of mine for the following reasons: 1st, to permit Genl. Sheaffe's retreat should he come my way that night; 2nd, to prevent the enemy from collecting the floating debris with which he might make rafts and effect a crossing. My views found acceptance — my orders were obeyed; a chieftain must necessarily be so clever!
>
> The planks of the bridge were therefore loosened and left in such a way that they could be at a moment's notice be removed; and at the first intimation of the approach of the enemy these planks were to be piled high in such a manner

as to offer a protection to sharpshooter, and in this way utilize them as a first line of defence. With the number of men I now had at my disposal this task could have been performed in about two minutes, for I must add that within a few hours my party was reinforced by the arrival of 40 militia men and 20 Indians .... I now placed six sentries in pairs, each 500 paces in advance of the other, while a dragoon was posted as a vidette still further in advance of these, I also sent out a few Indians as scouts.

During my absence on this duty, Lieut. LeCouteur had attended to my instructions with regard to the bridge, 20 feet of which could be removed "in the winking of an eye". On my return to my post I placed my men in that position they should occupy in the moment of need. I then caused a few fires to be lighted in the moment of need.

See Neilson, ed., *Reminiscences of the War of 1812-14,* 11-12.

[18] A gruff, impatient veteran of the Duke of Wellington's Peninsula army, Pearson had a ferocious reputation and was the source for many anecdotes. Surgeon Dunlop recalled that he was "as good a man, and as brave a soldier as ever drew a sword, but too much of a martinet to be a favourite with the militia." See William Dunlop, *Tiger Dunlop's Upper Canada* (Toronto, 1967) 27.

[19] Colonel Richard Cartwright (1759-1815), see DCB, V, 167-173. Commander of the Ist Regiment of Frontenac militia and of the militia of the Midland district, Cartwright was a Loyalist and one of the most prominent landowners and businessmen in eastern Upper Canada.

[20] Captain Neal McNeale, 8th Foot, killed at York, 27 April 1813, see NAC, RG 8 I, vol. 678, p. 195, Sheaffe to Prevost, 5 May 1813.

[21] For the official report of this action, see NAC, RG 8 I, vol. 678, p. 195, Sheaffe to Prevost, 5 May 1813.

[22] "Flankers." The two "flank" companies (the grenadier and light) of the 104th. "Flankers" can also mean light infantry or skirmishers in context.

[23] The Royal Newfoundland Regiment of Fencible Infantry. For a brief history, see E.A. Cruikshank, "Record of the Services of Canadian Regiments in the War of 1812. I. The Royal Newfoundland Regiment", *Canadian Military Institute, Selected Papers* 5 (1893-1894), 5-15.

[24] The Glengarry Light Infantry Fencible Regiment. Raised in the eastern counties of Upper Canada, the Glengarries specialized in skirmish warfare. See E.A. Cruikshank, "Record of the Services of Canadian Regiments in the War of 1812. II. The Glengarry Light Infantry," *Canadian Military Institute, Selected Papers* 6 (1894-1895), 9-23.

[25] Lieutenant Henry Nathaniel Moorsom, 104th Foot (d. 1814). Formerly with the 24th Foot, Moorsom joined the 104th in November 1812.

[26] "Breastwork." A field fortification of earth designed to provide cover for soldiers in a defended locality, sometimes reinforced with logs.

[27] "Abbatis." A field obstacle formed by cutting trees, placing them with branches towards the direction of a possible attack and entangling them as much as possible. Used to cover the approaches to fortifications.

[28] Major Robert Moodie, 104th Foot (1779-1837). A native of Fifeshire, Moodie joined the army in 1794 and served in several units until joining the 104th as a captain in 1803. He commanded the regiment from May until December 1813 and from August 1814 until it was disbanded. Moodie was married to Frances Sproule, the daughter of George Sproule, Surveyor General of New Brunswick. In the 1830s, he settled north of Toronto and was killed by a mob in 1837 at Montgomery's tavern on Yonge Street.

[29] Major Frederick G. Heriot, Canadian Voltiguers (1766-1844), see *DCB*, VII, 397-400. Like Le Couteur, Heriot was a Jerseyman and was seconded from the 49th Foot to the Voltiguers. Following the war he settled near Drummondville, Lower Canada.

[30] Probably Colonel William Johnston, commanding officer of the lst Regiment of Addington Militia.

[31] "Funky." *A Classical Dictionary of the Vulgar Tongue by Captain Francis Grose* (London, 1796; reprinted 1963) defines "funk" as "To smoke; figuratively, to smoke or stink through fear."

[32] "Ball cartridge." Live ammunition.

[33] In a letter to his wife dated 12 June 1813, Viger left a long and detailed account of the attack on Sackets Harbor. According to Viger, on 28 May 1813, the British cut off a flotilla of barges on its way to the Harbor capturing twelve of them and 140 men. See NAC, Microfilm M-8, Jacques Viger, "Ma Saberdache", 77-127.

[34] According to Viger, the troops embarked from the ships into boats at 10 P.M. on 28 May and "spent the whole night on the water, tossed by the wind and threatened with the very worst weather."

[35] This is a reference to a famous incident supposed to have taken place at the battle of Fontenoy, 11 May 1745. A regiment of French royal guards approached an English guards regiment. The English commander shouted for the French to open fire first but the French commander politely demurred, whereupon the English opened up and put the French to rout.

[36] "We little fellows would half of us been drowned." This is a reference to the fact that, traditionally, the light infantry were recruited from the smallest and most agile men while the grenadiers were recruited from largest and most steady men.

[37] Captain Richard Leonard, commander of the grenadier company, 104th Foot.

[38] Captain Sir James Lucas Yeo, RN (1782-1818), see *DCB*, V, 874-877. Yeo joined the Royal Navy in 1793 and was promoted lieutenant in 1797. He was made post captain in 1809 and in March 1813 was promoted commodore and assigned to command all British naval forces on the Great Lakes.

[39] USS *General Pike*, frigate, 28 guns. She was set on fire on the orders of the American naval commander at Sackets Harbor, Lieutenant Wolcott Chauncey, but was later repaired and launched. She was sold from the navy in 1825.

[40] "My Servant Mills." It was customary for each officer to have a private soldier as a manservant. The man in question was probably Private Cornelius Mills, 104th Foot, see Austin Squires, *The 104th Regiment of Foot* (Fredericton, 1962), 225.

[41] According to E.B. Brenton, *Some Account of the Public Life of the Late Lieutenant-General Sir George Prevost* (London, 1823), 83-86, although Prevost accompanied the landing force, it was commanded by Colonel Edward Baynes, the Adjutant-General of the forces in Canada.

[42] The official British report of this action is found in NAC, RG 8 I, vol. 678, p. 347, Baynes to Prevost, 30 May 1813.

[43] Le Couteur is using the word "young" here in the sense of "green" or "inexperienced." According to Viger, the "104th Regiment, a great number of which are Canadians, showed they were worthy of the leader [Drummond] who commanded them. It is the first fire this regiment had experienced and the test was no disgrace on it, that is certain."

[44] Captain Andrew Gray, Nova Scotia Fencibles.

[45] Ensign James Gray, 104th Foot (b. 1796).

[46] "No step." Vacancies among the officers of a unit caused by deaths in combat were filled by regimental seniority. If no deaths occurred, there were no "steps up" for junior officers.

[47] Lieutenant James De Lancey, 104th Foot, (1789-1813), born in Round Hill, Nova Scotia. As De Lancey died the following December, his wound might have been more serious than was thought.

[48] According to Charles Rainsford of the 104th grenadier company, the officers of the unit wounded during this attack were: "Captain Leonard, severely wounded in the gunboats; Major Drummond slightly wounded; Captain Shore, ditto; his brother, Lieutenant Andrew William Rainsford, who led the grenadier company into action, was shot in the abdomen, the ball knocking the sword out of his hand.... Lieut. James Delaney [*sic*] had a musket ball lodged in his arm, which was never extracted. He afterwards lost his life at Kingston. Lieut. and Adjt. Moore had his lower jaw badly shattered by a ball." See "Captain Charles Rainsford's Winter March across Lake Temiscouata" in *Saint John Daily Sun*, 23 August 1889.

[49] According to the official casualty return, the 104th lost 22 killed, and 7 officers and 61 men wounded, see NAC, CO 42, vol. 121, p. 245, Return of the Killed, Wounded & Missing in an Attack on Sackett's Harbour on the 28th of May, 1815.

According to the muster lists contained in Squires, *The 104th Regiment*, 196-229, 29 enlisted men of the 104th were killed at Sackets or died of wounds in the weeks that followed the attack.

[50] In the original text, Le Couteur left the figures blank. The numbers here have been extracted from Viger who, following the attack, questioned officers from the various units involved as to the number of troops present and the casualties suffered by each unit.

[51] William Robison (1789-1851), son of Mrs. Robison, "the Commodore's Widow."

[52] Ann Ellice Robison (1785-1856), the daughter of Mrs. Robison. In 1816, she married the Reverend George O. Stuart, later Archdeacon of Kingston.

[53] Although Drummond himself was wounded, Viger states that he came on board Viger's ship "in the course of the afternoon, to pay a visit to Mr. Moore, who had received a bullet in his mouth."

# Chapter Six

## "NO SURPRISES WITH NITCHIE ON THE LOOKOUT"

Action in the Niagara,
*June to October 1813*

***5 June [1813]***

The Grenadier and Light Companies were ordered to march to the Head of the Lake to join General Vincent's[1] division on the Niagara Frontier.[2] Major De Haren[3] of the Canadian Fencibles[4] was in command, he appointed me to [be] his Adjutant.[5] Sir Roger Hale Sheaffe,[6] an old acquaintance of my Father's, asked me to dine with Him on the 8th and we embarked in the afternoon in Batteaux, got to York by the 14th, and were pushed on to the Forty-Mile Creek on the 15th. The next day I was presented to General Vincent who asked me to dinner and enquired for my Father & Mother. I met Colonel Harvey,[7] our Adj[utan]t General,[8] and my kind Friend then, on the 17th, the Light Division, as we were called, was pushed on to the Twelve-Mile Creek where we joined the Light Company of the 8th, or King's Reg[iment]t., a company of the Glengarry [Light Infantry Fencibles] and a party of the 49th [Regiment] under Fitzgibbon.[9] We were again moved to the Ten-Mile Creek and then to the Crossroads. Here we had a Body of 550 Indians encamped with us. Our advance [was therefore] quite respectable — upwards of twelve hundred men.

***21 June***

On the 21st, Captain Shore & I, with Volunteer Winslow[10] and the Light Company, were sent to check a division of the enemy which was moving on Rohrbach's. Winslow came with me as [did] the Advance Section. We took the road to St. David's [by mistake] owing to the connecting file not watching the Company and, presently, we heard a sharp volley of musquetry in our rear, then a heavy roll of fire from six or seven hundred men, and again the sharp rattle of our Light Bobs. We were completely cut off. Our fellows killed one trooper and dismounted six more, then cut away from their ambuscade, which Shore had planned carefully, waiting till the rear of the column was in line with his left, when he fired into it. They sent a strong detachment to turn the position which forced our lads to decamp. We struck into the woods off the main road but it was dark before we found our way back & were warmly greeted for they thought us prisoner.

### *24 June*

About half an hour before day break, an Indian brought me a message from their Chief intimating that a strong force of the Enemy with Guns and Cavalry were moving upon us by De Cew's. I instantly ordered the turn out, as silently as possible, and ran to Major De Haren who desired the men to be formed instantly. The Indians had all gone off after their own Mode of warfare acting quite independently — we moved after them in a run towards the Beech woods.

Presently we heard one rapid, yet steady, roll of musquetry then a terrific Yell which sounded high above a roll of Artillery & small arms. The Major [ordered me] to gallop on and see how the affair stood, then return to bring the Light Division up to the best position. In a quarter of an hour, I got to the scene of action — some round shot came plunging along the road but the Indian yells were awful and ringing all around an extensive clearing — they concealed and lying down along the edges of the wood, the American force in the clearing in Line with their Guns on their Right and their Cavalry in reserve. The 49th [Regiment] I perceived to be to the Right of the Americans turning it. To these I rode when, immediately, a flag of truce was sent in with an offer to surrender to a British force.

Fitzgibbon wished them to surrender to Him but the American officer[11] said He would not to so small a force. I observed that "the Light Division, Seven hundred men under Major De Haren, was here." "The moment they are here and can protect us from the Indians, we will surrender." They came up in less than twenty minutes and Major De Haren ratified the treaty which Fitzgibbon had entered on. The Yankee Horsemen made a dash through the Indian fire and got off but we took Two Guns, a number of Volunteer officers, and 550 men.[12]

The Indians were very savage — one tomahawked an American close to me during the parley — they would have destroyed them all but for us. All the dead were scalped. Their heads divested of the scalp looked white and clean, some as if they had been washed. I got a capital black horse for a charger on this occasion, saddle & Bridle & Pistols and all.[13]

Major De Haren gave me charge of the [American] Com[man]d[ing] officer, Colonel Boerstler,[14] and the Field officers. Our Division was drawn up in line and presented arms to Him as He rode by. He admired the men greatly: "what fine, smart, well-disciplined Young Men." Then, as he passed the Indians and saw numbers of his poor men Scalped, He first asked: "Oh! What are those? What is that?" I made no answer but turned away my head for I felt for Him. He was badly wounded and seemed horror struck, the tears rolled down his handsome countenance. He was exceedingly sensible of the poor Courtesy which I had occasion to show Him and, when I left Him in the quarters allotted to Him, He was most friendly — a fine Gentlemanly Young man.[15]

The Indians were ticklish friends to deal with. I had for a few days been acting Commissary and Quartermaster as well as Adjutant to the Light Division, having to ride about the Country with an escort, buy Oxen, flour & Rum where I could get them, then do the distribution myself. One day, I refused to give a half-drunken Indian a Hide which He coveted over and above the Meat which had been issued to his tribe when he snatched his Tomahawk and made a motion as if to cut me down. In an instant, however, self-preservation had instinctively made me place my drawn Sword to his throat and He pretended it was a mere faint and, after a growl, [said] "Sago Nitchie".[16] Of course I shook hands with Him but my men would have bayoneted Him, if I had not prevented it. I complained to his Chief and He met with some Indian rebuff.

There was a poor unfortunate American Soldier, a Prisoner in the Indian camp. An old Mohawk Chief had lost his only Son in one of the late engagements and He kept this Young Man as a Victim — it was said to be immolated when He got Him into the back woods. The poor fellow implored us to ransom or rescue Him from his sad fate and shed many tears at the idea of being taken away from civilized man. We settled on a Subscription and offered the Old Chief a Considerable Sum to give Him up to us. No Sum would tempt Him — if the young Man behaved well, He would adopt Him as his Son! A delightful Compliment! Rescue Him we dared not, it would have lost us an alliance of seven hundred Indians, most invaluable allies they were — no surprises with Nitchie on the lookout.

After a few days Our Yankee friend was stripped of his Uniform and toggery of all sorts and clothed in an Indian dress. His hair was shaven, a tuft

*Watercolour by Le Couteur illustrating an incident from his journal. See the entry for 24 June 1813.*

left on it which was ornamented with Feathers and Horse hair and, though it was very lamentable to Him and excited our Sympathy, He looked irresistibly ludicrous. However we got the Old Chief, by Good humour and presents, to adopt Him as his Son which insured his life. He was, notwithstanding, incessantly watched both by night and day. We advised [him] not to attempt to escape till he had a year or two with them as any trick of the sort would cost his life.

### *28 June*

The Division made a general forward movement to St. David's. The 49th [Regiment] Flankers with two Guns joined us there. Johnston[17] deserted.

### *30 June*

General Baron De Rottenburg arrived at Head Quarters.

### *1 July [1813]*

Twaddle & Clarke[18] deserted from an advanced picquet at Queenston.

### *7 July*

A Detachment under Colonel Bisshopp[19] marched to attack Black Rock. They returned in two days after having taken three Field pieces and a large quantity of Stores but poor Col[one]l. Bisshopp, a highly promising Officer, returned mortally wounded with a loss of ten K[ille]d. & fifty wounded [and] missing; Capt[ain]. Saunders,[20] 41[st] F[oo]t., wounded, a Prisoner.[21]

### *17 July*

Our Indians intercepted a party of the enemy, scalped forty-five and brought in two officers and fourteen Prisoners. I *saw one Indian picking the flesh off a scalp.*[22]

### *18 July*

Our Light Division marched to the Crossroads where we found the American Picquets and drove them back after a sharp skirmish to the Second Ravine.

The next day we had a set off to our affair of yesterday as Major Chapin[23] and a body of Riflemen, supported by a about a hundred Oneida Indians, attacked our advance. I galloped down to see what was going on. Lieutenant Gladwin[24] of the 19th Light Dragoons came galloping along the road from a clearing, evidently badly wounded. He pulled up on coming to me and dropped into my arms. He had ridden among the American Indians, mistaking them for ours, shook hands with them, and "Sago Nitchee'd" them all around. They were greatly admiring his fine person and splendid Uniform when five or six riflemen rushed from the wood and shouted: "Seize Him! Stop Him!" Gladwin saw his error, turned around, and galloped off with his two orderly dragoons. The magnaminous Indians, having shaken hands with Him, did not fire a shot at Him or at his men but discharged their volley above them. The Riflemen, however, fired well — one hit Gladwin in the thighs and the others hit his corporal. We had two killed and five wounded in this fracas. Serjeant Ch[ase][25] deserted — from cowardice I suspect, He did not like fire.

At this time our division consisted of the 41st, 49th [Regiments], Flankers of the 104th, 8th [Regiment] Light Company, a troop of dragoons and Two field pieces, Sixes, under Lieut. Charlton[26] and about seven hundred Indians. The Picquets here were the

| | F.O.[27] | Cap | Subs | Sergts | Corp.& Privates |
|---|---|---|---|---|---|
| Advanced | 1 | 2 | 2 | 3 | 56 |
| Right flank | 0 | 1 | 1 | 2 | 36 |
| Left " | 0 | 1 | 1 | 2 | 30 |
| Balls [Farm] | 0 | 1 | 1 | 2 | 24 |
| Donaldsons | 0 | 1 | 1 | 2 | 24 |
| Quarter Guard | 0 | 1 | 1 | 2 | 21 |
| Rear Guard | 0 | 0 | 1 | 1 | 6 |
| | 1 | 7 | 8 | 14 | 197 |

The other morning Maj[or]. Dennis[28] of the 49th [Regiment], who was the field officer of the day, saw Norton,[29] the Chief of the Indians, making an attack upon the American advance. He told me to ride with Him to see what was going on. We rode to within fire of the skirmishers, and the gallant fire-eater began making his remarks on the irregular proceedings of the Indians when, lo, just 150 or 200 yards from us, was a Masked battery[30] which opened on us with grape [and] wounded the Major's charger which instantly galloped off, luckily homewards, with Him while I was extremely prepared to follow as hard as I could tear.

The Americans had the laugh at us, however, and threw out a Column to supplant their skirmishers. Our Guns, by this time, had awaked. Charlton came down with his two Guns and threw spherical case shot[31] with such beautiful precision over the Head of the Column as to make lanes in it. The men broke and would not follow their Commanding officer, a fine Man on a Grey charger, who was killed by Norton or one of his Indians. I never saw Artillery check an advance so completely.[32]

## *September [1813]*

Our light division was broken up and we rejoined the Regiment at the Four-Mile creek. While we were at St. David's, Sir George Prevost wished to reconnoitre the whole line of American piquets.[33] Major Moodie was in command of the battalion companies of the 104th [Regiment] on our left in front of Niagara. It was a little before day. Sir George ordered me to ride as fast as I could do so through the woods if I knew the road — I said I did — and to order Major Moodie to feel the picquets in his front, as far as the edge of the woods, to drive them into the plain, "but not to expose Himself to the Guns of Fort George on any account." Off I went at a gallop. Called back. "Repeat your orders, Sir, to me!" I did so. "Very well, Sir, Go off! Called back a second time. "Mind you give Him positive orders not to expose Himself!" "I know Moodie", I think He added in an undertone. This hesitation and uncertainty reminded me of Sackets Harbor.

Off I started in earnest. As I knew the woods perfectly, having ridden through them so often for orders, I got on well through the bush and forest, making a great noise, however, the horse breaking so many boughs. I began to hear gentle popping to my right and left in front, perhaps five hundred yards off on either side when, all at once, a musquet was fired in my very face as it were, the discharge almost burned me.

"You are a Cowardly rascal, who ever you are!" I shouted, "to fire without a challenge! Who are you?" "Who comes there?" one shouted. I had seen four or five bright barrels levelled at me, by the glance of light from the discharge. "You are a Cowardly set", I repeated, "to fire at a single man. I will not tell you who I am or give the Countersign till I know who *you are*!" I began to fancy they were Yankees, however, I made no resistance to a picquet. "We are a British Picquet!" "It can't be. British Soldiers would not have fired so! What Reg[imen]t. do you belong to? Who is your Col]onel] ? Who is the Captain of your Comp]an]y?" I then gave the Countersign and one put me into the right path. Away I galloped again.

Moodie was hotly pressing the American Picquets. I delivered my orders. "Gallop back to Sir George", He said presently — for I saw the defence was quite feeble, our men were absolutely making a running fire on the retreating foe — "Gallop to Sir George and tell Him if He will allow us to run in with the Americans, we may carry the Fort by a *coup de main*[34] "In

*Watercolour by Le Couteur illustrating an incident from his journal. See the entry for September 1813.*

the meantime, Major Moodie, remember the orders Sir George sent me to deliver to you are preemptory!" "Yes, Yes! Go!"

It was now day and I was back with Sir George in ten or twelve minutes. He was crazy when I delivered Moodie's message. "Yes, Sir George, I delivered Your Excellency's peremptory orders and Major Moodie said He would strictly obey them but sent me to know your further pleasure." "Go back faster then you came and reconfirm my first order!"

When I got back, Moodie was in a fury. He was a hot Soldier and might have taken the place, He had cleared the woods of every enemy. He had called at the outset for two Volunteers to bayonet the sentries. No one but Sergeant Avarne[35] stepped forward. "Well, Avarne", said Moodie, "Since no one Volunteers, I will go with you!" They two crept upon the *single* Sentry in front of the American picquet.

### *8 September*

Both the American and British fleets in sight. It was very exciting to behold, they looked so trim and wary of each other like two grim Bull dogs eyeing each other askance. We all ran down to the Lake shore to enjoy the heart stirring event that we expected would soon occur. Commodore Chauncey[36] came within a mile of us but He never fired a shot. The Yankee army we could see on parts of the shore as much on the lookout as ourselves — the Morass & Creek kept us well apart.

### *10 September*

General De Rottenburg sent me into the American camp, and into Fort George if I could get there, with a Flag of truce and two American Ladies, Prisoners *par mes garde*,[37] Mrs. Binsh and Miss Rogers. My instructions were to see all I could, the position of the American picquet on the Lake shore, how far from the morass, its strength, gather what force they had in our front etc., etc. — *espionage en Uniforme* with Major Andre's[38] fate before me.

The Sentry on the Shore levelled at the Boat though I waved my snowy pennon in his eye. "Don't shoot your own officer's wife and sweetheart, man alive! A Sentry need not fire at women!" He paused and shouldered his shooting iron. "You can't land, I guess!" "Then I calculate I won't but you've no orders to prevent women from landing. Go and shout for the officer or Serjeant of the Picquet and I will remain here!"

As I was dressed in No. One with a gay pair of wings,[39] He rather thought He must obey even a Britisher officer and He reluctantly went a little from his post & shouted so as to bring down the Subaltern of the Picquet. We got to be excellent friends in a Jiffy for I talked to Him as if He had been of our mess, asked Him how He liked it, how He roughed it and was so friendly that we both forgot the Ladies & walked pleasantly on. He sent off my request to Gen[eral]l. Wilkinson[40] to be allowed to have the honor of being presented to Him. His dinner came — a better one than I had smelt since I dined with Gen[eral]l. Vincent — Capital beef steaks, Potatoes, and a bottle of excellent brandy. "You'll picnic with me?" "With the greatest of pleasure?" — and avidly, I might have added.

Presently up came a nice looking blood in English shooting toggery, shooting Jacket, & gaiters as well made as if Buckmaster[41] had turned them out, a beautiful double-barrelled Joe Manton[42] and a fine setter. My friend Johnson introduced me to Mr. De Peyster[43] of the United States Artillery. "Oh the old story, You Artillery Gentlemen in the American Army, I perceive, take it quite as easily as ours do — fight when you're particularly wanted. When you can['t] shoot us, You go and shoot snipes and Woodcocks. Much pleasanter Sport, isn't it, than shooting one's own kindred and language."

"Indeed, Lieutenant, it is so, I assure you. Believe me when I tell you it so grieves my heart to fire my Guns on Your people that I have asked leave to return to Virginia or to serve elsewhere. Only think of my feelings. My Uncle, Col[onel]. De Peyster formerly commanded that old 8th or King's Reg[imen]t. which is now brigaded with you." I shook hands with Him at his nice feeling and we three young Men were like brother officers.

Just then, up came Major Forsyth,[44] the famous Rifle partisan, the field off[i]c[e]r. of the day. The Picquet turned out to Him & I counted forty-five or forty-six file. The instant He saw the red cloth He said in a low [voice]: "Never turn out when an Enemy's officer is by." He was perfectly courteous and chatty, made the General's apology for not receiving me as I should be put to the inconvenience of going so far blindfolded which, either riding or walking, was not pleasant. This I certainly felt because if my eyes were bandaged I could not investigate well and, as to screwing any intelligence out of worthy old Gen[era]l. WIlkinson's noddle, that was not within [a] Subaltern's grasp. So I made my bow, Having ascertained that here might be the 5th, 6th, 13th, 22nd, 23rd Reg[imen]ts., the Baltimore Blues, 200; Forsyth's riflemen, 250; Albany Republican Greens, 150; Volunteers, 200; Cavalry, 60; Capt[ain]. Christie, Watts & Bird, Light Artillery, 10 Guns. They had quartered about Niagara from the 27th June last.

*11 September*
General De Rottenburg sent me into the American lines with despatches. On this day more care was taken as to my seeing the Picquet or its position but several American officers rode from Fort George to chat to me: Colonels Cutting[45] and Preston,[46] Majors Malcom,[47] Cummings and Johnston, Captains Jones, Christie and Chapman. Strange indeed did it appear to me to find so many names, "familiar household words", as enemies — the very names of Officers in our own army. How uncomfortably like a civil war it seemed when we were in good-humoured friendly converse — far less animosity than between the Cavaliers and Roundheads.

*26 September*
Large reinforcements were seen marching past Lewiston towards Niagara both yesterday and this day. We received orders to strike our tents, parading in marching order.

*27 September*
On the advanced picket with Captain Armstrong.[48] A deserter came in and reported that the regulars had embarked in the American fleet and that the troops we observed moving Yesterday were reinforcements of militia.

*28 September*
Ran down to the Lakeshore in great excitement, the British and American fleets were just engaging about midday. I climbed into a tree with a good spy glass and reported to Col[onel]. Harvey what was going on. I saw the *Wolfe*, Sir James Yeo's ship, engage the American Commodore's vessel, the *Pike*, while the gallant Mulcaster[49] attacked the *Oneida*.[50] The Schooners were more distant in their civilities to each other. In about three hours, to my horror, I saw the *Wolfe's* Main and mizzen top Masts fall inboard and several of her Guns silent. I nearly fell out of the tree from agitation at the sight! Mulcaster had silenced the American brig — it was affirmed she struck her Colours — but at any rate, He had the chivalry to abandon his victory and ran in between his Commodore and the *Pike* and took the battle on Himself. At 1/2 past 3 the fleets separated but the *Royal George*[51] certainly saved the day.

*1 October [1813]*
I was on the advanced picquet when Major Moodie, the Field officer of the day, ordered me to take a dozen Men and to go forward to ascertain where

the American advanced picquet was posted, to retreat when I saw it, or was fired upon, but not to engage it. I called for twelve Volunteers when the whole of my Men stepped forward. I took those next to me, gave my Sword to a Sergeant and took my rifle. We crept along the edges of the road through the woods till I came where I saw the picquet must have been posted, then advanced very cautiously.

Presently I saw an American Soldier on the other side of the road at a half run, looking anxiously about Him. "Lie down, men, close!" I levelled my rifle at the man and, in a stifled voice: "Come over here, my man, or I shall shoot you." He was guided by my voice and saw my head and my rifle aimed at him. He came over, trembling. "Who are you?" "An American deserter, Sir." "Very well, you are quite safe if you tell me the truth, a dead man if you deceive me. Where's your Picquet?" "It marched into Fort George half an hour since." "Was it not relieved?" "No Sir, our Army is in full retreat for Fort Niagara and Sackets Harbor. It is said the British are going to make a fresh attack on Sackets. You can go safely to the clearing and see Fort George." "I will but, mind, your life is at stake if you deceive me." "Never mind me, Sir, I feel safe now with you. I do not wish to serve against the British."

I went and could see some of the distant American Picquets marching into Fort George from the direction of Queenston. I hastened back with this intelligence, found Lieut. Young[52] of the 8th [Regiment] come to relieve the 104th, marched to our Camp, found it bare, my tent, servant all gone. Our Regiment, the 49th and Voltiguers had marched suddenly for Kingston, making a corresponding move to the American Army. I had to march as far as the Twelve-Mile creek before I overtook the Regiment.

We were thoroughly rejoiced at getting out of the Black swamp. The exhalations of a morning from this pestiferous and noisome marsh were so heavy that I used to amuse myself by lifting my knees slowly when all the little globules of moisture used to run down my blanket into a small pool which I then emptied on my rich green carpet of verdant grass. Drains round the Tent were constructed so as to draw off the water to some stagnant receptacle. Fever and ague, with dysentery, prevailed to an alarming extent.[53] I escaped it by temperance and early habits.

### *[October 1813]*

At Burlington we were embarked in boats and pushed on with the greatest haste. On the 3rd [of October], we passed through the fleet and gave them three Jolly cheers. The Men-of-War's men returned the Compliment by manning their yards. We only reached York at 12 o'clock at night, wet and miserable, and started again at daybreak, cold and cheerless — indeed nothing could be more uncomfortable than our open flat-bottomed boats in an October morning with the cold at freezing.

*[6 October 1813]*

On the 6th it came on to blow a perfect storm and, although we were running along the shores of a fresh water Lake, it was 250 miles in length, and the seas were really if not mountainous in the sense of those of the Atlantic, were quite so for the description of vessels we were scudding with, so high that in our fleet, when two were in the trough of the Sea, the Crews entirely lost sight of each other. More than one exclamation "Here comes our finisher!" escaped some lips. We had to drive ashore before night came on, on a low flat peninsula which afforded us poor shelter but what we were all thankful for a rescue from imminent peril.

The following day, we got into the little lake where the water was as smooth as a mill pond though the wind continued high. Here we challenged a Grenadier's boat to a rowing match — Seven in a stretch from One point to another; the amount of our bet to be given to the winners. It was a capital trial of the pluck and bottom of the Light Bobs against the Grenadiers. Each boat pulling Eight oars, the men to relieve each other as they liked, but no two men to pull at a time. It was a Capital match, stem and stem, or neck and neck, to the last length, when one of [our] oars broke and we lost the match. The distance was pulled exactly in the hour.

We pushed on till 1 o'clock in the morning when we reached Kingston where every soul was asleep, barring the Sentries and Guards. I was glad to stretch myself on the carpet near the Stove at Thibodo's Hotel[54] — no bed to be had, indeed if I had got into one I question whether I could have slept in it, I had for so many months being accustomed to sleep harnessed, often not removing my belt.

## Notes

[1] Brigadier General John Vincent (1764-1848), see *DCB*, VII, 888-889. Former commander of the 49th Foot with thirty-two years of military service, Vincent was appointed to command the Niagara frontier of Upper Canada in February 1813.

[2] The orders for the two flank companies of 104th to move to the Niagara were dated 6 June 1813 and are found in NAC, RG 8 I, vol. 1203 1/2H, General Orders, Kingston, 6 June 1813. On 11 June, the battalion companies of the regiment were ordered to the Niagara under Major Moodie, see NAC, RG 8 I, vol. 1770, p. 241, General Order, Kingston 11 June 1813.

[3] Major Peter William De Haren, Canadian Fencibles (born c. 1776).

[4] A fencible infantry regiment raised in Lower Canada. For their history, see E.A. Cruikshank, "Record of the Service of Canadian Regiments in the War of 1812. VII: The Canadian Fencibles," *Canadian Military Institute, Selected Papers* 11 (1897-1899), 9-21.

[5] "Adjutant." An adjutant was an officer appointed to see that the orders of the commanding officer of a brigade or battalion were properly transmitted and obeyed. His principal task was to ease the burden of command by removing much of the detail work from his superior's shoulders. It was a responsible position and only intelligent and capable officers were chosen as adjutants. Le Couteur was rightfully proud of being selected as a brigade adjutant at the age of eighteen.

[6] Major General Sir Roger Hale Sheaffe (1763-1851), see *DCB*, VIII, 793-796. Born in Boston, the son of a British colonial official, Sheaffe succeeded to the command in Upper Canada in October 1812 on the death of Major General Sir Isaac Brock. He was replaced in June 1813 by Major General De Rottenburg.

[7] Lieutenant Colonel John Harvey (1778-1852), see *DCB*, VIII, 374-384. Harvey entered the army in 1794 and fought in Europe, the Cape of Good Hope, Egypt and India before being transferred to Canada as deputy adjutant-general. On 6 June 1813, he stopped an American force advancing on Burlington Bay at the confusing and hard-fought battle of Stoney Creek. Harvey later pursued a successful career as a colonial administrator and served, in turn, as Lieutenant-Governor of Prince Edward Island, New Brunswick and Newfoundland.

[8] "Adjutant General." An adjutant general was a senior staff officer who assisted the commanding general of a division or district. In effect, he functioned much as a modern chief of staff, removing much of the lower-level detail work of the commander and ensuring that his orders were carried out.

[9] Lieutenant James FitzGibbon, 49th Foot (1780-1863), see *DCB*, IX. A protégé of Brock's, FitzGibbon displayed considerable iniative as a commander of light infantry and irregular forces. He had a long and distinguished career as government

official in postwar Upper Canada. See Mary A. FitzGibbon, *A veteran of the War of 1812: the Life of James FitzGibbon* (Toronto, 1898).

[10] Volunteer John Winslow (1794-1856). John Winslow was the son of Edward Winslow, a Loyalist and Justice of the Supreme Court of New Brunswick. He was commissioned in the army in 1809 and, in 1812, was serving as a lieutenant in the 41st Foot when he got into a mess altercation with another officer. Brock insisted both officers resign their commissions. Winslow then joined the 104th as a volunteer (a private soldier who fought in the ranks but messed with the officers) hoping to be restored to his rank. With the support of Lieutenant Colonel Robert Moodie of the 104th and Major General Sheaffe, Winslow was granted a lieutenant's commission on half pay in 1819. He never again went on active service but was, for many years, Sheriff of Carleton County, New Brunswick.

On the Winslow case, see NAC, RG 8 I, vol. 676, Brock to Baynes, 23 July 1812; vol. 1218, p. 387, Prevost to Torrens, 24 September 1812; vol. 1026, p. 71, Memorial of John Winslow, 19 December 1816, pp. 74-76, Sheaffe to Winslow, 8 March 1816.

[11] The American officer was probably Captain Andrew McDowell, Regiment of Light Artillery, U.S. Army.

[12] For the British reports on the battle of Beaver Dams, see NAC, RG 8 I, vol. 679, p. 140, FitzGibbon to De Haren, 24 June 1813; 137, Return of Prisoners Taken, 138, Article of Capitulation, 24 June 1813 and Letter of Dominique Ducharme and other documents in *Doc. Hist.*, VI: 139-154. For the American side, see Boerstler, "Narrative of the Expedition from Fort George to the Beaver Dams, U.C." in *Doc. Hist.* VI: 130-137 and Isaac Roach, "Military Journal of the War of 1812," *Pennsylvania Magazine of History and Biography* 17 (1893), 281-315.

Le Couteur's account of the battle makes no mention of the role played by Laura Secord, a resident of Queenston, who overheard two American officers discussing a plan to surprise the British position at Beaver Dams and capture FitzGibbon. On 22 June, Secord set out to warn FitzGibbon and reached him, with the help of the Indians, that evening. FitzGibbon thereupon sent out Indian scouts who alerted him early on the 24th of the advance of Boerstler's column. See Ruth McKenzie, *Laura Secord, the Legend and the Lady* (Toronto, 1971).

[13] "Saddle & Bridle & Pistols and all." In 1813 it was customary for mounted troops to carry their pistol holsters attached to their saddles and not on a waist belt.

[14] Colonel Charles G. Boerstler, 14th Infantry, U.S. Army.

[15] Boerstler was acquitted for his actions at the battle of Beaver Dams at a court martial. He was promoted colonel but left the army in 1815.

[16] "Sago Nitchie." A corruption of the Ojibway salutation "Shaygo Niigii!" meaning "Hello friend!" or "Hello comrade!"

[17] Private James Johnson, 104th Foot, see Austin Squires, *The 104th Regiment* (Fredericton, 1962), 215.

[18] Privates George Twaddle and John Clark, see Squires, *The 104th Regiment*, 202, 236.

[19] Lieutenant Colonel Cecil Bisshopp, 98th Foot (1783-1813), see *DCB*, V, 82-83. Bisshopp is buried in Drummond Hill cemetery in Niagara Falls.

[20] Captain William Caulfield Saunders, 41st Foot (b. 1782).

[21] For the official British report on this raid, see NAC, RG 8 I, vol. 679, p. 234, Clark to Harvey, 12 July 1813. For the official American report, see Porter to Dearborn, 13 July 1813, in *Doc. Hist.*, VI: 223.

[22] Emphasis in the original text. There is an account of this action in *Doc. Hist.*, VI: 255, Thomas Ridout to Thomas Ridout, 20 July 1813. Of this skirmish, John Norton, the native leader, says "the whole army moved forward at Sun Rise, from St. David's to the Lake Shore" and, following the fight, "the enemy left many dead on the ground, the exact number we never ascertained." See Carl F. Klinck and James J. Talman, eds., *The Journal of Major John Norton* (Toronto, 1970), 336-337.

[23] Cyrenius Chapin was a medical doctor and resident of Buffalo who, in June 1813, formed a small corps of volunteers to "assist" the American army occupying Fort George. They were detested by the regular soldiers who called them "Dr. Chapin's Forty Thieves", see Roach, "Journal of the War of 1812", 144. Chapin was captured at Beaver Dams in June, 1813 but escaped while being taken by boat to Kingston. He was recaptured in December 1813 when the British burned Buffalo, NY.

[24] Lieutenant Henry Arthur Gladwin, 19th Light Dragoons (1789- c. 1869). Gladwin's wound was serious; he was sent on convalescent leave to England in October 1813 and only returned to Canada in November 1814.

[25] Squires, *The 104th Regiment*, 202, shows a Sergeant Thomas Lakeman Chase as having deserted on 25 August 1813. The high rate of desertion of the regular troops in the Niagara in general and from the 104th in particular was a matter of concern to senior officers. On 7 July 1813 Vincent reported to Sheaffe that fifteen men had deserted from the 104th in the previous few weeks, ten of whom were from the flank companies and "in consequence of the shameful conduct of this corps, the Royals [1st Foot] have been sent to relieve them." See NAC, RG 8 I, vol. 1024, p. 56, Vincent to Sheaffe, 7 July 1813. Sheaffe decided to make an example and, on 12 July, five privates of the 104th who had attempted to desert were sentenced by a court martial to be executed, see General Order, 18 July 1813, *Doc. Hist.*, VII: 251-252. It appears from the information contained in Squires's muster lists that only two soldiers, Privates James Bombard and John Wilson, were actually executed; the other three were transported for life.

[26] Lieutenant George William Charlton, RA (1794-1822).

[27] "F.O." Field officers: majors, lieutenant colonels and colonels.

[28] Brevet Major James Dennis, 49th Foot (1777-1855). Dennis had a distinguished career during the war, was knighted in 1844 and died a major general.

[29] John Norton, or the Snipe (c.1784-c. 1825), see *DCB*, VI, 550-553. Norton was the war chief of the Grand River Mohawks and, after Tecumseh, the most charismatic native leader of the war. He was also an educated and literate observer who left a valuable account of his wartime experiences, see Norton, *Journal*.

[30] "Masked battery". An artillery battery concealed from view by troop formations or terrain features and "unmasked" to open fire at the appropriate time.

[31] "Spherical case shot." A type of projectile used only by the Royal Artillery, this was an anti-personnel round invented by Lieutenant Henry Shrapnel and introduced into service in 1804. Spherical case, or shrapnel, consisted of a hollow shell filled with powder and small bullets that was exploded by a fuse at a predetermined point on its trajectory. If functioning properly, it produced an "air burst" with lethal effect on human targets.

[32] Unfortunately, Le Couteur's Journal breaks off at this point and does not resume until September 1813. During this period, the war in the Niagara continued on much as it had in the previous months with the British keeping the American army in Fort George and Newark (Niagara-on-the-Lake) penned up within their lines.

[33] According to Norton, this event took place on 24 August 1813 when Prevost "advanced with the whole Division, driving in the Enemy's picquets, until he had gained a position from whence he made a full reconnaisance of the Enemy's position." (*Journal*, 340.)

[34] "Coup de main." Surprise assault.

[35] The name of this man does not correspond with any of the names given in Squires, *The 104th Regiment*, 196-240. He could possibly have been Colour Sergeant Benoni Avery of the 104th.

[36] Commodore Isaac Chauncey, USN (1773-1840). Chauncey commanded the American naval forces on Lake Ontario.

[37] "Par mes garde." Under my guard or by my guard.

[38] Major John Andre (1751-1780). Andre was the adjutant general of the British Army in North America during the Revolutionary War and conducted secret negotiations with Benedict Arnold behind the American lines. Apprehended while wearing civilian clothes, Andre was executed as a spy.

[39] "Gay pair of wings." Light company officers such as Le Couteur wore elaborate metal wings on both shoulders. Le Couteur is wearing these appendages in his portrait. The American sentry mistook these wings for epaulettes, badges of rank, and assumed that Le Couteur was a major, as officers of that rank or above wore epaulettes on both shoulders.

[40] Major General James Wilkinson, U.S. Army (1757-1825). A veteran of the Revolutionary War who remained in the peacetime army, Wilkinson had an unsavoury reputation and is known to have acted as a paid agent of the Spanish government. His financial dealings made him the subject of numerous courts of inquiry and courts martial. His military prowess was not equal to his pecuniary acquisitiveness and he was known as the general "who never won a battle but never lost a court martial."

[41] Buckmaster of Bond Street, London, was a well-known tailor who had a considerable officer clientele, see Anthony Brett-James, *Life in Wellington's Army* (London, 1972), 77.

[42] Joseph Manton (1776-1835) of 27 Davies Street, London, was probably the best-known British gunsmith of this period.

[43] There was no officer of this name in the U.S. regular army during the war. He may possibly have been a militia officer. The DePeyster family was an old New York clan and Le Couteur may have been mistaken when he described the American as being from Virginia. The uncle referred to was Arent DePeyster (1736-1822), see *DCB*, VI, 189-191.

[44] Major Benjamin Forsyth, Rifle Regiment, U.S. Army (d. 1814). Forsyth joined the American army in 1808 and was prominent during the war as an aggressive leader in many raids and skirmishes along the border. Apparently Forsyth was not so cordial with all the visitors who came into the American camp under a flag of truce. Captain W.H. Merritt of the Niagara Dragoons recorded in his *Journal of Events Principally on the Detroit and Niagara Frontiers During the War of 1812* (St. Catharines, 1863), 36, that when he was sent into Fort George under a flag in early July 1813, his party were met by Forsyth and "abused in a most scurrilous manner".

[45] Lieutenant Colonel Jonas Cutting, 25th Infantry, U.S. Army.

[46] Colonel James Patton Preston, 23rd Infantry, U.S. Army. Badly wounded at the battle of Crysler's Farm, November 1813, Preston became governor of Virginia in 1816.

[47] Major Richard Montgomery Malcom, 13th Infantry, U.S. Army.

[48] Captain A. George Armstrong, 104th Foot (b.1780).

[49] Lieutenant and Commander William Howe Mulcaster (1785-1837) Mulcaster had formerly served as Yeo's first lieutenant in HMS *Confiance* and followed him to North America when Yeo was assigned there in 1813.

[50] USS *Oneida*, brig, 18 guns, launched 1810, sold 1825.

[51] HMS *Royal George*, sloop, 20 guns, launched Kingston, 1809, renamed *Niagara* in June 1814, sold 1837.

[52] Lieutenant Brooke Young, 8th Foot.

[53] This is no exaggeration. The 104th Foot suffered much from sickness during the 1813 Niagara campaign. On 15 September 1813, they reported 62 men sick out of a total of 194 at the Four-Mile Creek, see NAC, RG 8 I, vol. 1708, p. 34, Morning Sick Report, Centre Division of the Army, Four Mile Creek, 15 September 1813. The following day, 65 men were sick of 206 at the Four-Mile, see NAC, RG 8 I, vol. 1708, p. 36, Morning Sick Report, Centre division of the Army, Four Mile Creek, 16 September 1813.

[54] One of the larger inns in Kingston, Thibodo's was used as a ballroom and meeting place. In 1815 part of it was turned into a wax museum, see *Kingston Gazette*, 1 August 1815.

# Chapter Seven

## "THE CHEERING SOCIETY OF AN AMIABLE CIRCLE OF YOUNG GENTLEWOMEN"

Kingston,
*October 1813 to June 1814*

### *11 October [1813]*

Dear Mrs. Robison offered me a bedroom in her house with her former kindness but, as I was fearful of intruding on Her as She had friends in the house, I declined. Very distressing news of the defeat of General Proctor's[1] army, and the death of the Indian Hero Tecumseh,[2] reached us. Our army was said to be annihilated and the 41st [Regiment] cut to pieces.

### *18 October*

On the 18th dear Mrs. Robison having urged me to take my old room, I once more occupied my most comfortable and hospitable quarters.

### *19 October*

The next day, I was despatched under Captain Sabine's[3] orders to assist him in setting up Telegraphs[4] from the Islands to Kingston and Point Frederick. A most delightful [and] amiable companion was Captain Sabine, if I had appreciated Him fully, I should never have left his guidance.

### *21 October*

I entered my nineteenth year — too full of health, for I was painfully troubled with a succession of boils all along my legs and thighs, as a set off for the dysentery which I had escaped in the Black swamp. My fair friends sent me numbers of novels, Sir Charles Grandison who was to be my model, Self Control,[5] John of Lancaster,[6] some of these I read aloud of an evening, to a coterie of sweet girls, three or four, whom the old Lady permitted to listen to me. Major Hunter[7] called to see me. There are thirteen thousand American troops at Sackets Harbor with a design to attack this place — the defences along the Lake are good, but those about the Town amount to nothing.

Kingston, 24th October, 1813

My Dear Bouton,[8]

How to set about framing an excuse for my long silence to you, I know not. I shall trust to your generosity, and return you my Sincerest thanks for yours of the 11th June. I received it last month at Niagara and would have answered it from thence, had not an order from Sir George, for our proceeding to Kingston with the utmost dispatch, prevented it. You can not conceive how happy we all were at the Idea of leaving that detested place, where, only misery, wretchedness, Broken heads and no honour or credit can be met with.

I had not mentioned to any one of the family that we were employed against the Enemy's Indians, and although deserted by our own, owing to the mismanagement of our affairs of this at all events I am not a competent Judge, but I can assure you, that to us or our enemy's, is the Death whoop an agreeable sound. The Indians are cunning, cowardly and revengeful in the highest degree, *brave* only when their enemy is Broken or flying, and then the tomahawk and scalping knife are liberally made use of. I have witnessed it with horror, but an Indian if you face him, will never stand, this, we have well impressed on the minds of our men, and they fear them not. The Americans on the Ohio and Kentucky lands, are nearly Indians, they use the Scalping knife and Tomahawk, and are merely a civilized Savage, or rather without the Virtues of an Indian and all the vice and evil which civilized life sets forth. Some of the tribes, I have met with, are Brave, generous and honorable such as the Otawas, Cocknawagas and some others whose Jaw-breaking names I do not recollect. The Mohawks of whom we have all heard so much, are mostly cowards, thieves and dirty. They do not however make a practice of scalping which the others do, I shall endeavour to procure one as a *relic*.

One morning in a Skirmish after they had scalped 45 and taken 14, who were in no small terror of being similarly treated, they were dressing their scalps and some of them after picking of the flesh, eat it.[9] This a fact. Let the Ladies pass their comments, and rejoice that they are blessed in a country where such deeds were never heard of; happy little Island.

I had the pleasure, [illegible] of seeing the Grand Falls of Niagara. They gave me an impression I shall never forget or ever feel again, so sublimely grand you feel a terrible delight, a kind of horror, at the immense body of water forever falling, and the great lakes from which it flows. I crept to the edge of Table rock and looked over and almost shrunk back at the dreadful depth below me. The air was beautiful and the Sun shining on the Spray, made the beautiful rainbow. I had so much wished to see the charms of the Naiad of the Falls, Miss Willson, and her sprightly wit were the next object of our attention; after a cold collation prepared for us by the said Lady and well partaken of by your humble servant, We returned and 13 miles off, near the camp, we still heard the roaring Falls.

I am now, my dear Bouton, in about as comfortable quarters as a poor, wandering Soldier of fortune need be, at a Widow Lady's who has an agreeable daughter and lives in the handsome Style in Kingston. Thanks to my impudence & [illegible], and the kind hospitality of my Landlady Mrs. Robison. They are a Yankee family, and have several relatives in the American army and navy. Some hard, hitherto I have been fortunate in my acquaintances, I hope I shall continue so. I am just now, confined to the house by an inflammation on my knee which the Ladies have been very careful of, was much as I can walk about pretty well but have been in great distress for fear the enemy should make their attack before I can run about as usual.

By the by, the Americans have assembled a force of 13,000 men at Sackets Harbor under Gen[era]l. Wilkinson and intend attacking this, I trust we shall give them a warm and spirited reception, as they have no right or pretension whatever in attacking and disturbing the peaceable inhabitants of Kingston. The rascals, they are worse than Frenchmen, I would not give quarter to a [illegible] of them. Pardon my warmth. Their repulse I hope soon to write you an account of, perhaps they mean it only as a diversion and will attack Montreal.

It is very singular our Fleet and theirs have not yet come to a decisive engagement, all summer have they been growling and snapping at one another [illegible] Chauncey engaged Sir James last month; We saw the engagement take place and were not a little in expectation, it lasted nearly three hours and nothing on either side terminated. Chauncey had the weather gage, his long guns carried away the Wolfe's Main and fore top masts,[10] and they fell by the board, which for the time so disabled him, he could only make use of 5 guns, and the Navy say, Chauncey must either be a coward or a Jackass, for not capturing all our fleet which they have already done on the Upper Lakes after [word missing] battle. You will have heard the particulars long ago, I do not like repeating them, as I feel indignant at our proceedings. It will be a miracle if Poor Sir James does not get thrashed here also. He is not well supported — enough of Politics.

I feel proud, to hear of the progress in arms, made by the youth of my dear native Isle. Oh, if ever it is attacked, may I be there to share the honour of defending it. Pray give my kind regards and congratulations to Col[onel]. Touzel,[11] on the Subject nay, even to my friends the Inspectors, whom I hope to breakfast with again at Mrs. LaPerise. [Words missing] of the deeds of the 104th [Regiment], Bouton, as yet they have ever behaved gallantly, I am proud to say, but it is the Skeleton of a Reg[imen]t., my own compy. marched 95, fine lads from Fredericton and are now 25, The remains of as pretty a Light company as most reg[imen]ts. can boast of, I sicken when I think of it, it is truly mortifying. If DeCarteret[12] of the 96th [Regiment] is in Jersey yet, remember me most kindly to him, I expected to have seen him in this country, a report having reached us they were ordered out here.

I hope my Dear Grandpa and all the Family continues well in health, give them my kindest love and regards, as well as to all my fine friends in St. Aubins. [illegible] will have received my letter long since, I expect one from him soon. The day I received yours, I was greeted with one from my Mother dated 10th May and another June. They were all very well, Thank God, and had received your gazette which was a most agreeable treat.

Adieu my Dear Bouton, with my best wishes for your health and happiness, Believe me, ever yours faithfully and affectionately yours.

Le Couteur

### *28 October*

On the 28th at 8 o'clock at night the Bugles and drums sounded the alarm. I was quite lame from Boils, but I turned out and marched with my Servant some five miles through mud and water to Cataraqui to join my Company. My Captain was wonderstruck at seeing me and thought me mad — what the Light bobs defending Kingston and me not with them? I returned the next day, as it was a false alarm, and was rewarded for my patriotism by the approving smiles of my fair friends, with whom the dear old Lady made me stay to dinner.

What happy campaigning days for a young Soldier of fortune thrown upon a distant, new world a short time back — to be in the cheering Society of an amiable circle of young gentlewomen, all soundly educated in the useful pursuits of life, all intimate by relationships, with the lively frankness of American manner, all of singular piety with perfect cheerfulness.

### 7 *November [1813]*

Fresh alarms, the American army moving on the opposite shore. Our light bobs were sent down to Kingston Mills[13] all in a hurry to join Colonel Drummond's detachment at Ganonoque. But no sooner had we got there then He sent us back again — the Yankees having gone downwards.

### *10 November*

The 49th and 89th [Regiments] followed them down last night.

### *11 November*

Colonels Morrison,[14] Pearson and Harvey with eight or nine hundred men and a few Indians attacked the American army which had crossed to our side at Crysler's farm. The Yankees were three thousand strong commanded by Generals Boyd,[15] Lewis[16] and Covington.[17] They were defeated with the loss of Gen[era]l. Covington, Col[onel]. Preston, and a thousand men *hors de combat* & Prisoners. Our loss, only 1 Cap[t]. & 2 Subs. killed, 9 off[icer]s wounded and 150 Rank & file Killed & wounded. A creditable and highly brilliant affair.[18]

At this period I was very much troubled with boils, which confined me to the house. The dear old Lady was most kind and considerate to me in my sufferings. I was allowed to come down *en deshabille,*[19] and read to the circle. My bedroom reading was hard on the mind with Novels [and] drawing as a relief.

There was a relative of the family, an American Lady, who was often of the party. A fair gentle girl, she was about my own age, nineteen. A remarkable person anywhere, rather tall, pale, of a dazzling complexion, large blue eyes, very pensive, profuse light flaxen hair, most gentle in voice and manner, most firm of principle and character, an amazing reader, and far better read in history than any one I knew. It was impossible not to love Her for her sweetness and mind, yet I never could have had her as my bride. I was very attentive, very kind I am sure, and very much afraid of Her. She watched any stray expression and set it right, when it escaped me.

A very dear friend said to me: "Do You admire Miss _____ very much?" "She is the nicest girl I have met in America, very good & dear." "Is that all you think of Her?" "Oh Yes, what else could a poor Sub. like me think of?" "Then take care what you say and do, She has a heart as sensitive as it is good and you are making an undue impression upon it. Your courteous and frank manners are not what she has seen among her own people."

I was sensibly affected at the idea of constraint which I should have to put on suddenly with a person so engaging and instructive, who would not fail to perceive it instantly. I hardly credited my informant, or rather examiner, but a few evenings after at forfeits,[20] when I had to salute the young Lady as a forfeit, she trembled so much and looked so pale, though concealing her face as in a jest, that I felt more uneasy than Herself. This put me on my guard not be studiously attentive as I had previously been. Had I been Five and Twenty and a Captain, She would have been an admirable Mother to my, or to any other man's children who might have had the good luck to marry Her. As it was, she was far too educated and well read for any Sub. among us to worship. Yet, after Thirty years of the world's friction and all the nice young persons I may have met with, I can think of no one so well qualified to educate and direct children properly as that fair American.

There were three sweet children living in the house. A boy and girls,[21] the youngest of whom was my Godchild, sweet little Mary.[22] There was a secret sympathy between my fair friend and myself. She had observed that I never taught Dickey or said to the little girls any thing that was either rude or wrong though I was as playful as themselves and they all loved me dearly. She also, who was purity and delicacy combined, never said or did to them any thing but what was patient, gentle and instructive. How strange that not one of us young men ever thought we could fall in love with such a girl — she spoke like a book, as the Lads said, a good republican yet full of love and regard for the old Anglo-Saxon race from whom she came. The dear old Lady thought her perfection — she called her the sweetest girl she had ever known.

It was delightful to see the fine, old, well-dressed Gentlewoman, whose figure was like Mrs. Siddons, so loving and tender towards all these young persons, myself among the number. William Robison, who was stone blind, was amazingly well read, and had a prodigious memory, recollecting every thing He heard, read or spoken. His ear had that peculiar delicacy, which blind persons possess, of recognizing persons at a distance by their step or tread. He was a good carpenter and very ingenious — a very good companion in private life. Miss Robison was about thirty, a most excellent person, a more pious, loving devoted daughter and Sister never existed. Kind and distant at first, but very sincere in giving me advice or a lecture whenever I might deserve it with all the frankness of a Sister. She gave me a Bible, with her invocation for my welfare, which I possess to this hour. If I had repaid this family with proper gratitude, I should have returned to America to visit them. I sent them trifles which I fear never reached.

*27 November*

Dined with Commodore Sir James Yeo, Captains O'Connor[23] & Groves[24] of the party. Sir James knew my Uncle Capt[ain]. Dumaresq and Phil[ip] Pipon,[25] the latter He said had the reputation of a crack Officer, and of having a Frigate in the smartest order in the navy.

How very frank and pleasant these marine big wigs are on shore and what awful tyrants some of them are on board ship. I have seen a Captain of a Man of War fling a round shot, an 18 or 24 pounder, I forget which, at his mens' legs to make them trot round the windlass faster — flinging his speaking trumpet at them as a joke. Yet this tyrant could be most winning in the society of strangers on shore. The Captains of our freshwater fleet had a very snug little mess perfectly organized — their pastry and sweets were equal to Farranas. They cost me Calomel,[26] however, as I was unwell when I went to them. Port wine alone restored the tone of my stomach after the attacks of dysentery and subsequent boils.

*7 December [1813]*

I dined with the Captain of the Main Guard who took me to his mess, the De Watteville's[27] a very good, rather foreign dinner, but not half the plate or style of our messes. They mostly spoke Swiss or German, several of them French. I afterwards got very intimate with Fauche,[28] a very nice well-educated Swiss Gentleman, Late of the Light Company. We constantly spoke French in private.

*8 December*

I received a long letter from my dear Father of only two months' date from Jamaica. My dear Mother, Gordon & Himself were all well — his were quite Angel letters, few and far between!

*18 December*

A day of alarm. Just as I was plumed for Parade, the Adjutant came to me.

"Johnny, You are to be placed in arrest!" "What for?" "Not being present for picquet at Guard mounting today. Colonel Fischer[29] of De Watteville's, a regular old Martinet, the Field officer of the day, has ordered you to be placed in arrest — so you better run out of the way before I come to do it officially as I am not dressed!" The dear good fellow had given me that chance. "I was not warned. Moore, the Orderly, never brought me the Orders yesterday." "Run and tell him so after you have seen the Orderly Corporal!" I found the man who owned before witnesses that He had omitted to warn me through inadvertence — away I went to old Fish.

I sent my card up. Col[onel]. F[ischer].: "Vat you vant, sare?" "I have come to make my excuses to you Sir, as Field officer of the day, for not having been present for picquet at Guard mounting to day and ..." — interruption — "I cannot help dat Sare, You are close to de enemie and You are absent from yor dutie. I have ordered you in arrest! I can hear no more!" "But Colonel Fischer, I was not warned!" "Dat is not true, sare!"

My blood was up and I forgot myself: "Colonel Fischer, I do not know what the rules of Your service may be, but a British officer cannot speak an untruth. I am the son of a British General Officer now in the command of a district in Jamaica, if I am placed in arrest at any time, I shall have to quit the King's Service. I have never failed to do my duty in my life, ask Major Moodie and I give you my word of honor the Corporal forget to warn me. He told me so this morning."

"Young Gentleman, You are very impertinent to speak to me in soche disrespectful manniere, but if You were not warnd, dat is anoder ting. I will speak to Major Moodie."

"I assure you, Colonel Fischer, I meant no disrespect whatever to you but the loss of my honor, and of my commission together made me forget myself undoubtedly — I respectfully beg your pardon!" My being the Son of a General and a certain anxiety His experienced eye read in my countenance that the love of duty was there, saved me.

Moodie, to whom I went, instantly went off and vouched for the honor of his Sub. The fine old Warrior sent me an *invitation to dine* with Him as an atonement, and we were as great friends as a boy Sub. and a quasi-General of fifty years' service could be afterwards. He did me the honor to dine with me, as well as Sir James Yeo, and Commissary General Turquand[30] — which were thought great stretches of hospitality in a Sub. But *our mess was* the mess of the day — conducted on guest days like the table of a Nobleman — every thing of the best - no noise among waiters or officers, all aiding one another to do honor to the Guests, never mind whose they were. Often and often have I been asked by my three Commanding officers to take charge of one of their friends and they have courteously returned the attention. It was a happy mess of brotherhood that jolly, gentlemanlike 104th for four years. After that, two, I was going to say Villains, disturbed its harmony. Milton makes one destroy perfect felicity for ever — no wonder that a couple of the same destroyer's agents should have done mischief among an unsuspecting set of, till then, frank friendly-hearted Young Men.

I received a letter from M[ajor] Gen[era[l] Sir Tho[ma]s Saumarez some time since dated 28 Sept[ember]. stating that he had succeeded my friend Gen[era]l G. Stracey Smyth as L[ieutenan]t. Gov[erno]r. of New Brunswick. He has got to Fredericton where He says "Everybody here speak of you as you are spoken of every where you go; It is perhaps as well You did not continue much longer as it might have spoiled you as a Soldier, and you would not have seen so much service which will be of infinite use to you as long as you live." Sir James Saumarez has rec[eive]d the grand Swedish order of the Sword and my Uncle Phil, his Captain, an inferior order.

### *25 December*

Xmas day. How I looked back with sorrowful delight to those happy Merry Xmas days our family had enjoyed together at St. Peter's where my dear Grandfather, Sir John Dumaresq, a pattern of the fine old English Gentleman, used to receive his Children, his Grandchildren, his Nephews and Nieces and more distant branches with the most joyous hospitality. As a College boy I used to look forward to that day for months with bright anticipation to enjoy his dear bright countenance which ever received me with the most bland smiles. When I carry my recollections back to when we returned from Scotland, at that time I was Six years old, when dear old "Ma Luzon" Colas, his housekeeper, my own Mother, and my Nurse received me from the gig, the day we arrived in Jersey, and clasping me in her arms at the entrance to the Lawn [said:] "*Man chier P'tit, Je te tiens aguèrre un faie, tu ne me requitteras pont!*"[31] I had been to the frozen North but my little heart had not chilled to her warm embrace! What a pattern of Love, truth, devotion, activity and independence was that admirable and much loved Person to all the family.

Then, my Grandfather's person was in the beauty of elderly manhood. He was rather above five feet, Six Inches high, of admirable form for any feat of activity or strength. His step light and airy with an inexpressible grace of manner. He used to whip me up on his shoulder, and run or march about the lawn, or room, to the tune of the "British Grenadiers" — "Some talk of

Alexander, and some of Hercules"[32] — which I verily believe did more to inspire me with the early love military than any one thing. Then his beautiful face was so sweet in expression, his features rather small but almost faultless, a front of Jove, with a rich hazel elongated eye and fringed eye lashes, under which, if roused the fire would sparkle with immense power. He had been Captain of Winchester school, his talents, manner and attractive look would have placed Him at the head of any University, so said better Judges than I. He received high polish at the French Court whither he was sent – and became without a Compeer, the first Jerseyman of his age: a fine Gentleman, of splendid eloquence as a Patriot, and an able advocate. Later he filled the Bench with honor and dignity. He was named to the Royal Commissioners as a great Lawyer — authority!

Though some thousand miles from dear St. Peters, The Gentleman Cadet was in very happy quarters for any Xmas day. Dear Mrs. Robison had invited me to dine with a merry family party — it was my duty and my privilege to endeavour to amuse.

After tea well over and arrangements were making for forfeits or some amusement to be fixed upon, I slipped out with Miss Ph____s, an ally who lent me one of Her Mother's dresses. In a short time I was fully equipped, slipped out of the back door, knocked at the front door, and requested to speak to the kind old Lady as a decayed Gentlewoman requiring aid. Miss Ph. was of course sent out to hear my story and thought it would be better the poor Lady should tell her own story to the whole party who might become interested in her welfare. This was reported and the decayed Lady told her piteous tale, loss of Husband, children, fortune. The old Lady Herself was completely won and a large sum was preparing for her relief but a certain occasional twinkling in the unfortunate Lady's eye led one or two of the fair sparklers [to] suspect the truth — a whisper went about and screams of laughter following, the poor Lady had to cut and run.

Florella was there. We drank a toast to the glorious captors of Fort Niagara which was taken, or rather carried, by surprise and storm on Sunday last, my friend Dawson[33] leading the assault, it will make him a Captain so everybody say.

On Picquet sat up all night with Captain Shore and Bass. What a horrible round we had in going the circuit of Kingston there were no roads or even paths of a snowy night to be found, so that visiting rounds en Masse — officer, corporal and File of men were lost for an hour occasionally. I have often been out above two hours on these necessary and unavoidable duties, always between the hours of 12 and daylight. On this occasion a kind friend, Miss R[obison]. sent us a nice hot supper which was highly acceptable.

### *1 January [1814]*

This is a great day of festivity in Upper Canada as well as elsewhere. It is the visiting day *par excellence*. The Ladies sit in state, like girls sitting as Bridesmaids at home to receive wedding suits. Cake and Wine and Kisses are privileged to be taken together — many a young fellow has lost his heart on this great day when the too near contact of eyes and lips has formed the first link of a chain destined never to be broken. Red Coats were not deemed sufficiently intimate for the blessing, generally, but I managed now and then to succeed by commencing an attack upon some respectable dowager as a Hornwork.[34]

### *4 January*

Heard the news of the capture of Black Rock and Buffalo[35] which was hailed with a jolly three times three after dinner.[36] Our elegant and pretty friend Mrs. Markland[37] gave us a handsome ball. The Colonel and a lot of us went there together but, instead of introducing us, He made me enter first and introduce Himself and the unknown of our party. "Johnny, you are the master of ceremonies on these occasions."

### *6 January*

Dined with Colonel Drummond and Commissary General Turquand, the latter an old friend of my Father and Mother at Jamaica. They live *en garçons, en grand, et en bon gout*.[38]

### *7 January*

Mr. and Mrs. Robison went home to the Napanee Mills today. He is a worthy man; She is a very nice person, a devoted Mama and must have been a beauty but like many American women has lost one of the chief attractions behind ruby lips. Sweet little Martha, my Godchild,[39] is the only playfellow left, Richard & Elizabeth being at home.

### *9 January*

Shore rowed me for being a little late for parade but He admitted I had a *fair* excuse. I was running to keep myself warm at the Square when I perceived a fair Lady Captain — of the 100th Regt, wife — very smartly got up with an Umbrella feeling for a point where to cross a little shallow stream which intercepted her progress. I was on the very point of jumping when she cast an imploring look at me. She was rosy, fair and *en bon point*, a very nice armful. I did not know the lady; I could scarcely offer to take Her up on an embrace and carry Her over. It was too wide to jump Her across. I could still less offer to take Her up as they land you at low water in Jersey, on my back.

Now all this was very perplexing, I was sure it was time for me to be telling off the Light bobs and I was looking at a pretty Lady and doing nothing. "I beg your pardon, Madam, you seem at a loss to cross that brook, allow me." I placed my nice clean boot, foot and all into the middle of the running water. "Now Madam if You will favor me with your hand, and place Your pretty foot upon my instep, You may skip over dry shod." Over she flew. "How very gallant I declare, thank you, to whom am I indebted for this happy expedient." "L[ieutenan]t. Le C. of the 104th. By your pardon but I am late for Parade" & off I flew. The funniest story I ever heard belonged to this Lady afterwards.[40]

*10 January*

Major Moodie drills our Regt[iment]. on the ice — it is very disgusting. When we are in close column, the ice cracks with reports like young pistols, one fancies the whole regiment is going into four fathoms at a plunge, when He stands, 30 yards off, safe enough. Even when we Light bobs are skirmishing, the ice made hideous noises. As I passed in skating the other day, I declare it feels uncomfortable, though it is pretended it is best when it does so.

*21 January*

General Drummond,[41] afterwards Sir Gordon, arrived with his suite.

*23 January*

W[illia]m. Robison dined at the mess with me. He brought his family from the Napanee Mills with Him today.

*6 February [1814]*

No church to day, Our Rector having gone to York to celebrate the wedding of Captain Loring[42] of ours and Miss Campbell,[43] a pretty person of Nineteen.

*8 February*

On the main guard with a Captain of De Watteville's who could just make out English enough for broken words of command. He asked me to *dinniere* somehow which I understood sufficiently, and my French made it agreeable to me in a Swiss German Society.

*12 February*

Took a walk in my snowshoes, we having had some very heavy falls of snow — there may be a couple of feet of it in the open fields.

### *16 February*

Captain Popham[44] invited me to their Navy mess, a first rate one both for style and company — all Captains and select society. The shipping are getting fitted rapidly and will be ready when the ice breaks.

### *17 February*

Captain Henry Alexander Stewart Dobbs RN,[45] a prime Sailor and Gentleman, having invited our Rector, the Reverend Mr. Stuart to attend for the occasion, He was united in marriage to dear rattle, Mary Cartwright, the daughter of Colonel Cartwright and niece of W[illia]m. Robison, at Eight o'clock this evening. The happy couple were to have gone to Montreal for their honeymoon but a rumour of an Attack coming to ear this morning, Hymen had to yield to Mars, and no leave could be thought of. It is of no use to give one wedding cake to dream on, if you have been dancing desperately a whole night. Sleep comes on like a dead weight.

### *25 February*

It is thawing fast, symptoms of spring. The Sun is getting high, it freezes at night and thaws by Day.

### 7 *March [1814]*

Returned from the Napanee Mills where I enjoyed two very pleasant days with W[illia]m. & Mrs. Robison, Mrs. Cartwright, Stevens and M[is]s. Smith there. On Sunday we went to the Mohawk Church.[46] The Minister or reader was an Indian Chief, the Squaws were on one side and the Indian Men on the other. None looked up as we entered though my Red uniform was enough to attract notice in some Churches that I have entered. The reader had a fine sonorous voice and read very impressively. After having witnessed these men scalping, looting, Yelling and carousing in the Upper part of the Province, it was very striking and imposing to behold them listening to the Divine truths of Christianity. I believe it was a translation of St. John's Gospel into the Mohawk language — one of the many blessings conferred on the American race by the glorious British and Foreign Bible Society.[47] The Squaws sung their hymns sweetly, plaintively.

### *14 March*

Miss R[obison]. being away, Florella is keeping house for Her. How quiet and methodical she is in all things — what a well constituted mind she possesses! The dear old Lady asked me one day whether I could not love such a being? I could if I dared but she was far above my range of intellect. I could admire rather than love. Love Her in the Christian as everybody who had the privilege to know Her, must do.

### *3 April [1814]*

The Ice is getting very dangerous. I went over to Points Henry and Frederick Yesterday and found it very sloppy in returning. The new ships are nearly completed. News of the affair at Odell Town and La Colle Mill.[48] The Enemy under Macomb[49] & Wilkinson attacked our troops on the 30th last, but received a severe repulse. The 13th [Regiment of Foot] under Sir W[illia]m. Williams[50] and some Marines, and Militia behaved very well. The force was com[mande]d. by Gen[era]l Vincent.

### *10 April*

This morning, on jumping out of my bed, a singular sight presented itself to my view. The *Sidney*[51] was floating out of the harbour in a large cake of ice, with all the Bushes and trees also a part of the road which led to Her. She was helpless in the stocks while the *Beresford*[52] was *sailing* after Her to her assistance. She was brought up about half a mile from the harbour, having rigged a cable and anchor by that time, I suppose. The next day the *Wolfe and Melville*[53] were released from their torpid state, and the harbour and Lake begins to wear a European Aspect while the now full-rigged ships enliven it and form a bright contrast to the miserable appearance they had while unrigged and laid up in ice bergs like ill-shapen block houses. They would have been ugly customers to attack with their jolly crews to defend them — *batteries a fleur de glace.*[54]

### *14 April*

Hearing that our two ships of war were to be launched to day at 3 P.M. I got over by one o'clock to witness the preparations but at three the ways for the smaller vessel were not yet finished so we, a large concourse of Ladies, Gentlemen & others, had to endure a drizzly rain. Captain Popham took Martin & I to the Navy Mess where we enjoyed a good lunch and at 1/2 past 5, the blocks were knocked away and the pretty Frigate *Princess Charlotte*[55] glided into the smooth fresh water, dashing the white foam before Her in her plunge. The gallant Mulcaster, her Captain, was launched with Her. Half an hour later, The *Regent,*[56] a Noble Sixty-gun Frigate followed the *Princess,* as a Lover to guard his Belle. He, not *she*, went off beautifully, plunging into the calm waters then rode in Triumph a real Lord of the Lake. It was a very exciting day, for the Americans have a war of Carpenters with us at Sackets Harbor.

*Marginal sketches from Le Couteur's journal, showing ...*

*... HMS Prince Regent, the fifty-six gun frigate launched at Kingston, 14 April 1814. See the journal entry for that date.*

*... the type of coach in which he travelled through New York in January 1816. With "four capital trotters [it] brought us along at a rate of Ten miles an hour - a jolly pace."*

### *23 April*

Walked out to McLean's to witness the effect of rockets on a picketed fence which had been erected for occasion. These Congreve rockets[57] explode a shell at a given distance and when accurately fired, which is rarely the case, are very destructive. One of them struck the picketing and carried away a great part of it, a fragment of the shell came back & fell near Col[onel]. Fischer. The last that was fired mounted into the air perpendicularly and, for some moments, the spectators were in doubt whether it would not fall among them. We all agreed that the rushing noise of them would frighten any Cavalry.

### *1 May [1814]*

Sunday. May day. I had the happiness to receive letters from my dear Mother from Jamaica dated two months later than the last — They were all well — and one from my Aunt Betsy Pipon.

### *2 May*

Sir James Yeo hoisted the Commodore's broad pennant[58] today to act as Rear Admiral on the Lakes with a Captain.[59]

### *3 May*

An expedition in embryo. In hopes we were to join it but it was confined to De Watteville's [Regiment], the Glengarries & Marines, with some Artillery & Rockets, under the command of Col[onel]. Fischer.

### *4 May*

The Fleet sailed this morning. The *Regent* looks a Superb ship on the water, going out in grand style under a Royal salute. They did not get out of Sight all day for want of wind.

### *5 May*

The wind having been fair during the night, the business must be all over. At half past four we could hear the discharge of the heavy guns quite plainly, firing it seemed by Vollies. Intense anxiety prevailing till Saturday 5 P.M. when the *Regent* hove in sight followed by the Squadron. It was a proud sight to see the noble ship entering the harbour with the American below the Broad pendant, signalling Victory. Captain Jervoise[60] came on shore soon and gave the history of the taking of Oswego. They landed about twelve yesterday under a heavy fire of artillery and musketry and carried the Fort by storm. They captured ten long 32-pounders, the Cable and lower rigging of their new ship, and upwards of one thousand barrels of Flour & salt etc., etc. Our loss amounted to 1 Captain, Holtaway,[61] Killed an15 men, 2 off[icer]s and 60 men wounded.[62] Poor Capt[ain]. Mulcaster was very dangerously wounded — it is said He saw the shot and could not get away from it. Poor Victor May[63] is mortally wounded. On Sunday we buried poor Holtaway.

### *10 May*

The flower of De Watteville's Reg[imen]t., De May, died this morn. His brother, the Colonel, is in the deepest distress and was forced to be torn from his body. His interment took place on Wednesday, the whole of the garrison attended.

### *24 May*

Up at five for a Muster. Our Colonel is an early bird with a Vengeance. Received a letter from my dear Gordy dated Jamaica Dec[ember] 7 last — it has been five months and a half coming through the adj[utant]. Gen[era]l's Office in London. My Father was much pleased at my having been acting as Adj[utan]t. to the Light division. He desires me to buy a horse, etc. They were in a nice house prettily situated close to the barracks. Gordon writes very nicely for a Lad of thirteen. He says:

> The Park camp[64] as it is called, where the barracks are, is a fine flat piece of ground, when we came here first it was full of holes and the weeds were so high that you could not see anybody, but since Papa has had command of the Brigade, he has set the black pioneers[65] to work and now it looks as well as a gentleman's park. Since He has done that the Soldiers are much more healthy, and many less have died this year than before. Papa gets up every morning at day break, gives the pioneers a task. He shows them how to weed, and if they do all that He tells them, they get two holidays instead of one.

He contrasts the conduct of my Father with that of some other General officers who lay a bed all the morning till it is time to go to the Clubs. He talks of the Youngsters of the army drinking very hard. The Packet had been taken and the mail lost. They were all well.

### *4 June [1814]*

Our good old King completed his 76th Year. As many guns were fired from the Forts as a Royal salute. We had the very disgusting intelligence that my friend, Captain Popham, and Capt[ain]. Spilsbury[66] with two hundred men were taken Prisoners in Sandy Creek the day before Yesterday. So much for taking boats full of men up a wooded creek with hidden enemies on each side shooting into the boats as at Targets[67] — Sir James in a horrible rage at their imprudence.

### *6 June*

Col[onel]. Drummond resumed the command of the Reg[iment]t., being quite recovered from his wound.[68]

### *9 June*

My excellent friend, Capt[ain]. Philip Dennis,[69] left us for England on sick leave, the climate being too cold for Him. My Kind Mentor, as they called Him, left his Telemachus,[70] as the wags called me, his beautiful sabre as a Keepsake — I was often allowed to wear it as a *dress* sabre.

Col[onel]. Drummond amused Himself by teaching us to load on *our backs.* Our light bobs did not at all enjoy scratching their nice bright pouches and dirtying their Jackets. Carter[71] of the Artillery and Gray[72] of the 8th [Regiment] dined with me this week.

### *13 June*

I received a long letter from Sir Tho[ma]s. Saumarez Yesterday which I answered at once telling Him the news of the day. Vice President of the Mess this week. *Nine* Doctors dined with us today — it was enough to breed a plague. Pleasant fellows they are, nevertheless, the most educated among us all. The fleet having completed their provisions, sailed with reinforcements for the Royals, King's, 100th & 103rd [Regiments] on the Niagara frontier — 250 men.

### *16 June*

The *whole* of our Regiment ordered to work at the new Line-of-battle Ship, 104 Guns — in compliment to our number of course she sh[oul]d be called the 104th — a pleasant job for Soldiers. We have been Canoemen, woodsmen, snowshoemen, batteaux men, Gunboat men, and now shipbuilders — what next? It is very amusing and interesting however, in *fine* weather, to watch the various workmen in a dockyard. It is whispered that some Yankees are working among us and will set the vessel on fire some jolly night. We are sharp on Sentry however!

I have received a very kind letter from Sir Thomas Saumarez informing me of his project of raising a Regiment of Blacks and "in case I raise a Corps, I shall have my applications from various quarters, and if so I would reserve a Company for You, and apply immed[ia]t[e]ly for you to join me." I wrote to thank Him very sincerely and that I would gladly accept his offer. Would I had done so when General Coffin offered me a company for *Four hundred* pounds last year, when He was raising the New Brunswick Fencibles. The other is not so certain as that would have been. It was cruel my being advised to refuse the rank, a Captain at eighteen![73] — what a chance lost!

### *17 June*

Captain Shore returned from Sick leave and took command of the Light Bobs. We witnessed a lively Sight this morning. Mr. McGillivray,[74] one of the Heads of the North West Fur Company, started for the far lakes in his noble Canoe this morning. She is the finest Canoe I ever saw — I should fancy Five and twenty feet long, very broad, light and strong. He has to visit his posts *Twelve* hundred miles off and is to perform the distance in twelve days, putting aside bad weather, nothing but very high winds stop Him. He had twelve Jean Baptistes[75] or woodsmen as a crew, fine active fellows. These paddle all day long from 3 in the morning to 9 at night, from 100 to 120 miles in a day, along the rivers and lakes. They carry the Canoe over the portages.

### *20 June*

My excellent and respected friend Colonel Cartwright lost his youngest Son this day, a sweet youth,[76] the fourth child this excellent man has lost in three years. I attended as a pall bearer — the good colonel told me that hard as was the trial, He could bear the dispensations of Providence with resignation, He had been sadly tried, but his children were all good — their death left no pang, but sorrow.

### *26 June*

Sunday. The regiment was inspected this morning at *half past five*. Old General Stovin[77] is yet earlier than his Turkies. After the review, He examined the interior economy[78] of our *well regulated* corps, found our books, barracks etc. at 11, and expressed high approbation of all. Generals Drummond, Stovin and the Commodore dined with us. The General's ADC, Captain Jervoise, is a very agreeable young man.

Replied to my dear Mother's letter of the 26 April — they were all well.

Went to Cataraqui in Moore's Canoe - we were about half an hour paddling the *three miles and more.* Much pleased with the encampment. Our mens' huts of bark are laid out in a Square and the whole is enclosed with a neat fence. The huts do not admit a drop of rain and the situation is very healthy. Paddy Coyne[79] declares He is so snug He must get spliced.[80] It blew very hard when we returned, which made a bobbery of a nasty short Sea. I was very pleased to get out of the Canoe unducked.

### *1 July [1814]*

Heard of the arrival of two thousand of the Duke of Wellington's late army at Quebec — the 6th, 82d and 90th [Regiments].

Gen[era]l. Stovin ordered "all officers off duty to attend the Guard Mounting, at Six o'clock every morning" — the Lazy ones fiercely annoyed.

We have to thank the Turkey stealers for this. The worthy General does not patronize the flower of the army — we Subs — at his dinners. I have dined with him, however. But He is a turkey and poultry fancier, feeds some on barley, some on wheat, some on rice, tis said, and the flavours of the meat varies, more or less succulent, juicy or dry, which the Big Wigs and Gourmands discuss but the Subs only hear of. Now the Story goes that, although there was a sentry over or near to the Poultry yards, some military foxes scaled the fences and captured the Turkies, making a confidential report to Him on the barlied, wheated or riced meats.

### *6 July*

The Yankee army crossed the Niagara on the 3rd opposite Black Rock. Six thousand men with a train of Artillery. On Mississaga picquet — the duty comes round every third night.

### *7 July*

Part of the 89th [Regiment] arrived today — sent on to York. Rumours that the Yankees are threatening the Upper Country again in consequence of the sharp action between Gen[era]l. Riall[81] & the Yankees at Chippawa on the 5th.[82]

## Notes

[1] Brigadier General Henry Proctor (1763-1822), see *DCB*, VI, 616-618. Proctor commanded the Right Division of the British Army and was decisively defeated by the American Major General William Henry Harrison at the Battle of the Thames in October, 1813. Proctor was later courtmartialled for his actions during the battle. He was acquitted but reprimanded and this ended his active career.

[2] Tecumseh (1768-1813), see *DCB*, V, 795-801. The charismatic head of the Indian confederation of the old Northwest, Tecumseh was the most powerful native leader during the war. His death at the battle of the Thames spelled the end of the dream of an independent Indian state in North America. For recent studies, see John Sugden, *Tecumseh's Last Stand* (Norman, 1985) and R. David Edwards, *Tecumseh and the Quest for Indian Leadership* (Toronto, 1984).

[3] Captain Edward Sabine, RA (1788-1883), see *DCB*, XI, 798-800. Sabine became a very distinguished scientist.

[4] Le Couteur uses the word "telegraph" here in its early nineteenth century meaning of a semaphore.

[5] Mary Brunton, *Self-Control, a novel* (Edinburgh, 1811).

[6] Richard Cumberland, *John of Lancaster, a novel* (3 vols., London, 1809).

[7] Major Thomas Hunter, 104th Foot (b.1782). Hunter was in command of the 104th from January to June 1814.

[8] Le Couteur placed this letter in the text at this point. The addressee, Philip Bouton, was the husband of his Aunt Louisa.

[9] Le Couteur's mentions this incident in the text of the Journal, see entry for 17 July 1813.

[10] This description of the damage suffered by the *Wolfe* disagrees with the Le Couteur's Journal entry for 28 September 1813 when he states that she lost her main and mizzen top masts.

[11] Lieutenant Colonel Helier Touzel, Inspector of Militia at Jersey.

[12] Lieutenant John Dan De Carteret, 96th Foot.

[13] Kingston Mills was located near the present-day site of the Kingston Mills lock of the Rideau Canal five miles north of the centre of the town.

[14] Lieutenant Colonel Joseph Wanton Morrison, 89th Foot (1783-1826), see *DCB*, VI, 520-521. A fine soldier and the victor of Crysler's Farm, 11 November 1813. See William Patterson, "A Forgotten Hero in a Forgotten War," *Journal of the Society for Army Historical Research* LXVIII (Spring, 1990), 7.

[15] Brigadier General John Parker Boyd, U.S. Army (1764-1830). A former soldier of fortune in India, Boyd joined the American army in 1808.

[16] Major General Morgan Lewis, U.S. Army (1754-1844). A veteran of the Revolutionary war, Lewis served progressively as Attorney General, Chief Justice and Governor of New York state. A brother-in-law of U.S. Secretary of War John Armstrong, he was appointed a brigadier general in 1812 and promoted to major general the following year.

[17] Colonel Leonard Covington, U.S. Army (1768-1813). A veteran of the Indian wars of the 1790s and a former member of Congress, Covington joined the U.S. Army in 1809 and was killed at the battle of Crysler's Farm, 11 November 1813.

[18] According to NAC, RG 8 I, vol. 681, p. 59, Corrected Return of the Killed, Wounded ... 12 November, 1813, British casualties at Crysler's Farm were 22 killed, 148 wounded and 9 missing. For the British report of this action, see NAC, RG 8 I, vol. 681, p. 78, Morrison to De Rottenburg, 11 November, 1813.

[19] "En dehashibille". In a state of relaxed dress.

[20] Forfeits was a popular nineteenth and early twentieth century parlour game involving the transfer of an article which a player gave up as a penalty and tried to redeem by performing some silly task.

[21] These were the children of Mrs. Robison's son, Richard, who had married Mary Secord in 1803 and who resided in Napanee. They were Richard, age 9 or 10, Elizabeth, age 8 and Martha, age 6.

[22] Le Couteur's memory is at fault here. His goddaughter, Mary, was not born until 3 October 1814, see Journal entry for 2 January 1815. The little girl he is referring to is actually Martha Smith Robison, born 14 March 1808.

[23] Lieutenant and Commander Richard O'Conor, RN, Yeo's flag captain: lieutenant, 1806; commander, 1810; captain, 1814.

[24] Either Lieutenant and Commander Thomas S. Groves, RN: lieutenant, 1796; commander, 1810; or James Groves, lieutenant, 1802; commander, 1814.

[25] Captain Philip Pipon, RN (d. 1819) the brother-in-law of Le Couteur's mother: lieutenant, 1794; commander, 1802; captain, 1808.

[26] "Cost me calomel." Caused him to ingest mercurous chloride, a laxative.

[27] De Watteville's regiment was a foreign regiment in the pay of the British crown. Nominally Swiss, it actually recruited men from every European nation. For a history of this unit, see John P. Martin, "The Regiment De Watteville: its Services and Settlement in Upper Canada," *Ontario Historical Society, Papers and Records* 62 (1960), 17-30.

[28] Le Couteur's memory is playing tricks with him here. There was no officer named Fauche serving in De Watteville's regiment in 1814. There was, however, a Lieutenant Gaspard Fauche (b. 1795) serving in De Meuron's regiment with whom Le Couteur socialized in Montreal in 1815.

[29] Lieutenant Colonel Carl Viktor Fischer, De Watteville's Regiment (1766-1821).

Fischer had seen much action against the French and was seriously wounded during the assault on Fort Erie, 15 August 1814.

[30] Deputy Commissary General Peter Turquand.

[31] "Man chier P'tit, Je te tiens aguèrre un faie, tu ne me requitteras pas." My dear little one, I've got you and I won't let you go.

[32] This is the first line of the "British Grenadiers," perhaps the most famous British march, which dates from the late seventeenth or early eighteenth centuries. See Lewis Winstock, *Songs and Music of the Redcoats. 1642-1902* (London, 1970), 29-31.

[33] Captain Thomas Dawson, 100th Foot (1790-1838). For the British report on the capture of Fort Niagara, see NAC, RG 8 I, vol. 681, p. 253, Drummond to Prevost, 20 December 1813.

[34] "Hornwork." A type of outerwork in fortresses.

[35] The villages of Black Rock and Buffalo, NY, were captured and burned by a British force under Major General Phineas Riall in retaliation for the American burning of the Canadian village of Newark (Niagara-on-the-Lake). For the official British report of these actions, see NAC, RG 8 I, vol. 681, p. 319, Drummond to Prevost, 30 December 1813.

[36] "Three time three." "Hip, hip, hurrah!" repeated thrice.

[37] Catherine (Herchmer) Markland, the wife of Thomas Markland, captain in the militia and second only to Richard Cartwright as a leading citizen in the social and economic life of Kingston, see *DCB*, VII, 583-586.

[38] "En garcons, en grand, et en bon gout." Like bachelors but in good style and taste.

[39] Again, Le Couteur's memory is false. It was not Martha Smith Robison who was his godchild but Mary who was not born until October 1814.

[40] Unfortunately, Le Couteur does not see fit to share the story with his readers.

[41] Lieutenant General Gordon Drummond, Commander, Upper Canada (1771-1854), see *DCB*, VIII, 236-239. Drummond assumed this post in December 1813 and held it until 1815 when he succeeded Prevost as commander in chief, British North America.

[42] Captain Robert Loring, 104th Foot (1789-1848), see *DCB*, VII, 517-518. Loring was Drummond's personal ADC and remained in Canada after the war holding a series of staff appointments.

[43] Mary Ann Campbell, daughter of Judge William Campbell of York.

[44] Lieutenant and Commander Stephen Popham, RN (d. 1842): lieutenant, 1805; commander, 1810; captain, 1814.

[45] Lieutenant and Commander Alexander T. Dobbs, RN: lieutenant, 1804; commander, 1814.

[46] The Mohawk Chapel was built with the assistance of the Society for the Propagation of the Gospel in 1791 and was located in the Indian grant given to the Loyalist Mohawks in the vicinity of the modern town of Deseronto, Ontario on the north shore of the Bay of Quinte. The chapel Le Couteur saw was not the present structure which was erected in 1843. For the early history of this settlement, see M. Eleanor Harrington, "Captain John Deserontyn and the Mohawk Settlement at Deseronto," *Queen's Quarterly* 29 (1921), 165-180.

[47] Le Couteur is unaware that this translation was made by John Norton, the same Indian leader he records as having been a ferocious fighter during the recent campaign in the Niagara, see entry for 18 July 1813. Norton's translation was published in an edition of two thousand copies by the British and Foreign Bible Society in 1805. Norton was active in the work of this society which was devoted to the extension of Christian missions and the abolition of slavery.

[48] The battle of LaColle Mill fought on 31 March 1814, was a victory for the British. For the official British report, see NAC, RG 8 I, vol. 682, p. 289, Williams to Vincent, 31 March 1814.

[49] Brigadier General Alexander Macomb, U.S. Army (d. 1841). Macomb defeated a British army under Sir George Prevost at Plattsburgh in September 1814. He was chief of the U.S. Army from 1828 to 1841.

[50] Lieutenant Colonel William Williams, 13th Foot, (1776-1832). One of the best light infantry commanders in the British army, Williams had fought in the West Indies, Egypt and Spain.

[51] HMS *Sir Sidney Smith*, schooner, 14 guns. Launched in 1806, she was renamed the *Magnet* in 1814 and burned to prevent her falling into American hands.

[52] HMS *General Beresford*, schooner, 12 guns, launched in 1812, renamed the *Netley* in 1814.

[53] HMS *Lord Melville*, brig, 14 guns. Launched in Kingston, 1813. she was renamed the *Star* in 1814.

[54] "Batteries a fleur de glace." Literally ice-flowered batteries.

[55] HMS *Princess Charlotte*, frigate, 43 guns, launched Kingston, April 1814.

[56] HMS *Prince Regent*, frigate, 56 guns, launched Kingston, April 1814.

[57] Introduced into service in 1805, Congreve rockets were a military adaptation of the civilian skyrocket. They were notoriously inaccurate and, as one commentator said, were useful if you wanted to hit a large city as they would strike it "somewhere or other, and no doubt set fire to the town; but the part of the town you could not very well choose." See George Larpent, ed., *Private Journal of Judge Advocate Larpent* (London, 1854), 354-355.

[58] "Broad pennant." The distinguishing pennant of a naval officer of commodore's rank which was flown from the mast of his flagship.

[59] Yeo's appointment as commodore meant that he no longer would have to command his own ship as well as command the fleet but would now have a "flag captain" (a captain of his flag ship) to perform this duty.

[60] Captain William Jervoise, 57th Foot (1782-1862), ADC to Lieutenant General Gordon Drummond, British commander in Upper Canada in 1814.

[61] Captain William Holtaway, Royal Marines.

[62] According to the official casualty lists (NAC, RG 8 I, vol. 683, p. 113, Return of Casualties, 6 May 1814 and List of Officers, Seamen & Marines Killed and Wounded, 6 May 1814 in W.H. Wood, *Select British Documents of the American War of 1812* (4 vols., Toronto, 1920-1928) III: 1, 64, the British losses were 24 killed and 98 wounded. For the official British report on this battle, see NAC, RG 8 I, vol. 683, p. 105, Drummond to Prevost, 7 May 1814.

[63] Lieutenant Franz Ludwig Viktor May, De Watteville's Regiment (1791-1814).

[64] This is Up Park Camp near Kingston, Jamaica. It is still used as an active military base by the Jamaican armed forces

[65] "Pioneers." Each infantry battalion contained a number of pioneers who were soldiers equipped and trained to clear obstacles and underbrush and construct simple bridges.

[66] Lieutenant and Commander Francis Brockell Spilsbury, RN (1784-1830), see *DCB*, VI, 730-731: lieutenant, 1805; commander, 1811; captain, 1815. Spilsbury remained in Upper Canada after the war, settling in the Newcastle District.

[67] The official British report of this action is NAC, RG 8 I, vol. 683, p. 226, Drummond to Prevost, 2 June 1814.

[68] Le Couteur is in error here. Drummond was wounded at Sackets Harbor in May 1813 but recovered quickly. In June of that year, he was appointed Deputy Quarter Master General of the forces in Upper Canada, a staff appointment that kept him away from 104th for a year. See NAC, RG 8 I, vol. 1203 1/2 I, General Orders, 13 June 1813; vol. 1171, p. 265, General Orders, 9 May 1814. On William Drummond, see Donald E. Graves, "William Drummond and the Battle of Fort Erie," *Canadian Military History* I (1992), 25-43.

[69] Captain Philip or Petit Dennis (b. 1794).

[70] Telemachus was a character in Homer's Odyssey. The son of Ulysses and Penelope, he searched for his father and protected his mother. He was advised by the goddess of wisdom in the form of his father's friend, Mentor.

[71] Lieutenant Thomas Carter, RA.

[72] Lieutenant James Gray, 8th Foot.

[73] According to the *General Regulations and Orders for the Army, 1811*, (London, 1816), 37, "No Officer shall be promoted to the Rank of Captain, until he has been

Three Years a Subaltern." Le Couteur had not yet completed this required period in November 1813, when Saumarez offered him a company.

[74] One of the numerous McGillivray clan connected with the North West Company, possibly either Simon (1783-1840), see *DCB*, VII, 561-562, or William (1764-1825), see *DCB*, VI, 454-457.

[75] A period term for French Canadians.

[76] Stephen Henry Cartwright (1801-1814).

[77] Major General Richard Stovin, a veteran of thirty-three years service and, in the spring of 1814, commander of the Centre Division of the British Army in Canada.

[78] "Interior oeconomy." The internal administration of the unit, its books, records and accounts.

[79] Ensign James Coyne, 104th Foot (1789-1816).

[80] "Must get spliced." Should get married.

[81] Major General Phineas Riall (1775-1850), see *DCB*, VII, 744-746. Riall was the commander of the Right Division of the British Army in Canada in the spring of 1814.

[82] For Riall's official report of the action at Chippawa, see NAC, RG 8 I, vol. 684, p. 51, Riall to Drummond, 6 July 1814.

# Chapter Eight

"A SOLDIER'S LIFE IS VERY HORRID SOMETIMES"
The Battle of Lundy's Lane
*25 July 1814*

### *9 July [1814]*

Saturday. Received sudden orders for the Flank[1] companies under Colonel Drummond to embark in bateaux tomorrow morning at six for Upper Canada. Had every thing prepared — dear Mrs. Robison had some nice biscuits baked for my journey.

### *10 July*

Sunday. Not yet off. Wrote to my dear Mother and to My Uncle Tom Dumaresq — not to leave till this evening. God grant that the Yankees may not attack Kingston! Sunday — thc Flank companies, 120 men, under Lieutenant Colonel Drummond, embarked in Bateaux for thc Uppcr Country. The 89th [Regiment] to move upwards also this evening.

### *11 July*

Owing to a headwind, we could not proceed last night. It continued very heavy till midday. When at 12 o'clock We tipped the "girls we left behind Us" Three cheers, and pulled off in good style. Got to Fairfield's, Ten miles, about 6 o'clock — the men wet and weary from having pulled hard against wind and rain. After a good supper and some rest started at 4 A.M. the wind still heading us. Rested the men at Widow Fincie's where the subs got up a dance together for sheer fun's sake, vulgarly called a Bulldance, to the Colonel's enjoyment who joined in it with his boys. Anything to make service light!

Off again and passed the Upper Gap which is formed by the Head of Isle Sante and Indian Point, the Commencement of the beautiful bay of Quinte, a rich fertile country — the water smooth and transparent as glass. It was common to see fish gliding about, and the stones clear at twenty feet depth, or more. Pulled on to twenty-five miles for our day's work. Opposite Van Allstein's Mills, where we landed and pitched our Tent — Shore, Coates,[2] Considine, Woodford[3] & I. The Grenadiers had theirs close by.

We continued the same daily work getting on some twenty miles or more till Sunday 17th. It was raining heavily we all got very wet, when about 3 o'clock, on the clearing off of a thick fog - we saw apparently a large Yankee Gun boat, coming out from under the high land and standing for us. The Grenadiers who were considerably ahead pulled for the shore. We light bobs with Col[onel]. Drummond, being more under the tongue of land that was ahead, ran for the beach, landed, and mounted a high ridge of land that overlooked the enemy, taking up a few Congreve rockets with us.

Seeing that the Grannies[4] had fired on the Stranger, as she refused to show her Colours, Drummond mounted a [Congreve] Rocket, which was fired and dashing over the woods in an oblique direction, fell within a hundred yards of the Gun boat. She evidently took the hint, sheered off, and still would show no colours, on which we were assured of her hostility. Out with another Rocket, this on being fired, went off hissingly and whizzingly, but just as it should have cleared the wood, its tail touched a bough and it came flying back towards us, putting us all to the rout. The enemy saw the rocket rise, but did not witness its freaks, when presently We saw them hoist a *red* coat, for a Colour, then we soon learned the pleasing intelligence that we had been firing at some of our wounded men, going down to Kingston.

We pulled hard all day and reached York about 5 P.M. and pitched our tents near the Fort. Found the *Melville* here - and heard that the De Watteville's [Regiment] were marching up.

### *20 July*

A heavy cannonade heard all this morning in the direction of Fort George. The Shaws,[5] and Jarvises[6] were very kind asking us to dine. We were so short of luxury, in our march that, on going to dress for dinner at Mrs. Shaw's, Pat C[onsidine] called to his servant: "Butler, my boots and bring my toothbrush" — the absence of Day and Martin[7] and the substitute for it, set us in a regular roar. The two columns of smoke which were seen were the melancholy intimation of the burning of Queenston and St. David's by the Americans.

Pushed on to the army on the 22nd and pulled twelve miles beyond Burlington heights opposite to the Forty-Mile Creek, where we halted for the night. Up before day, and rowed across the bay to the Forty-Mile Creek before 8 A.M., halted to breakfast & rest till ten — and started with a fair wind — in four hours reached the Twelve-Mile Creek. Waited for orders.

*24 July, Sunday*

Started early and marched to the position at Shipman's. Found the Glengarry Light Inf[antr]y and about one hundred Indians encamped there. Marched on to the roar of the Artillery. We were not long under their protection, but were moved on eleven miles and passed the Incorporated Militia,[8] the 8th, 103rd, and 1st Royals [Regiments], in succession. We began to fancy our Flankers were to attack "Uncle Sam" the moment the 89th and De Watteville's [Regiments] arrived.

At last we were halted at Pratt's over the ravine, all wet through, drenched with perspiration and rain. Pitched our tents in the very advance, comfortably enough, and eat a hearty and frugal dinner of bread and butter! Nought else to be had! The enemy from Six to Ten thousand strong with Cavalry and Artillery, their Volunteers on Queenston Heights and the regulars along Queenston plain about five thousand. Their Indians, Tuscaroras and Oneidas, some Hurons too, and their Militia have left them. So much the better if they have, the scalping Knife is a nasty adjunct.

*Monday, 25[th] July*

Roused at 3 o'clock. The 89th [Regiment] came up last night. We received *false information* that the enemy had recrossed to the United States at Chippewa. We snatched up a breakfast near the 103rd [Regiment], who were with us waiting for orders to move.

12 Noon. Moved to the Twelve-Mile Creek, where we made ourselves comfortable and got a good dinner. [At] 4 o'clock, received pressing orders to hurry on to Lundy's Lane where the enemy were already engaged with the 89th and Glengarry [Regiments]. It would be difficult to describe the feelings of us young Soldiers hurrying into action, with the roar of Artillery and Musketry pealing in Our front, sometimes rattling in heavy surges, sometimes scant, as if troops pressed were retiring. The echo through the woods too as we were not marching, but running up, for our anxiety to aid our hard-pressed comrades became painful and short breathed. Some old Hero talked of "this flesh trembling at the dangers his Spirit would launch it into." I am persuaded that many of us had that feeling.

It was near 8 o'clock and getting dark as we reached the battle field. I made my usual prayers to God to grant me his protection and my life, ready though I was to lay that down for my country, at his pleasure, but hoping that no worse than a wound might befall me — nor a fall into the hands of the Savages - death we thought preferable.

They were hard at it. A staff officer placed our Companies in rear of the Centre of the 89th [Regiment] as we came up. Drummond finding us very much exposed to all the shots that missed the 89th, moved us on about twenty yards where there was a cross railed fence behind which he ordered us to lie down till we were wanted. It was funny and very satisfactory too to hear the balls rattling against the rails just over our heads, without hitting any of us.

An incident or two in war I must relate. As we marched up, to my utter astonishment, I saw the Captain of Artillery passing me. "What, in the name of fortune, brings you from your guns?" "Two of them were taken at the Bayonet's point and my Gunners are despatched. They made me a Prisoner, shoved me into the church above there, but as I saw a window at the other end and no one watching. I jumped out and here I am."[9] Captain Glew[10] of the 41st [Regiment] Light Company who was on the left under the crest of the hill, saw all this. When Jonathan thought He had the Guns safe, and like a raw fool had bayonetted the horses as well as what men he could catch, and fancied the centre of the battle won — bold Capt[ain]. Glew charged them with his gallant light bobs and retook our Guns, and one from the enemy.[11] He ought to have been made a Knight Bannaret or a Major on the spot.[12]

Another. While we were under this fire, Lieutenant Colonel Drummond was seated on his war horse like a knightly man of valour as He was exposed to a ragged fire from hundreds of brave Yankees who were pressing our brave 89th [Regiment]. It was an illumination of musquetry in our left front. Capt[ain]. Shore's servant, Nickerson,[13] a short active highlander, was lying down, or on his knee often as I was peeking at the fray, when presently He stood bolt up. "Nic, Lie down!" Down He came. Presently up again. "Don't you hear the shot all around you, lie down!" "Yas Sur!" Down again. Up again in five minutes. "What's the use of my speaking to you, and your disobeying my orders - this is no place to be finding fault with a good Soldier!" "Wall Sir, do ye no see Col[onel]. Drummond sitting on that great horse, up there amongst all the balls - and sale I be laying down, sneaking whan he's exposed — Noe I wunt!" "Please yourself then!" — for I could not but admire the fellow's generous heroism!

The battle ceased in our front, while the enemy withdrew to make fresh dispositions. We were moved on, in first line, to the right of the 103rd [Regiment], the Royals on our Right. Just then, a curious event in war occurred. The Glengarry light Infantry, who had been covering the extreme right, were recalled into line. Suddenly our line saw a black line rising over the hill in our front, when we poured in a rolling volley on them. L[ieutenan]t. Colonel Battersby[14] in the most daring manner rode down and shouted: "We're British!" Happily the rise of the hill and the darkness favoured them, and few if any were hurt.

Immediately after this, the enemy, having reformed and obtained reinforcements, came forward in great strength continuing his efforts to take the hill till midnight. The Centre of the 89th [Regiment] was literally charged five times. Capt[ain]. Spunner,[15] on seeing L[ieutenan]t. Latham[16] fall, seized the King's Color which He had carried, and shouted "My boys, would you desert this color!" The fine fellows rallied to the color — but poor Spunner was killed. One heavy column, which crossed our front, I heard receive the word, "Form Subdivisions" and the officers repeating the words — into which we poured some heavy vollies till they retreated. Two [British] officers were taken Prisoner in our front by the Americans, on being questioned, answering: "We are the Glengarry and Royals" and walking up to them. [They] did not return.

One circumstance I have never forgot, as a lesson in war. Gen[era]l. Drummond rode up to the 103rd [Regiment]. "My lads *will you* charge the Americans?" He *put a question* instead of *giving the order* — they fired instead of charging.

About midnight the whole of the American army had retired, while we kept the field. As there was a rumour that General Brown was coming to renew his attack on our small but victorious army, twenty-five hundred to three thousand at most, Lieutenant Colonel Drummond made us draw all the dead horses into a line on the crest of our position and, if attacked, to kneel behind them as a breastwork, a capital one it would have proved.

I was on duty that night. What a dismal night. There were three hundred dead on the Niagara side of the hillock, and about a hundred of ours, besides several hundred wounded. The miserable badly-wounded were groaning and imploring us for water, the Indians prowling about them and scalping or plundering. Close by me lay a fine young man, the son of the American general Hull.[17] He was mortally wounded, and I gave him some brandy and water, and wished Him to give me his watch, rings and anything He wished sent to his family. He told me much about Himself and to come to Him in the morning when He would give them to me in charge. When I got to Him, He was a beautiful Corpse, stripped stark naked, amidst a host of friends and foes.[18]

Our Mens' heads and those of the Americans were within a few yards of each other at this spot, so close had been the deadly strife at this point — a magnificent man, a Field Officer of the Yankee army, lay close by Him. One old Yankee, who I relieved much, told me it was a judgement on Him for leaving his happy home, wife & Children. I sent an American Captain to the rear on a litter, shot through both legs.

The scene of the morning was not more pleasant than the night's horrors. We had to wait on our slaughterhouse till 11 before we got a mouthful — when a great Camp Kettle full of thick chocolate revived us surprisingly, though we devoured it among dead bodies in all directions.

Poor Moorsom of ours, the D[eputy]. Ass[ist]ant. Adj[utant] General was killed early in the action, the last of four or five brothers killed in the Service. We had the mortification to see the smoke rising in minute column from Street's Mills,[19] which the enemy burned in his retreat, for, although our Cavalry, Indians and light troops followed them, we were not in force sufficient to punish them farther. We accordingly moved down to Queenston. The 41st [Regiment] marched on to Ft. George.

### *27th [July]*

We buried our excellent friend Moorsom at Queenston this day by the side of the gallant General Brock.[20] Coates as a Clergyman's Son, I directed to read the funeral Service while I commanded the firing party. On parting from his Sister, He had written these beautiful lines in her scrapbook:

> Thou didst with honor, press th' ensanguined plain,
> But not unhonored lie amidst the slain,
> By noble Brock's, thy gallant body rests,
> Thy worth and virtues in thy comrades' breasts.[21]

[Le Couteur to William Robison, 27 July 1814][22]

Queenston, 27th July, 1814

My Dear William,

As I conceive Your Good Mother, will be anxious to know how I am after our late action, and that I owe her a letter *at least*, for all her kindness to me, I take the opportunity of Walker's going down with Poor Loring's horses, as a safe one.

*View of the Niagara River looking north from Queenston Heights by Gardner D. Engleheart, circa 1860. On 27 July 1814, Le Couteur buried one of his fellow officers of the 104th Foot near the place where the artist sketched this landscape.* G.D. Engleheart/National Archives of Canada/C-100116

After this prelude, I commence my detail. We reached the army on the 24th, the 89th [Regiment] the morning after, when General Drumond immediately advanced, with them, and the Glengarry whom the enemy attacked about six o'clock in the evening of the 25th. The heavy columns of the enemy of course drove them in, but they still kept up the action till our division came up, consisting of the Royals, 103d, and ourselves. The Kings and Flank companies of the 41st [Regiment] came up at the same time. It was then quite dark about eight o'clock.

The 103d [Regiment] and us formed line, on the right Flank of the Royals and 89th, who were formed in line, and keeping a very heavy fire on the enemy, who also returned it in very good style. We were told the enemy were advancing on our Front, and soon after saw a Column coming right down upon us, we were then ordered to commence, and we raffled away. A Man ran down from them and called, we were firing on the Glengarry Regiment, imagine to yourself, the Consternation we were in, at this misfortune, which had also happened to the 89th and 41st [Regiments], our lads instantly ceased, but the l03d fired another volley, not knowing it so soon.

Just after, we were told General Riall was taken prisoner and wounded, and that Three pieces of artillery which we had just brought up were charged and carried by the enemy. They had driven on to the enemy, without knowing, where they were taken. Affairs just then looked very ill on our side, the Yankees were behaving nobly, and the 89th [Regiment] were giving way a little. The General rallied them himself, and made them and the Royals advance to within 50 yards of the enemy's line, we and the Grenadiers of the 103d [Regiment] on their right and the Glengarry on their left at the same time giving Three cheers, we poured in a terrible fire on them for an hour, when they began to give way, and finally ran.

Until the morning we were not aware of our Victory's being so complete. Near three hundred of the enemy lay dead on the field of battle, besides a great many wounded. Mrs. Willson[23] reckoned Sixty waggon loads of wounded that passed her house, and Thirty officers were in her house early in the action. But our Victory was a [illegible] one. We have Fifty officers killed, wounded, and missing, most of them Prisoner, from going in among the enemy in the Dark, and from speaking the same language, once separated, we could not distinguish friends from foe. There were [word missing] officers killed and about 18 wounded. Poor Moorsom was killed, whilst cheering [words missing] the Royals. Loring was made Pr[isoner] carrying orders and getting among [words missing] instead of our own troops. An American [word missing] fell into our hands in the same way, as [words missing] inferior officers. The loss among the Troops was [word missing] K[ille]d., 404 w[ounde]d., and 140 missing & Prisoners.

I assure you, I never passed so awful a night as that of the action. The stillness of the evening after the firing ceased, the Groans of the dying and wounded, I went to several of them and got a Captain taken away. I could not sleep tho' I was quite fatigued and weak from 36 hours marching, fasting and Fighting. I was cold and wretched, what must not have been the misery of those Unfortunates who remained on the Field. A Soldier's life is very horrid sometimes.

You must excuse this letter, my Dear William. It is quite dark, I am writing on a board, out of doors, give my very best regards to Mrs Robison and [illegible] my best respects to Mr. & Mrs. Cartwright, Kiss my dear Elizabeth, Martha & Dicky for me. God bless you [illegible] My Dear William & believe me your very affectionate and faithful,

Le Couteur

### *29 July*

Queenston. The Royals and 103rd [Regiment] marched towards Chippawa at daylight this morning and the 89th to Fort George, four hundred of DeWatteville's [Regiment] joined down there.

### *30 July*

We marched for Bridgewater and arrived there about 9 A.M. Coates and I walked to have a view of the Falls from the Table Rock, then attempted to go below them but did not find the safe path. I betted Considine Five pounds that the Yankees would make peace with us by this day Six months.[24] The Yankee army still at Fort Erie, our advance within a mile and a half of them. General Conran[25] joined us Sunday.

### *31 July*

The Light Division formed of the 41st Flankers, 89th and 100th [Regiments] Light Co[mpan]ys and our two Companies of Flankers, marched at 10 o'clock during the heat of the day to Palmer's, six miles from Fort Erie.

## Notes

[1] That is to say, the light infantry and grenadier companies of the 104th Foot.

[2] Lieutenant James Coates, 104th Foot (b.1794).

[3] Assistant Surgeon William Woodford or Woodeforde, 104th Foot (1792-1856). Woodford married Lucy Anne Miller of Fredericton and practised medicine there after the war. He returned to the army in 1832 but resigned in 1835, subsequently taking over the family estate in Somerset.

[4] "Grannies." Grenadiers.

[5] Colonel Aeneas Shaw (d. 1814), see *DCB*, V, 752, and his wife, Margaret. A Loyalist and former member of Simcoe's Rangers, Shaw came to Upper Canada as an officer in the Queen's Rangers who cleared the site of the town of York in the 1790s. He retired from the army and was appointed a member of the Legislative Council and later Adjutant General of the Upper Canada militia. Shaw commanded the York militia at the attack on that place in 1813.

[6] William Jarvis (1756-1817) and his wife, Hannah (Peters) Jarvis (1763-1845), see *DCB*, V, 452-453. A Loyalist, Jarvis was Secretary and Registrar of Upper Canada. He and his wife resided in a handsome estate on the outskirts of York.

[7] This is possibly a reference to the London firm of Day and Martin, well-known manufacturers of shoe blacking. The idea is that the only way Considine would have been able to simulate a well-polished boot was to use his toothbrush on it.

[8] The Incorporated Militia Battalion of Upper Canada was a militia unit embodied for the duration of the war. Trained, uniformed, equipped and armed as regular infantry, it fought throughout the 1814 campaign. For a history of this unit, see E. A. Cruikshank, "Record of the Services of Canadian Regiments in the War of 1812. V, The Incorporated Militia," *Canadian Military Institute, Selected Papers* 9 (1897-99), 70-80.

[9] From Le Couteur's description of the sequence of events, this officer was probably Captain James Mackonachie, RA, who had accompanied Colonel Hercules Scott's brigade with his guns.

[10] Captain Joseph Barry Glew, 41st Foot (1783-1838).

[11] Another witness to this incident was Private Shadrach Byfield, 41st Foot. See John Gellner, ed., *Recollections of the War of 1812* (Toronto, 1964), 38.

[12] This account of the recapture of British artillery by force of arms during the battle of Lundy's Lane solves an apparent contradiction in the historical evidence for this action. Most British and Canadian authors state that Drummond's artillery, which was taken by an American attack midway through the battle, was recaptured by the British at the end of the battle. The account of Shadrach Byfield, a private in Glew's company, is usually cited as evidence of this statement. The preponderance of evidence, however, suggests that, at the end of the battle, all the British artillery was

in American hands and was abandoned by them when they left the ground, only to be discovered by the British the next morning. On this subject, see Donald E. Graves, *The Battle of Lundy's Lane, 1814* (Baltimore, 1993).

From Le Couteur's account, we know that Glew did recapture some pieces of the British artillery but that this took place *midway during the action,* not at the end of the battle. What Le Couteur could not know, as he did not see it, was that these guns were recaptured by an American counterattack.

[13] Probably Private Nathaniel Nickerson, 104th Foot.

[14] Lieutenant Colonel Francis Battersby (1775-1845), Glengarry Light Infantry Fencibles.

[15] Captain Robert Spunner, 89th Foot. Spunner was buried on the battlefield but his remains, along with some other British casualties, were disinterred in the late nineteenth century and placed in the vault under the memorial to the battle erected in Drummond Hill Cemetery, Niagara Falls, Canada.

[16] Lieutenant John Latham, 89th Foot. Latham's remains are today interred in the vault under the battle memorial erected in Drummond Hill Cemetery, Niagara Falls, Canada.

[17] Captain Abraham Hull, 9th Infantry, U.S. Army, son of Brigadier General William Hull.

[18] Hull lies buried today in Drummond Hill Cemetery on Lundy's Lane in the modern city of Niagara Falls, Canada.

[19] A reference to the hamlet, more commonly known as Bridgewater Mills, which lay on the Niagara River between Chippawa and Lundy's Lane. It was burnt by American troops on 26 July 1814.

[20] Le Couteur is in error here. Moorsom could not have been buried alongside Brock in 1814 as the latter's remains were at Fort George and were not transferred from there to Queenston Heights until 1824.

[21] Unless Moorsom was unusually prescient, he could not have known before his death that Brock's body would be interred on Queenston Heights in 1824. This factual error casts doubt on the authenticity of this poem.

[22] This letter is contained in the collections of the Clements Library, University of Michigan, War of 1812 Papers, M-1907.

[23] Debora Willson operated a tavern near the Table Rock overlooking the falls of Niagara that was popular with the officers of both armies during the war. See Chapter 6, Le Couteur to Bouton, 24 October 1813.

[24] As the Treaty of Ghent, which ended the war, was signed on 24 December 1814, Le Couteur would have won this wager.

[25] Major General Henry Conran (1767-1829). Conran was appointed second-in-command of the Right Division in August 1814 but was incapacitated by a fall from his horse.

# Chapter Nine

## "A DISGRACEFUL DAY FOR OLD ENGLAND"

Conjocta Creek and Fort Erie

*August and September, 1814*

***2 August [1814]***

Yesterday we moved to Miller's after a wretched, wet night, rain & thunder. At eleven last night the Colonel routed us and desired us to see that our Men had Brown Bess[1] in trim by their Side, an attack being expected about 2 in the morning. A cow breaking over a fence was construed into Jonathan upon our right flank and the division had to turn out under arms till about 5 when we were allowed to rest. Capt[ain]. Basden[2] and the light company of the 89th [Regiment] joined us again. The army advanced and took up a position opposite Black Rock.

At 11 [in the morning] the Light division under Brigadier Shindy[3] (Col T[ucker])[4] were suddenly ordered to embark in bateaux at 11 P.M. [on] a dark night for some secret expedition, in embryo. All in expectation of making lots of prize money, *plunder* etc. Reached the Yankee side shortly and landed about two miles below Black Rock about midnight — no sleep in an enemy's country.

About a little before daylight we moved on, left in front, *without an* advanced guard or any apparent precaution. When I mentioned it to Col[onel]. Drummond, he said it was no business of his — the Brigadier might please himself.

Just before day, the men in our front of another corps began firing in a shameful style and ran past us. I halted my Subdivision and came to the charge[5] to keep the others off. Capt[ain]. Shore formed upon me. Col[onel]. D[rummond] sent me on with a Sergeant [illegible] and a file of men to see, cautiously, what was in our front. There was a little firing too far off to hurt anything, when I heard the word given behind me, vizt. "Ready, Present!" I shouted: "throw yourselves down or you're dead men" and laid flat. The volley passed over my head but my poor gallant Sergeant was killed by my side. We crept back after finding ourselves between two fires.

Day now dawned and we advanced extended but the surprise was at an end thro' the misconduct of our Commander. There was a broad and deep creek in our front with a broken bridge or it — two beams alone remained entire. Behind it was a heavy breastwork lined by a company of riflemen who shot every Fool that came near the Bridge and defied our Field Guns. After keep[ing] us in check till 7, we had the vexation to retire with the loss of twenty men, when we recrossed unmolested. The failure was owing to Col[onel]. Tucker's total want of military command.[6]

We were pushed on, at 4 o'clock, to within a thousand yards of Fort Erie when the enemy complimented us with some rounds of shot & grape to make us take care of ourselves during a reconnaissance of about an hour. In my opinion the Fort is only to be taken by assault. No impression is likely to be made by an attempt at breaking a mud fort.

### *4 August*

The troops bivouacked last night. Jonathan appears to be throwing up a battery on the opposite shore. Charlton gave them a few shots where they were unloading a boat and killed a man at a Cart's tail which stopped their amusement for the day. Turned out at daylight, a very severe order issued blaming the misconduct of one Regiment & praising us for the Black Rock affair.[7]

Appointed an Acting Engineer till some Engineer Sub comes up. Constructed a battery on our left, facing that of the enemy. Col[onel]. Harvey gave me carte blanche as to the numbers of men — thus I had a Gun mounted in the day behind a half-moon battery.

### *6 August*

Constructed the front of a two-gun battery within one thousand yards of Fort Erie last night as the first breaching battery — a mortar, one 18 and one 24-Pdr. [gun] mounted. The American fleet in sight off Fort Niagara last evening. Had a sharp skirmish with the enemy's riflemen in our right advance about four today. Their object was to turn our right but our picquets were well placed — they were driven off soon. Our loss about twenty killed & w[ounde]d. The enemy got our range and the shot came plunking into our battery pretty hotly.

*7 August*

Sunday. Up till ten last night, hard at work making fascines[8] a mile off and taking them to the battery. At work again before daylight — it rained so hard that we were wet through nearly all night. Completed two embrasures of the battery by 12 o'clock. Several shots from the Schooners fell about us, but without effect.

*8 August*

Phillpott[9] kept me at work. From 6 till 3 in the morning hard at it. Came to camp thoroughly fagged & slept till 1/2 past seven. Down at the battery from nine till five. The Schooners fired at us the whole day long. Threw up an "epaulement"[10] to guard the men from a flank fire without orders from the Engineer, though with Colonel Scott's entire approbation and aid. It secured the men's lives but when Lieutenant Ph[illpott] came down at night and saw what had been done, He got into a violent passion and wanted me to take it down again, which I declared I would not certainly do as He chose to be absent all day and the Field Officer of the day could testify how many lives it must have saved. I had made it about seven feet high and eighteen feet thick, a secure work which covered the very rear of the Battery. We had such high words that I said I would no longer serve under his orders and the next day I rejoined the company.

Col[onel]. Drummond told me that Gen[era]l. Drummond was very displeased with me for having done so as Col[onel]. Scott had spoken most highly of my zeal and ability. I had worked in my shirt like the men! The General would have continued me on that duty, but he *sent the Engineer to the rear.*[11] I was very sorry afterwards for my hasty decision — it lost me a staff appointment which the Lieut[enant]. Gen[era]l. told Drummond he would have given to me, but for that. "He must learn that young men may be blamed unjustly and must bear it." He gave the appointment to L[ieutenan]t. Solomon,[12] my junior — Ten shillings a day extra, two horses and a Guinea a week lodging money — £400 a year lost!.[13]

*9 August*

In the woods all day with the company on duty making abbatis for our entrenchments. The Yankees did not fire at us all day for a wonder! When the Gen[era]l. went down about 7, they spied him or his staff and saluted him with five shots.

### *10 August*

The Guns placed in battery last night. The Yankees are doing the same on our flank over the river — those guns will enfilade our battery & picquets at a long range - twelve hundred to two thousand yards, I think.

Writing to my Mother. About 9 o'clock the enemy attempted our battery but the abbatis checked their advance and a heavy fire forced them to retire with severe loss. Lieut[enant]. McGregor[14] of the Royals killed. They fired about twenty shots from the Schooners at anchor off the Fort at our picquets but no one was hurt.

### *12 August*

On the advance picquet last evening. I had the left picquet, Capt[ain]. Shore the Centre, and L[ieutenan]t. Considine the right. The battery being complete, we expected the Guns would open to day, it being the sovereign's birthday.[15] However the General put it off, and the Yankees enable us to keep it differently. It was about 1 o'clock in the day when Considine & I had gone to Shore's picquet to eat, or snatch, our dinners with Him. We heard the drums beat to arms, or the volunteer drums as we called them, in Fort Erie — an ominous sound of preparation for attack. Shore desired us to return to our picquets and place our men in readiness.

The picquet in my charge was placed behind a stout breastwork with a heavy abbatis in its front about thirty yards off, it would be a difficult matter to pull it aside, or cut it down under the fire of forty or fifty men. The woods in which we were posted were part of an endless forest marching to the North pole, for ought we knew, some of the trees of the growth of centuries, with their heads in the Clouds.

Some time about three, I heard "bang, bang" far on the right - the well-known sharp ring of the American rifle. I instantly placed my men under cover all along the breastwork and made them place their caps on it away from themselves. I then heard two more shots — then the music began to gather like a girl playing preludes, now it came on, all along the right towards the Captain's picquet. Just then, I saw my poor brother Sub., Considine, supported by a soldier passing by the rear of my picquet badly wounded. "What's the matter my boy?", I ran up. "I got it here, and it came out there", pointing to a wound received over one hip and emerging over the other. "God bless you!" I thought it was all over with him and ran back to my men.

The fire was ragged and closing on me fast past the center, a rifle ball just grazed my whisker as I came up. One of the men said "Mr LC [illegible] yourself or you will be hit." "Steady my lads, not a shot till I tell you to fire — level every man at a rifleman and wait till we see lots of them close to the attack — now my boys!" and a steady roll brought down a lot of them. The riflemen knocked the men's caps over nicely — which greatly amused my men. The enemy made a desperate attempt to turn our flank but after an hour's hard fighting they were driven back with serious loss, leaving many of their dead and rifles along our front.

I did not lose a man. When the men who were on the right advance [illegible], were examined they were found to have met instant death — though both on the alert and in the act of levelling. One was shot over the left arm and in the left eye, the other near the waist and shot through the heart, both their firelocks were cocked and neither trigger pulled. Death had been instantaneous in both cases. Considine went to see what was coming and got the third shot, the fourth missed his Corporal. We lost several men in the other two picquets — my having concealed my men saved them all while our own fire was deadly — they never passed me to get towards that battery — and I got praised. I was glad nevertheless to have got out of the Scrape alive. Made a hearty supper and turned in thankful.[16]

### *13 August*

Saturday. This morning after daybreak the Cannonade began in earnest on both sides. How it did echo through those ancient forests! No more sleep this morning. 6 A.M., heard that my friend Cap[tain]. Dobbs [RN] had cut out two of the American schooners from under the guns of Fort Erie last night. Lieut. Shalch[17] was killed in boarding.

### *14 August*

Sunday. Last evening the Volunteers, consisting of men from the King's, Wattevilles, 89th, 100th & 104th [Regiment] flankers under Colonels Fischer and Drummond, 104th, marched to attack Snake Hill in high spirits and certain of Conquest. After we had got to [the] Plateaux, the General's Aid de Camp, Coore, overtook us with a Counterorder. Colonel Drummond had told me that the General had an idea of taking the flints from the mens' arms. I observed that "such a proceeding must ensure defeat, if troops could not be trusted with their flints they had better leave their arms behind them. I won't answer for our men. If ordered not to load, not a man would think of it but if placed by accident in a position where they might [be] required to use them and find it impossible to charge, they might be destroyed without offering any opposition." He agreed with me and said He would "object to

*This depiction of the American attack on Fort George, 27 May 1813, shows the relative positions of Fort Niagara on the left and Fort George on the right. Le Couteur served around Fort George in the summers of 1813 and 1814.* Artist unknown/National Archives of Canada/C-23675

it". Our light Brigade for piquet at 12 o'clock. Slept till the cannonade roused me.

About sunset Col[onel]. Drummond told Coates & me that our Flankers were to form the Storming party with the 103rd [Regiment] under Col[onel]. Scott and two companies of the Royals, to move at 2 o'clock in the morning on Fort Erie by Signal from a Rocket. That the Snake Hill works were to by stormed by De Wattevilles, the King's, the 89th and 100th [Regiment] Light Companies at the same moment.

I shall never forget the solemn tone in which our good, kind and gallant Col[onel]. Drummond took leave of us. He told me that it was probable we should never meet again, something whispered this would be his last day. He must not impart any fears for Him in my mind because He would lead on his men as usual. I urged on Him His many escapes, to look cheerfully upon this attack, we might all meet happily — under Providence! He desired me to tell Bedel his Servant to send his Trinkets & Papers to Mrs. Drummond and took a most affectionate farewell of us both which brought tears to my eyes. "Remember the honor of the Regiment, dear Boys, God Bless You!"[18]

To give some idea of the fort we had to attack, I will endeavour to describe it. It was neither Badajoz[19] or St. Sebastian,[20] nor anything of such strength, yet it was an ugly Customer for fifteen hundred men to attack Six thousand, it was said, placed behind breastworks and ramparts, with guns and a blockhouse bristling in every direction. The fort was of irregular form, with demi-bastions that flanked the ditches. The faces were of earth, but the embrasures seemed to me to be of masonry — at any rate our fire, instead of affecting a breach, seemed to me and others to ram the earth harder.

### *15 August*

Monday. There was a strong blockhouse in the rear of the Curtain or in the body of the place, which was full of men. The distance from the woods which afforded us cover, our point of entry, on to the plain to the ditch of the fort might be three hundred yards. About an hour before daylight, our Columns led by Cols. Drummond and Scott marched as silently as death — not a whisper — presently we got within two hundred yards we were discovered. As we heard the roll of fire to our right by the attack on Snake hill — in an instant, a blaze of musquetry and Artillery opened upon us — happily considerably too high.

We still marched at a rapid but steady pace, in a few minutes the head of the column, or rather the forlorn hope, got to the ditch, jumped in , reared the Scaling ladders and cheered us as they mounted. We increased our pace and cheered loudly, defying the fire of the enemy. I jumped with our Company into the ditch. It was slow work to get up the ladders — of which there was not one quarter enough — there were palisades to be cut away, while a galling flank fire from a Gun and musquetry annoyed us sadly. Still, on we pressed, cheering.

I had mounted the ladder, got over one palisade into an embrasure and was in the act of jumping into the place when I saw it full of combatants. Our men had carried the Fort, all but the Block house from which I heard them firing and shouting: "Come over you rascals, we're British deserters and Irish rebels" when, just then, I remember seeing a black volume rise from the earth and I lost my senses.

After I recovered them, I was lying in the ditch fifteen or twenty feet down where I had been thrown by a tremendous explosion of gunpowder which cleared the Fort of three hundred men in an Instant. The platform had been blown over and a great beam had jammed me to the earth but it was resting on the Scarp. I got from under it with ease, bruised but otherwise unhurt.

But what a horrid sight presented itself. Some three hundred men lay roasted, mangled, burned, wounded, black, hideous to view. On getting upon my legs, I trod on poor L[ieutenan]t. Horrens[21] broke leg of the 103rd [Regiment], which made me shudder to my marrow. In placing my hand on Captain Shore's back to steady myself from treading on some other poor mangled person, for the ditch was so crowded with bodies it was almost unavoidable, I found my hand in a mass of blood and brains — it was sickening.

But lively notions quickly followed. The explosion had caused a cessation of hostilities on both sides for a few minutes — then the Americans finding but a handful of men in the Fort, rushed to their Guns and then turned a Six pounder on the ditch in which we stood and gave us a round of grape shot. I, happily for me, had seen them preparing and had proposed to Shore to form and try to carry the Gun but it was impossible to maintain order, or to enforce obedience. So I made myself as pancake like as possible against the scarp while the grape shot flew by. Some of the men shouted: "They are going to spring another mine!" when all rushed to escape. The Yankees yelled, fired and cheered.

I turned to Shore & Major Elliot.[22] "I will not stay to be made a Prisoner, I shall run across the Plain & take my chance — Good bye!" Away I started, bringing with me a steel-mounted scabbard which I picked up from the ditch to replace my own, burnt on picquet by accident which had obliged me to carry a naked sword for a month so that the wags had called me "bloody-minded Johnny". However, in that horrid melee, I got a memento which now hangs on my Light Infantry sabre at Belle Vue.

I dashed across the Plain under such a roar of voices, Musquetry & Artillery as I never desire to run from again. Just as I had cleared half the distance, L[ieutenan]t. Fallon[23] of the 103rd [Regiment] Grenadiers was close before me, staggering, his sling belt caught [in] a stump. "Oh" he exclaimed, "I am caught at last." "No, Jack, my boy", I said, "you're not caught, its a tree." "Oh Johnny, I'm so dreadfully wounded in two places, I can't get on, I'm so weak." As we spoke, a grist of grape shot scattered at our feet. We escaped, as all of us have seen a Sparrow escape from a charge of No. 4.[24] "Never fear, place your arm over my Neck and I'll take your waist, I'll run you in and not desert you — hurrah!" And we got to our batteries safely.

After handing my wounded friend to some of his own men, I looked for some of mine. Sorrow and despair took hold of me. Forgetting where I was, I threw my sword down on the battery, weeping: "this is a disgraceful day for Old England!" I had noticed no one, it was a sort of soliloquy, an escape of feeling. Col[onel]. M[yers] said: "For shame, Mr. Le Couteur, cannot you conceal your feelings, is it not enough to meet defeat without adding despair to it before the men?" Col[onel]. P[earson] called out: "No, no, Myers, it's not that, it is the generous feeling of a young Soldier's disappointment!" and He took me kindly by the hand as I picked up my Sword.

To my confusion and regret I saw General Drummond and his Staff close to me. The General called me to Him. "Do you know anything about Y[ou]r Colonel?" I could not articulate for grief. "Killed, Sir." "Col[onel]. Scott?" "Shot thro' the head, Sir, Your Grenadiers are bringing Him in, Major Leonard & Maclauchlan wounded & Capt[ain]. Shore a prisoner." The General felt for me and said "Never mind, Cheer up. You are wanted here. Fall in any men of any regiment as they come up, to line our batteries for fear of an attack." Duty instantly set me to rights and I was actively employed cheering & ranging the men as they came in.

Our men behaved admirably, two mistakes leading to the failure. The two Col[onel]s, Scott & Drummond, went in with the forlorn hopes, or leading men, and were both killed — hence all direction ceased. Then the Block-house was impregnable to us — the doors below had been removed, the staircases or ladders also — so that when our men got in with a view to assault the garrison, they were shot through the loop-holed floors. It should have been destroyed by hot shot before the assault. But the explosion which we thought was designed, they declare was accidental. It cleared the Fort of three or four hundred men at a blast.[25]

It was a fearful list of hors de Combat — Killed, wounded & missing, burned or Prisoner.

| Lt. Cols. | Majs. | Capts. | Subs. | Staff | Sgts. | Privates |
|---|---|---|---|---|---|---|
| 2 | 1 | 10 | 21 | 2 | 64 | 903 |

— or one strong regiment put out of the way.[26]

When calling the roll of the company on the evening of that sad day, myself and twenty-three of us [who remained] out of seventy-seven all burst into tears together.

Later in the evening, my Captain joined us, having made his escape on seeing me get safe across the plain but he went towards Snake Hill and lost his way in the woods. Our gallant Colonel killed, Captains Leonard and MacLauchlan[27] I found badly wounded in the tent, en route to the rear. I was so tired and worn out that I could hardly move but I went on Piquet and remained till 12 at night.

It appeared that the Snake Hill party were repulsed owing to their flints having been removed, a scandalous want of confidence in the brave men who formed the assaulting party. Basden and Barstow[28] told me that they got round to the edge of the lake quite unperceived, that De Wattevilles behaved admirably but that the ladders were so short they could not reach the top of the parapet. The Americans at last finding only cheers to oppose them, got on top of the parapet and shot the unarmed men — unarmed because they had no flints — like so many sheep. The small fire of the Light Companies having no effect on the heavy body of Infantry and the Artillery that was belching forth death, they had to retreat perforce.

### *16 August*

Tuesday. Turned in and got to sleep till daylight when a heavy cannonade roused me. Heard that our poor Colonel had been bayonetted. We recovered his Gun and the beads[29] He wore round his neck — some of them I have now. The Yankees had buried 140 officers & men left in their Fort.

### *17 August*

Wednesday. On Picquet again tonight, got off it safe. Cap[tain] McMillan[30] of the Glengarry and I were seated on a stump when a round shot from across the river passed between his head and mine, made us both draw back. A man was lying on his back in front of us and the picquet was spread about behind the breastwork. The ball, after passing us, struck the sleeping man's pouch from under Him, exploded the Cartridges and struck the balls among the Men, who jumped in all directions, thinking it to be a shell. I flew to the poor fellow next me, who was unable to rise after a violent jump which He gave on the ball passing under Him. It had not grazed his skin but He was totally paralyzed. We placed Him on a blanket & sent Him to the rear. My Captain took me to dine with Him after being relieved, and gave me a treat of Port wine which was all expended in the 104th long since.

*18 August*

The Right wing of the 82nd and the 89th [Regiments] joined yesterday. The remains of the 103rd ordered to Fort George. A heavy skirmish in the bush. Philpott reconnoitering where to place another battery within five hundred yards of the Fort.

*19 August*

Another skirmish in the advance, they dispute our constructing batteries very decidedly.

*20 August*

Came off picquet — a wretched night, constant rain. We had a very sharp skirmish with them. Our men got ten of their rifles, of which I obtained one. No sooner had we driven them off, then the Fort opened and pelted us with shot and shell the whole afternoon. We kept quietly in the ditch, nevertheless got one man wounded in our battery.

The General moved our Camp more to the rear out of reach of shells or roundshot which were very uncomfortable visitors in the former camp — the Yankees sending them occasionally at random to vex us.

*22 August*

The 82nd and 89th [Regiment] Bands enliven our dreary existence. I played S[hore] a trick by dressing in a couple of night shirts, with a silk Handkerchief for a shawl, and a Cap arranged for the purpose, sent to say a young Lady wished to see Him and when He became gallant, I took to my heels with Him following in full chase to the infinite amusement of the wags who were in [on] the Secret. Received a letter from my dear Mother dated 22 May last, all well.

*23 August*
Our light Brigade on picquet last night. It was wretchedly cold. On a covering party, we were within five hundred yards of the fort, throwing up a breastwork and digging trenches to cover us from their grapeshot. They dropped three shells filled with bullets near to us but without their bursting or having *the effect of shrapnels.* They fired a great many shots at our battery as usual. Relieved and sent to the reserve, very well pleased for our poor company is a skeleton.

*24 August*
The left wing of the 82nd [Regiment] arrived this morning — a very nice corps. We have cautioned them against exposing themselves rashly to the rifleman's fire. It is not like open warfare as they have been used to against the French. If their men expose themselves in bush or forest fighting, the Americans will punish them. They laugh at the idea. Jonathan tried to throw shells into our present camp. We hear them drop a little way off in the woods, a sound unmusical [except] to Volscian[31] ears!

*25 August*
No rest for reserves yet. Our Brigade once more for picquets. Quiet enough.

*26 August*
Friday. The enemy attacked our picquets last night by way of trying what the Duke's old Soldiers are made of and what we are at. The 82nd [Regiment] lost two killed and thirteen wounded. The Yankees lost a Captain & left several killed behind them. The 82nd not yet aware of the value of *treeing.*

In our last heavy skirmish, the old hands, the Glengarrys, killed and wounded fifty of the Americans and only lost one man. Shore & I on the battery picquet, Jonathan cannonaded us until two in the morning. It was so cold I could not sleep. At daylight we commenced our fire. Sabine came down and enjoyed a whole day's practice at the Fort while they repaid the salute in kind. Very amusing to us Frogs in the ditches. Came off picquet with a *thundering* headache.

*29 August*
On Picquet last night, no rain and quiet for a wonder. A deserter came in and reported that their Riflemen had crossed over to the States, that our shells are very destructive and had wounded General Gaines[32] severely. The new Battery to be finished tonight.

### *31 August*

On Picquet. A deserter reports that our new battery has annoyed them much already. Heard that McDouall had repulsed an American attack on Mackinac.[33]

### *1 September [1814]*

The 104th [Regiment] ordered to do duty with the Engineer department. A deserter reported that forty men were K[illed] or W[ounded] in the Fort Yesterday. On the reserve picquet last night, only a few shots fired. Some brought on ourselves by Basden, Brown & I telling stories in turn which made us, men and all, laugh so loud that the Fort fired at us and the Field officer of the night came up and gave us a precious wigging for risking the mens' lives unnecessarily.

### *2 September*

Basserer joined last night & L[ieutenan]t. Leonard[34] today, the latter Capt[ain]. Shore sent to Fort George to take charge of the invalids.

### *4 September*

Sunday. Our Brigade on duty, we all off the roster. A severe skirmish from 1 P.M. till near 7, the enemy having made a desperate attempt to force our new battery which annoys them greatly, a tremendous rain and thunder storm broke over the combatants about 5 [P.M.] and tended to cool both parties. They were repulsed. The rain lasted all night, we lucky to be under shelter. The Casualties were about twenty. L[ieutenan]t. Marsh,[35] a fine young man, was killed.

Captain Jobling and L[ieutenan]t. Kelly,[36] 104th [Regiment], joined us — a most ridiculous blunder at our head quarters. We are Eight officers to Eighteen men, the debris of our two flank companies, four officers having been sent up, quite out of all place and time.

### *5 September*

Monday. Walked round all the batteries and picquets with my old light company Chum, Cap[tain]. Jobling, as bold a fire-eating Northumbrian as any man in this army. The Fort and the Enemy's fleet at anchor off it, looked very gay. Wrote a long letter to my dear Mother. Reports that the enemy are building batteaux, in secret, behind Squaw Island. They are either planning some expedition or a move for the Fort.

### *8 September*

The 100th [Regiment] Light comp[an]y marched for Fort George and, at dinner time, we had orders to march tomorrow for Chippawa & Queenston to occupy the latter until F[urther] O[rders].

## Notes

[1] "Brown Bess." The British soldier's traditional name for his issue musket.

[2] Captain James Lewis Basden, 89th Foot (1785-1856).

[3] "Shindy." The *Lexicon Baliconitrum, or Dictionary of Buckish Slang, University Wit and Pickpocket Eloquence* (London, 1811) defines shindy as a dance. Tucker's army nickname of "Brigadier Shindy" implies that he was excitable and not steady in action.

[4] Colonel John Goulston Price Tucker, 41st Foot, commander of Fort Niagara.

[5] "Came to the charge." Presented bayonets.

[6] For the official British report on this action, see NAC, RG 8 I, vol. 685, p. 34, Tucker to Conran, 4 August 1814.

[7] See Ontario Archives, MU 2052, Harvey Papers, District General Order, Fort Erie, 5 August 1814. This strongly worded order by Drummond forbade the soldiers of the Right Division to duck or flinch from American rifle fire when in formation and threatened the penalty of death for any man who retreated without orders in action.

[8] Fascines were tied bundles of wood used in the construction of fieldworks.

[9] Lieutenant George Phillpott, RE (d. 1853).

[10] An epaulement, in nineteenth century fortification terminology, was a fieldwork erected to provide shelter from enemy fire with no provision for firing over or through it.

[11] Actually, the engineer sent to the rear was Captain Samuel Romilly who Drummond regarded as incompetent, see NAC, RG 8 I, vol. 685, p. 49, Drummond to Prevost, 12 August, 1814.

[12] Lieutenant Edward Wentworth Solomon, 104th Foot (1795-1828), a Haligonian.

[13] Le Couteur exaggerates here; his increase in pay would have actually been £238.

[14] Lieutenant Gregor McGregor, 1st Foot (1785-1814).

[15] It was actually the birthday of the Prince Regent, the future George IV. The birthday of George III was 4 June.

[16] For an account of this action from the American side, see *Doc. Hist.*, I, 135, Gaines to Secretary of War, 13 August 1814. Although Le Couteur could not know it, the American commander at the battle of Conjocta Creek, Major Ludowick Morgan, was killed during the fighting that took place this day.

[17] This is incorrect. The British officer killed during the cutting out of the two American schooners was Lieutenant and Commander Charles Radcliffe, RN.

[18] Drummond's presentiment of death is confirmed by the account of Surgeon William Dunlop of the 89th Foot. Dunlop remembered that:

> We breakfasted at eight; Colonel Drummond was in high spirits – it has

sometimes struck me since unnaturally high, — but that idea might have proceeded from the result....

We sat apparently by common consent long after breakfast was over. Drummond told some capital stories, which kept us in such a roar that we seemed more like an after dinner than an after breakfast party. At last the bugles sounded the turn-out, and we rose to depart for our stations; Drummond called us back, and his face assuming an unwonted solemnity, he said, "Now boys! we never will all meet together here again; at least I will never again meet you. I feel it and am certain of it; let us all shake hands, and then every man do his duty, and I know you all too well to suppose for a moment that any of you will flinch it." We shook hands accordingly, all round, and with a feeling very different from what we had experienced for the last two hours, fell into our places.

See William Dunlop, *Tiger Dunlop's Upper Canada* (Toronto, 1967), 51.

[19] A fortress in Spain unsuccessfully attacked by Wellington in 1811 and finally captured with great loss the following year.

[20] A fortress in Spain attacked and carried by Wellington in 1813.

[21] This is perhaps a typographical error. Le Couteur possibly meant Captain S.B. Torrens, 1st Foot, ADC to General Conran, or Lieutenant George Hazen, 103rd Foot (1786-1836).

[22] Captain G.A. Eliot, 103rd Foot (1785-1835), Deputy Assistant Quartermaster General.

[23] Lieutenant John Fallon, 103rd Foot (1790-1820).

[24] "Charge of No. 4." Fine buckshot used to hunt birds.

[25] For the British official reports of this action, see NAC, RG 8 I, vol. 685, p. 94, Drummond to Prevost, 15 August 1814 and p. 101, same to same, 16 August 1814. For a recent study of this ill-fated assault, see Donald E. Graves, "William Drummond and the Battle of Fort Erie," *Canadian Military History* I (1992), 25-44.

[26] The official casualty return for the assault on Fort Erie is found in NAC, CO 42, vol. 128-1, p. 182a, Return of Killed, Wounded & Missing. It lists a total of 905 casualties.

[27] Lieutenant James A. McLauchlan, 104th Foot (1796-1865).

[28] Lieutenant Charles Barstow, 8th Foot.

[29] It was Drummond's custom to carry a double-barrelled gun, possibly a shotgun, into battle and to wear strings of beads presented to him by the native warriors of Upper Canada who admired his courage.

[30] Captain Alexander McMillan, Glengarry Light Infantry.

[31] "Volscian ears." The Volscians were an ancient and warlike Italian tribe conquered by the Romans in the fourth century B.C. As they resided in a volcanic area of the

Italian peninsula, Le Couteur's reference possibly means that, only to Volscian (or warlike) ears would the sound of an exploding shell that *missed* its target be unmusical.

[32] Brigadier General Edmund P. Gaines, U.S. Army (d. 1849). Gaines was promoted a major general for repulsing the British attack of 15 August 1814.

[33] Lieutenant Colonel Robert McDouall (1774-1848), commander of the British post on Mackinac Island, see *DCB*, VII, 556-557.

[34] Lieutenant Thomas Leonard, 104th Foot (b. 1794).

[35] Lieutenant John Marsh, Royal Marine Artillery.

[36] Ensign Waldron Kelly, 104th Foot.

*The King's bridge and the village of Chippawa, Upper Canada, by George Heriot, circa 1805. Le Couteur was stationed here briefly in September 1814.* G. Heriot/National Archives of Canada/C-12768

# *Chapter Ten*

## "THE PRETTIEST LITTLE AFFAIR ANY OF US HAD EVER SEEN"

On the Lines of Communication

*September and October, 1814*

***9 September [1814]***

We marched at 6 A.M. in beautiful weather and got to the Chippawa Creek by 11. Here we received orders to halt and both companies to remain there with positive orders to hold the posts, and not to give it up to any force whatever.

Chippawa Creek at its confluence with the River Niagara, is about fifty yards wide, the banks are low, only two or three feet above the water. It is navigable for some distance, the Schooners are about a mile up.[1] It is very defensible as it can only be attacked in Front openly, the Niagara below it being very rapid, and so near the Falls, about a mile, that it would be foolhardy to attempt a landing.

***10 September***

A violent thunderstorm and rain prevented us from stirring.

***11 September***

Still raining.

***12 September***

Solomon went down to order up the 97th [Regiment of Foot], says the men in camp are getting sickly. On Patrol last night, had a twelve-mile walk, or ride rather, for I got a horse for eight of them.

### *13 September*

Occupied myself in a dismal raining day by putting in Shingles instead of panes of glass in the window frames, the Yankees having broke nearly all the glass. My performance as Glazier made our bed room very comfortable, for the wind last night had blown into it with a whistle all night long. We called in Brisland[2] our fiddler and got up a Bull dance, taking it in turn to do Lady.

### *16 September*

The 97th [Regiment of Foot] under Col McCarthy,[3] about five hundred strong, marched by. We gave the officers a dinner *à la Tête de pont*.[4]

### *17 September*

On Picquet. A dry night, for a wonder, till daylight when it came on to rain. A Body of the Enemy moved down from Buffalo to Schlosser.

### *18 September*

Sunday. The Enemy surprised our batteries yesterday about 3 o'clock during the heavy rain and were fortunate to carry three of them. De Wattevilles and the Kings, the troops on duty, were forced [back] before the Supports could arrive. The 6th and 82nd [Regiments] recovered [Battery] No. 2, with the Bayonet, and the Glengarry, Royals and 89th [Regiment of Foot] retook the others. We had six hundred men *hors de Combat*, the Americans double that number. Poor Jack Barstow, my friend and fellow Campaigner, was killed. It was a very savage affair, our Men bayonetted every Soul in No. 2 battery, it was full of corpses. We took many Officers and 170 Prisoners.[5]

### *19 September*

Monday. The Yankee Officers came down, thirteen in number. We were just seated to dinner when they were announced and we all rose to give them our seats. They looked very downcast and wretched. However, as we offered them such comforts in washing & preparation as we might, then placed them at our table, they were quite struck with our hospitality and Kindness, and were soon perfectly gay and at their ease. I had to escort Six of them quite alone to Mrs. Willson's [Tavern] at the Falls, upon their Parole not to escape, rescue or no rescue. It was a dark night, raining hard. We had given some of them caps, as they had lost theirs in the fight. I was very glad to get safe with my Prisoners to their quarters and insisted on getting beds for them. One told me "it was the first time He had ever been in an engagement and it should be the last."

### *20 September*

Shot and Shells coming down in batteaux. Smells of a retreat. The Yankees spiked and broke the trunnions of a 24- P[d]r. [gun] and two 18's while in possession of our batteries one short half hour. On Picquet. Heard that Chippawa Creek is navigable for Vessels of sixty tons, thirty miles up, and for Batteaux, sixty-two miles, within five miles of Burlington where the 103rd [Regiment] marched to this day.[6]

### *22 September*

The 8th or King's [Regiment] marched by for Fort George. The Army retired to Frenchman's Creek. Several Officers, Sabine, Sheppard,[7] etc. dined with us.

### *23 September*

Called up at 11 o'clock last night and sent up with Batteaux for stores [at] Black Creek. Got there 2 in the morning and walked a mile through mud and water to Colonel Myers for orders. The Quarter Master General sent me back to take up my quarters in the commissariat store where I laid down in my harness, slept till 6, awoke half frozen and half dry. Comm[issar]y. General Turquand and my friend Jack Ashworth[8] treated me to an excellent breakfast which tended not a little to revive me.

After sending off the batteaux as they were loaded, and supplied with a good lunch, I started at three with three or four of the last boats of my brigade. I ordered them to keep in my wake exactly as I had the river Pilot on board with me. The last boat, instead of obeying My orders, tried to pull past some of the others and got out into the Stream. I shouted, we all shouted to them, but it was too late. She had got into the horrid, rapid Current of the everlasting Falls — We got along perfectly safely. Saw the men straining every nerve to pull back towards us but, alas, they only made the matter worse by bad steering and the boat was going down broadside on. Some of the men then lost courage to pull, stripped and jumped into the stream to swim for it. One did get to Drake's Island, one got to the shore, the other was hurried over the Falls!! The Corporal, a brave fellow, left two oars out, pulled first on one Side, then on the other, then somehow steered and shoved his great batteau on Drake's Island so that we soon sent native boatsmen to bring Him and the boat off. It was a dismal sight, but entirely proceeded from disobedience of orders so I was not at all blamed.

Our men were marching off for Queenston as Coates & I got in. We found our excellent friend Capt[ain]. Sabine at Rohrbach's. He gave us a

Most hearty welcome, a capital dinner and a bottle of port, a luxury we had not enjoyed for a length of time. Indeed, the table seemed so nicely laid out with a clean table cloth and snuggeries that we hardly knew how to behave.

### *24 September*

Saturday. Got to Queenston. A lovely day, but shining dismally on that lovely village — it will be long before it is restored to its peaceable attractions. It is melancholy to see such wanton destruction as the broom of war has made in it, it is a palace of desolation. We are in quiet possession of Colonel Dickson's[9] fine large house, with the 89th [Regiment] light bobs, it being the only one with windows left in it. As the big wigs were sure to take the best rooms, I mounted at once to the garret where the Yankees had broken nothing, the doors & other windows being safe & the room snug. At night I turned down, not in, all standing, with my blankets above & bearskin below me.

Just as I was dropping to sleep, I heard a strange cry close by me. I listened, surely no one is being murdered? — another faint plaintive cry! "Hallow, that's no mistake", I grasped my sword, "Who's there?" Another cry! In the very room I could have sworn. "Who's there?" I shouted, determined to be heard. "Say what are You? Where are you?" Another cry like a dying child's! Good God, this is horrid and no answer, no candle and quite dark. I thought it wisest then to grope my way out, find my Servant, and bring a Candle, convinced that some person dying was concealed in the garret.

My Servant soon procured a light and up we came, listened, no sound, looked everywhere. Presently we both heard a faint cry. "It's a child, Sir!" "Where can it be hid?" At length I noticed small closets or recesses under the attic. We opened the little door and placed the candle inside, then, came another cry — looked in for our baby and saw a bright pair of glistening eyes, faintly looking at the light for help. Gentle, compassionate, tender-hearted reader, the dear, sweet, soft baby was a tabby. A beautiful, starved, tortoise-shell kitten - so weak that it could not stir.

I had heard that Cats were not grateful, I was resolved to try! St. Germain,[10] my man, would have ended it of its misery, by "il faut la jetter par la fenêtre, Monsieur[11]" "Non, non", I said "Nous l'avon sauvée, il faut la secourir, allez me chercher un peu de pain et du lait, ou de l'eau au moins."[12] I brought the poor bag of bones out and rubbed Her gently to give her warmth and circulation. St. Germain brought me a little bread & milk in a Tin and poor Pussy lapped up as much as I would let Her have. I then placed Her at the foot of my blanket and in the morning found my patient enjoying sound repose just where I had placed Her, gave Her some more milk &

bread. She was a crop, no ears nor tail.

On telling my story to the mess at breakfast time, the Doctor declared that I had treated the case of starvation, with Aesculapian skills — friction, warmth and light diet in small portions. "Johnny, you have mistaken your trade, You should have been one of us." "No, No, Woody, no poisoner, thank you." "Let's see your patient." "No I'll be hanged if I do, till she can walk." "Oh Johnny Johnny, its a girl you've got upstairs — we must see to believe!" "I'm the Lady with the Cat's face in the Pantomine. If You all promise not to hurt Her, I'll bring Her down." They did, and I brought down poor pussy, she excited everyone's pity. She could not walk from weakness.

In a few days, however, what a change — she became a lively beauty, so grateful, so fond, so faithful. No one could Coax Her from me, but worse than all — She followed me to Parades. "Look" said the Light bobs, "see Mr. Le Couteur and his Cat coming to Parade." Queeney became the wonder and delight of the Light company when St. Germain had told the awful story. In the good old superstitious days of Queen Bess, no one would have remained in, or revisited that chamber at night. Even my friend St. G[ermain] had a very respectable awe-struck countenance when he heard the first groan. Dear Grateful Pussy.

The Surgeon's wife was very fond of a pet cat and had just lost one. She was twelve hundred miles off in New Brunswick and Woody begged Her of me for his wife who would take special care of Her for my sake and her own. As I could not bring my fair friend back to Jersey conveniently, I made a graceful effort and our Doctor took Her the whole way to Fredericton in a suitable carriage of her own where I heard of her health and progeny long after!!

### *26 September*

A valuable officer, Col[onel]. Gordon[13] of the Royals, died last night of his wounds. No sugar or milk to be had. Coates and I walked round the Orchards or Gardens and got a quantity of nice peaches for our Mess off Standard trees, like our apple trees at home. Jobling was robbed of £21, luckily money is not wanted much now.

### *27 September*

On Picquet last night. Very quiet, no enemy to be seen on the opposite or Lewiston side. Walked out towards St David's on a shooting excursion, saw one quail, no game.

***1 October [1814]***
My brother's 13th birthday, may He have many happy returns of this day in more peace and quiet than I have enjoyed lately.

***2 October***
Sunday. Major Clifford[14] read prayers to us — the first time since we left Kingston.

***3 October***
Basserer & I went out fishing just below the whirlpool where we caught Black and white Bass & Pickerel — the former & latter excellent fish. N.B.: A Yankee Rifleman fired at Basserer and me and drove us from our fishing. We have a very pleasant and quiet post here — good fishing but bad shooting.

***6 October***
Change of scene. Woodford came from the heights about 9 A.M. in a great hurry — "the Yankee army is encamped above Lewiston; supposed to be General Izard's[15] from Sackets Harbor" put us all on the "Qui vive". About 2 o'clock we observed the General and his Staff reconnoitring us all along the Banks of the river — lots of 'em about the banks all day. I do not think that they will attempt the crossing in our teeth, it would be a dangerous experiment with such a rapid current and only a narrow landing place, well-watched and defended. Looking out very sharp all night, nought but their camp fires to be seen.

***7 October***
The 100th marched in to reinforce us, the Marquis of Tweeddale[16] commands here, the guards to my sorrow not to be relieved till Sundown — not to be seen, no doubt.

***8 October***
An alarm last night — the luggage of the 100th coming in mistaken for Izard's army crossing.

***9 October***
The American army moving towards Schlosser, their rear Guard disappeared about 9 A.M. Convinced that it [is] only a demonstration and that they have no notion of crossing — probably to form a junction with Brown's army at Erie.

***10 October***

Martin lent me his Horse to ride to Fort George. It appears to be a very weak fort and under the guns of Fort Niagara. There is a ditch, palisading and ramparts. Crossed over to visit Fort Niagara which has the appearance of a much stronger Fort and seems to be very tenable. The stone houses should prevent an enemy from holding it even if He entered the enceinte. The Quarters in it are wretched. Mississaga on our side near the lake is a pretty little Fort and would prevent vessels from coming up the river. Dined with Sabine at the Artillery mess and got back after ten.

***11 October***

Leyden,[17] Hewson,[18] Brown,[19] Gugy,[20] Martin & I walked to the Heights among the Chestnut woods, and felled a tree to get at the chestnuts which we gathered in plenty at the expence of our fingers, to send Capt[ain]. Dobbs, RN, who declared if we did not send Him a bag full, He would not give us a passage to Kingston.

***12 October***

On Picquet last night, the Marquis [of Tweeddale] is wonderfully vigilant. He sits up with us and watches by the hour. A fine Gentleman and Soldier — something like our dear Drummond. Have had my eyes straining since daylight at sundry Yankees on the other bank. Izard's army went up to Erie & is crossing to our side. Deserters say they menace another move upon us. They will never force the [Chippawa] Creek, in my opinion, if we protect the right well by the Glengarry, Militia and Indians.

***14 October***

The Alarm guns fired early and the 100th, 89th [Regiments] and us marched up to Lundy's lane. Obliged to bivouac & sleep without blankets — a cold berth. Gen[era]ls. Brown and Izard with eight thousand men advanced to Street's creek. They fired a few shots and shells at the Glengarrys.

***15 October***

Moved on about two miles and quartered ourselves. No sooner were we snug [then] the 100th [Regiment] came up and the Marquis sent us on. We halted and occupied a tavern by Lundy's Lane, for the day we hope. Walked over the deathful and dearly disputed ground of our battle on the 25th [of July 1814]. It was very good position. If the church had been occupied and loop-holed, the position would have been impregnable and of easy defence — propose to sketch it tomorrow! Never trust to tomorrow young Soldier.[21]

### *16 October*

Turned out last night at 8 and moved on, halted in rear of the entrenchments at Chippewa. Half frozen all night through from the intense cold, obliged to stand up as the ground was too wet to sleep on. A few shots fired by the Americans at some (four) of their deserters coming to us. After daylight we observed a body of the enemy near a mile off over the creek, a strong piquet probably. The main force is in the woods and probably moving up to attempt getting round our right. Do not think they will attempt the battery plan again, our *tête de Pont* is a stout one.[22]

### *17 October*

The Americans are at some mischief, we cannot yet divine it — fancy they are cutting a road thro' the woods, some miles to the right. We are very alert.

### *18 October*

Wretchedly cold last night for, though we are in a house, there are no doors or windows left to it. Turned out about three and marched off in a hurry to Olsen's — the Yankees being expected forthwith. We can comprehend the nature of the roads we may move on in their direction as we have been marching ankle deep in mud. It must have been a false alarm for we were moved back in time for our dinner.

### *19 October*

We had hardly laid down and got into sound sleep the night before last Wednesday, when Coates ran down & awoke me, "Le C. dont flatter yourself you are going to sleep, rouse up, we are going to surprise a picquet!" Packed up my haversack and off in a Jiffy to Olsen's — it is hardly worth repeating that we were marching knee deep in mud in a pitch dark night — over rough and smooth — an exquisite enjoyment for those who have never tried it. We slept in the wet for about half an hour while the 100th [Regiment] and others were crossing the river in batteaux. They then halted. We awoke cold and shivering & crossed, then marched on rapidly about nine miles through a horrid, swampy road, then halted on a sort of clearing at P___. Ordered to light camp fires, cook and sleep — we did both with a will.

### *20 October*

In the morning found the Glengarries were there. They gave us a hearty breakfast and saved us from famishing. About 7, we all moved on and joined the 82nd [Regiment] then advanced, a dashing little division under our gallant Marquis Tweeddale, and Colonel Myers.[23] Reached Cook's Mill's about 8 when the Glens [Glengarries] became suddenly engaged in our front. The Ground was a fine large clearing with the Chippawa Creek on our left, a gentle slope to the front and bank of the creek. About a mile in front were woods and to the extreme left we could perceive the American Army moving over a pontoon or temporary bridge which they had thrown over the river.

About four hundred of them had engaged our advance, the 82nd and 100th [Regiments] were formed into line. We were thrown in extended order on the left and in support of Carter[24] with a Field piece and four Rockets. The Americans getting stronger and their fire overpowering the Glens, we were ordered to advance, extended, to turn the American right. Our men dashed into the ravine in good style and engaged the Yankees in our front, who soon gave way, for a short distance.

But they, in turn, being supported by about four hundred fresh troops, We had to give way in turn and retreated in good order a little way, when the 82nd [Regiment] Light bobs came to our aid, when both companies cheered and checked the enemy again. The rocket brigade was then brought up very opportunely and a volley plunging into a Column not yet deployed threw it into confusion, as well they might. This checked their further advance. Our Gun was very ill-placed behind a little wood and only barked without biting. We halted for a short while, drawn up securely behind a rail fence, a capital protection, when soon after the Marquis ordered us to retire by alternate wings.

The line formed, and we flankers extended on the Flanks, covering the line, Rockets and Gun. The Americans came out of the woods. Officers and men did not fire and I verily believe cheered us while admiring the beautiful Military movement we were executing in slow time. It was altogether the prettiest little affair any of us had ever seen. The Uncle Sams were about eighteen hundred men, yet after the check, they would not advance to attack our seven hundred in position. The Americans retired on finding their project at surprise had failed, as our rear was strong. They had watched us moving alternately to the rear for a Mile, when we filed off and marched to Cumming's, Six miles, wet, weary and hungry.[25]

The misery was of short duration for we were given a splendid breakfast by Cumming, rested the men there and learned Casualties. Ours: 3 killed, 1 Serg[ean]t. & 3 wounded. The others: 17 killed and 28 wounded. Capt[ain]. MacMillan [of the Glengarry Light Infantry] was wounded with our lads, while in the bushes. He had a hand-to-hand fight with a Yankee, the Sword against the Musket, & cut down the man.

We continued our retrograde march to Olsen's, and crossed the Creek and were quartered for the night about a quarter of a mile on — no bedding, not a thing to eat. Sent an imploring message to the 89th [Regiment] for relief but found that they were quite as miserably off as ourselves. Gave it up in despair when our Noble Marquis, hearing of our distress, saved us from starvation by sending us a fine shoulder of mutton and a loaf of bread which were divided by my little sharp sabre, there not being one Knife, much less a fork, among us.

### *21 October*

A dreadful cold night of suffering was the last, no blankets, the fire out, and frost on the ground. I verily believe that the enemy were not coming down to our right but merely intended to burn Cook's Mills as they supply most parts of the country with Planks, flour etc. About 2 o'clock we got orders to march for Fort George in order to embark for Kingston. I completed my twentieth year this day and am thankful to God for having preserved me in safety through many dangers.

### *22 October*

Halted by our old field of battle for the night and marched into Fort George and took up quarters with Walker of the Commissariat.[26]

### *23 October*

Sunday. Ordered to embark all in a hurry at 8 A.M. without our breakfast, right happy to do so — Huzza!, Huzza!

### *24 October*

The Old King's[27] as suddenly embarked as we were yesterday, all in the *Niagara*,[28] Sloop of War, Captain Collier.[29] This morning off Long point, the King's were removed to the *Charlotte*. A fine breeze, jolly sailing on fresh water. Yet the sailing is like that in the Channel, a short sea, but a much longer run than from Jersey to England. It seemed funny to see the Sailors throw a bucket overboard, and drink from it. The Ducks in sight at 2 o'clock — no signs of Jonathan Chauncey's fleet. 5 P.M., passed the Ducks and anchored inside the Gap about eight. Wind foul.

***25 October***

Sailed at daylight. Obliged to beat in, off Nine Mile point when the wind became fair — got a view of Old Kingston about twelve. We flattered ourselves we should dine on shore. Anchored about four and received a mortifying order not to land till a signal was made. In expectation all the evening ending in disappointment.

## Notes

[1] Le Couteur is here referring to the two American schooners captured on 13 August 1814.

[2] Private Michael Brisland, 104th Foot.

[3] Lieutenant Colonel William McCarthy (b. 1771), 97th Foot.

[4] "Dinner à la tête de pont." A tête de pont is a fieldwork constructed to protect the end of a bridge. Le Couteur is making a pun.

[5] The official British report on the sortie of 17 September is found in CO 42, vol. 128-2, p. 271, De Watteville to Drummond, 18 September 1814.

[6] Le Couteur could not know it but, in the 1820s, the first Welland Canal would join Lake Ontario to Lake Erie by way of the Chippawa River.

[7] Lieutenant Edmund Sheppard, RA (d. 1840).

[8] John Ashworth, Deputy Assistant Commissary General, Commissariat Department.

[9] Lieutenant Colonel Thomas Dickson (1775-1825), commanding officer of the 2nd Lincoln Militia Regiment, see *DCB*, VI, 211-212. Dickson was a prominent merchant, Collector of Customs and ferry owner in Queenston.

[10] Le Couteur's memory is playing tricks here. His servant at this time could not have been Private Joseph St. Germain of the 104th Foot as this individual was captured during the assault on Fort Erie on 15 August 1814 and not released until the end of the war in 1815. See Austin Squires, *The 104th Regiment* (Fredericton, 1962), 232.

[11] "Il faut la jetter par la fenêtre, Monsieur." We should throw it out the window, Sir.

[12] "Non, Non. Nous l'avons sauvée, il faut la secourir, allez me chercher un peu de pain et du lait, ou de l'eau au moins." No, no. We have saved it, we have to revive it, go find a piece of bread and some milk, or at least some water.

[13] Lieutenant Colonel John Gordon, 1st Foot. Gordon had been badly wounded at the battle of Chippawa, 5 July 1814 and mortally wounded at the sortie of 17 September.

[14] Major Miller Clifford, 89th Foot.

[15] Major General George Izard, U.S. Army (d. 1828). Izard was the commander of the Right Division of the American army at Plattsburgh. In August 1814, against his protests, he was ordered to march his army west to reinforce Brown's Left Division at Fort Erie.

[16] Lieutenant Colonel George Hay, Eighth Marquis of Tweeddale (1787-1876). A twice-wounded veteran of Wellington's army, Tweeddale came to Canada in 1813 to command the 100th Foot. Wounded again at the battle of Chippawa, he returned to duty before he was able to walk to command a brigade offered to him by Drummond. On Tweeddale, see "Recollections of the War of 1812 by George

Hay, Eighth Marquis of Tweeddale," *American Historical Review* 32 (1926-1927), 69-78.

[17] This is a typographical error. The officer in question is probably Ensign William Leaden, 89th Foot (1793-1832).

[18] Lieutenant John Milliquet Hewson or Hewetson, 89th Foot (1797-1869).

[19] Probably Lieutenant Daniel Browne, 89th Foot (1782-1843).

[20] Lieutenant Thomas Gugy, Glengarry Light Infantry (c. 1796-1825).

[21] It is unfortunate that Le Couteur did not leave a pictorial record of the battlefield at Lundy's Lane as it looked during the war. The area over which the battle was fought is now part of the city of Niagara Falls, Canada.

[22] "Battery plan." A reference to the American attack on the British siege batteries at Fort Erie on 17 September 1814.

[23] Lieutenant Colonel Christopher Myers, 100th Foot (d. 1817), Deputy Quartermaster General, Upper Canada.

[24] Lieutenant Thomas Carter, RA.

[25] For the British report on the action at Cook's Mills, see NAC, RG 8 I, vol. 686, p. 70, Myers to Drummond, 19 October 1814.

[26] Thomas Walker, Deputy Assistant Commissary General, Commissariat Department.

[27] "The Old King's." The 8th (or King's) Regiment of Foot, one of the senior regiments of the army and a mainstay of the defence of Upper Canada during the war.

[28] HMS *Niagara*, sloop of war, 22 guns, launched at Kingston in 1809 as the *Royal George*.

[29] Captain Edward Collier, RN: lieutenant, 1803; commander, 1810; captain, 1814.

# *Chapter Eleven*

## "THE CLOSE OF A HOT AND UNNATURAL WAR"
## Garrison Duty at Kingston
*October 1814 to March 1815*

***26 October [1814]***
Landed this morning at six and found dear little Jem ready for my luggage, waiting to take me to dear Mrs. Robison who gave me a maternal welcome, re-echoed by all her family — most happy to find them all well. Called to see her brother Col[onel]. Cartwright and her Nephew, Dr. Smith,[1] & families.

***27 October***
Found a Guernsey man, Major Brock[2] of the 37th, here, a nice person, dined with me at our mess.

***28 October***
Capt[ain]. Dobbs invited me to dine with them at Judge Cartwright's. Mrs D. looking well.

***29 October***
Rode to Cataraqui to see Bradley[3] — sorry as usual. Two Marlow men of the 9th, Seward[4] and Scargill,[5] dined with me — old chums.

***31 October***
Sir James Kempt[6] & staff, L[ieutenan]t. Gore[7] and Capt[ain]. Dumaresq,[8] a relative who bears a high reputation for gallantry and ability, dined with our Mess. Sir James was pleased to say that He had never seen a mess so like the establishment of a private family of distinction.

### *1 November [1814]*
The fleet sailed with the 37th [Regiment of Foot] and detachments for Niagara. Kingston has been greatly strengthened since we left it last, there are Six blockhouses and a stout picketing all round it besides the batteries — it is safe from a *coup de main* without the fleet.

### *3 November*
A dance at Mrs. R[obison's]. — very gay. Much rain this week.

### *10 November*
The fleet returned from Niagara with the 41st [Regiment] and King's L[igh]t C[ompan]y. [The] 41st moved on in batteaux for Montreal.

### *13 November*
My rascal M[ills][9] played me and my friend Mrs. [Shore] a vile trick by getting her maid in the family way. I and He wished to marry her but Cap. S[hore]. never would consent to it which I was exceedingly angry at. However both the poor girl & child died. He was very penitent and really wished to do what He ought but was prevented — shamefully, I think.

### *16 November*
Suffering from a violent attack of Rheumatism — beginning to pay for my good health while campaigning. Poorly to the 20th, could not go to Mess.

### *23 November*
Attacked with dysentery, and poorly to the 4th Dec[embe]r. Confined to my room with fever and dysentery to the 11th, very weak. Took a walk.

### *12 December [1814]*
The dysentery returned.

### *16 December*
Pretty well recovered, began to visit again. Reading *Elegant Extracts*[10] then [illegible]. Twenty-four Ladies and one hundred Gent[leme]n at the assembly[11] last night. Girls up! Market high!

### *18 December*
Sun[day]. Heard a very good sermon from our Minister, took a ride to exercise man & horse.

*View of Kingston, Upper Canada, 1819 by John J. Bigsby, after an unknown artist. Le Couteur spent part of the late spring of 1813, and the winters of 1813-14 and 1814-15 in garrison in this town.* J.J. Bigsby/National Archives of Canada/C-20885

***23 December***

Mr. & Mrs. Robison & children came down from the Napanee Mills to spend their Xmas holidays in town. The dear children a great amusement for me.

***25 December***

Sunday 25th, Xmas Day. Wrote a long letter to my dear Grandfather in pursuance of a time-honoured custom of my younger days. Freezing very hard, obliged to parade in our Ear Caps, the river is nearly frozen over. I was invited to join Mrs. Robison's family dinner, which I greatly enjoyed with the dear family. Sweet little Martha coaxed me to know whether I would stand Godfather to the little baby, to be called Mary, a name doubly dear to me being my own beloved Mother's.

***26 December***

A Str[ong] wind has broken up the fine skating ice. The *Psyche*,[12] a fine 38-Gun frigate, was launched today. Snow everywhere.

***31 December***

Singular weather these last four days. It is nearly as warm as Summer and all the Snow in the Town is off the Streets. Very unhealthy. Mr. Robison dined with me at our Mess.

***1 January [1815]***

My New Year's day not very auspicious, being very ill from my old disorder — dysentery. Marched to Church, however, before breakfast.

***2 January***

My God daughter, Mary Robison, was baptised, christened I should say. Was to have been named Mary Jane, but was called Mary in Compliment to my dear Mother. Born 3 Oct[ober], 1814.

| | | |
|---|---|---|
| 1. Richard Cartwright Robison was born | | 20th Jan. 1809 (died) |
| 2. Elizabeth Anne | " | 8 Dec. 1806 (died) |
| 3. Martha Smith | " | 14 March 1808 |
| 4. Thomas Weeks | " | 10 Nov. 1811 |
| 5. Mary, My Godchild | " | 3 Oct. 1814 (died) |

*3 January*
The heavy rain seemed likely to spoil the chance of a good assembly this evening but the ladies of Kingston like small difficulties to show their spirit in surmounting them.

*7 January*
Suffering from my old complaint. Capt[ains]. Bowles[13] & Jackson[14] dined with me. Sent an excuse to Seward of the 9th as I was too poorly. Freezing hard and three inches of snow on the ground.

*8 January*
Took a long walk with the hope of walking off my disease. The Surgeons attribute the prevalence of dysentery to the changeable state of the weather. Today the rain has melted all the snow. It is dreadfully wet and sloppy.

*12 January*
Freezing hard — the Ice is taken, as far as Long Island. Went out skating.

*13 January*
Fine ice. Skated over the river to Point Frederick and round the Fleet. A curious feeling to be able to glide close up to ships of War, reduced to wooden fortresses on a field of ice. They break the ice all round at night, to keep a sort of ditch round them but, in the depth of winter, that will be impossible.

*15 January*
At Church.

*16 January*
Monday. A Sergeant and Ten men of the 81st Regiment deserted last night with arms, clothing, appointments and 60 rounds of ball cartridge. Sent off with thirteen men of the Light Company and a Guide after them. We crossed over to Long, or Wolfe's, Island, due South nearly. The ice was very thin and, in some spots, the water came thro' the hot springs. I made the Guide move first, then followed, and made all the Men follow in Indian file. It was a ticklish walk of nearly three miles, there were about three inches of Snow on the ground, and we moved on across to Mill Bay, where I halted the men to dine about 12 o'clock. We had just then fallen on the track of two or three men which we, of course, made sure was that of some of the deserters. The guide

had gone a little way from us. I had ordered my men, should we come on the Deserters suddenly, to desire them to surrender — if they hesitated, to give them a volley and charge them. The mens' arms were loaded ready for action.

All at once We heard the Guide roaring for help lustily. I fell in the men and charged towards Him. To my surprise I saw Him chased by a Soldier across an arm of the Lake. I ordered one Man to give Him a shot and rushed at Him, Sword in hand. As I neared Him I saw two men at the edge of the lake aiming at me. I shouted: "Surrender to the 104th, or you're a dead man!" He dropped on his Knees and said: "I surrender Sir — Your men almost shot me." "Who are You?" "I am a Sergeant, Sir, sent after a deserter from the Marines. I have a couple of men with me." I was very happy the poor fellow had escaped [but] I made Him show me his orders.

We then moved on, sometimes through brushwood, sometimes over Cranberry Swamps, a most laborious march with no tracks of any thing human, till we had, it was said, walked thirty-nine miles, to the passage Point, opposite the American shore. It was blowing a gale and dreadfully cold. My men made an immense fire and cut down a quantity of Pine boughs and a few planks [and saying] that I was still suffering from the Ill effects of dysentery, insisted on covering me with their Great Coats.

Just as I was lying down, as some of the men had gone to the lake shore for water, We heard a great shouting and one came up to say a man in a Canoe was struggling through the ice to reach the Shore & they were Cheering Him on. Soon they brought the poor fellow up to me — wet and almost at death's door from exhaustion and cold.

He was Sir James Yeo's Coxswain, had been taken with Captain Popham in the boat affair.[15] He had been, in turns, coaxed, flattered, offered rewards, [and] offered a higher post to induce Him to desert his allegiance — then they placed Him in a Prison with other Englishmen. They had put Him on poor diet and in close confinement, and still offered Him rewards to become a traitor but the noble fellow was a true Jack Tar.

He determined to escape. Another man & Himself managed to tear their sheets into strips and one night, seeing an opportunity, they let themelves down from the top of the blockhouse. He went for the Lakeshore, and walking close to the edge where He could not be tracked, had got all the way round from Sackets Harbor till He found a broken canoe of wood. In this, with a bit of plank, the heroic sailor took his chance, sometimes partly afloat, sometimes shoving his frail bark over the ice, just hard enough to bear Him. Providentially, our fire directed Him to Salvation for, without that intervention, He would have perished from fatigue and cold, poor fellow. He shed tears of joy at this happy meeting, as He was known to me and others. The men took off some of their dry clothes to give Him warmth.

We had a quiet bivouac and started homewards at daylight. In our way, a Magnificent deer with Antlers of splendid growth started across our path. I gave Him a volley without effect. Soldiers are not dead shots at a flying object with a single ball.

When we got to the Lake shore, we had the horror to notice that the Ice had rotted. The guide thought it scarcely safe to cross! What were [we] to do? Starve there without provisions? I told Him to cut two or three long poles, we would give them to Himself and the heaviest men — if they popped through their poles would save them, and we should halt till they found a better spot. So wc acted. All went well with us, We saw Coates's party, who had gone round the East end of the Island, crossing below us.

Presently One of Coates's men went through, another went to help Him, He went in, then a third went through the ice. All three were drowned! It was a fearfully nervous spectacle for us all. I ordered the men, if any of us went through, to extend their arms and wait till the man with a Pole came to Him. Happily We had no occasion for them. If Coates had adopted the same precaution, his men would have been saved probably. As it was, half Kingston had turned out in deep anxiety to witness our perilous walk and, when we got near the shore, planks were pushed out in the bad places to secure our landing.

### *24 January*

This afternoon at Mess, on eating a small bit of cheese, I felt it as it were settling down my intestines, when I was taken with such violent and sudden pain in my side that I was obliged to hurry away. I remained in horrid agony for an hour or more, took large doses of castor oil and dear Mrs. Robison made them apply flannel bags with hot salt to my side and which at length gave relief. I have never felt such agony, as I was doubled up & rolling on the floor from it. It is weakness of stomach, the dysentery, a violent colic.

### *2 February [1815]*

Attended the Assembly, the most crowded I ever saw, could only manage two dances — out of spirits. Finished *Sir Ch[arles]. Grandison.*

### *6 February*

Took a long ride. In coming home, I saw a man knock a woman down and gallantly jumped off my horse and knocked Him down. Up jumped the woman and took her Husband's part so off I sneaked promptly. Captain

Rainsford brought his bride, the late Miss Clarke from Montreal, a very pretty person.

***8 February***
The 9th and 81st Light Companies marched for Prescott. The Yankees are said to be in large force about Ogdensburgh.

***11 February***
Busy at the Q[uarter] M[aster] Gen[era]l's Office with Craufield[16] drawing a plan of Fort Erie to compare it [to] my own sketch of it.

***15 February***
Dismal news of the defeat of our army at New Orleans.

***19 February***
Blessed reports of Peace from an Albany paper of the 18th. Hope they are true as we are all tired of the war. Finished reading Wilson's *Egypt*.[17]

***21 February***
Increasing rumours of peace.

***22 February***
Went to the Country Picnic with Dickson — very nice young people there, the pleasantest party I have been at this long while.

***24 February***
Heard the American official news of peace!!!

***25 February***
Several American officers came over from Sackets Harbour with the news. We received them very well, gave them a dinner, and made our Band play "Yankee Doodle" on drinking the President's health which gave them great pleasure.

This I heard from my brother officers for Col[onel]. Moodie came to my quarters and asked me at what time I could start express for Montreal with the dispatches and news of Peace. "In five minutes" I said. "Good. Well Johnny, You shall have a quarter of an hour. I'll go and send a Sleigh for you and bring you the despatches." I was writing a long letter to my dear Mother, put it under cover, and wrote "the Ratification of Peace by Mr.

Madison just arrived from Sackets harbour and I am sent express to Montreal with the news. Adieu, Le Couteur."

I saw the first shot-holes in the Sails and hull of the *Belvidera* Frigate when she came into Halifax on the [26th June 1812] and I witnessed the Second engagement between our Sloop-of-War's boat and the *Rover* of Salem the following week and now I am the bearer of the blessed News of Peace at the close of a hot and unnatural war between kindred people. Thank God!

I was provided with a Quarter Master General's route[18] and order to impress drivers, Sleighs and horses wherever they were to be had and, hastily packing a change of uniform and half a dozen shirts in My Portmanteau, with a hearty leaving taking for a week of my dear friends, the Robisons. The Sleigh soon came to the door and I, well enveloped in Furs, started at Speed. I had no great difficulty to obtain conveyance by day but, after midnight, it was *une autre affaire*.

When I got down among the Dutch settlers about 2 o'clock in the morning, My driver told me He did not know where to drive for a conveyance, the Inn to which we had gone having none and his horses were so jaded they could not proceed. He knew of a rich Dutch farmer who had famous Cattle. "Drive there!"

It was a fine large farm I could see as I drove up the avenue to it. The watch dogs barked at me furiously. I shouted & knocked. At last the Old Farmer appeared at an upper window. "Vats all dat! Vat de teufel mak's you mak dat noise!" The Old farmer was holding a light in rear of his right, wondering whether it might not be a Yankee inroad while all the younger branches, Male and female, were arming or in alarm. "I want horses to take me on to Prescott! I am travelling with Gov[ermen]t. despatches express!" "I got no horsen, vat de teufel, you come fraiten de hause vor? I got no horsen." "I must insist upon having horses, I am carrying the news of Peace." "Vat you say, Vat you say?" was repeated by Father, Mother Children. "Peace, Peace — Yes Peace with America" "Oh I zall zee my two boys dat are in de Militia. Oh My boys, my boys! Horsen! Yees, You zall have de best horsen, Mysell I will droive You! Yes, Yes, My boys, thank God, Peace!"[19]

The whole family ran down half clad to get me a warm meal, Schiedam,[20] horses, blessings. A superb pair of nearly thorough bred horses, a fine sleigh well-lined with fine furs, to carry me Sixteen miles in an hour and Twenty minutes — good kind people to the Messenger of peace!

I saw Aubin[21] of the 57th for a moment at Prescott. He wished me to dine, but I was off in ten minutes with all the diligence I could use. So difficult was it in some places to obtain horses that I was forty-three hours in getting to Montreal.

It was about six in the morning when I disturbed good old General De Rottenburg who sent me word I was very welcome with my official despatches but He had received private intelligence of the Peace the previous night. I called again at the official hour and was presented to the pretty Mrs. De Rottenburg — then about the period of Fat, Fair & Forty, scarcely a wrinkle on her lively brilliant countenance.[22] I asked for three or four days leave to visit my friends, which were readily granted. A day or two after, I received an intimation that, the Regiment being ordered to move down the Country, I might remain at Montreal.

On the 16th of March I wrote My Father urging Him, now that the war was over, to apply to the Duke of York[23] to be allowed to join him at Curaçao either on his staff or on leave. The Regiment was under orders for New Brunswick, it was said, either to be reduced or to be garrisoned there. I was anxious to quit a country of which I had seen all I desired but I would go through the States to see the domestic habits of the people to whom we had been opposed and were old anglo-Saxons. They had turned out very good soldiers. Their officers were gallant and enterprizing, and altho' our Engineers said they do not understand Fortification, they had shown that the rules of common Sense and effectual defence guided them. They would have a fine army ten years hence and [because of] that, we should Keep twenty thousand men in Canada.

## Notes

[1] Dr. W. Anson Smith was the son-in-law of Mrs. Robison, having married her daughter Martha in 1807.

[2] Major George Brock of the 37th Foot.

[3] Captain William Brown Bradley, 104th Foot (1771-1850).

[4] Lieutenant William Seward, 9th Foot (1792-1857).

[5] Lieutenant James Scargill, 9th Foot (1793-1875).

[6] Major General Sir James Kempt (1765-1854), see *DCB*, VIII, 458-465. A 21-year veteran of the army, Kempt fought throughout the Peninsula war. In 1820 he was appointed Lieutenant Governor of Nova Scotia and, from 1828-1830, was Governor General of Canada.

[7] Lieutenant Charles Gore, 43rd Foot, Kempt's ADC.

[8] Captain Henry Dumaresq, 9th Foot (d. 1838), Deputy Assistant Quartermaster General.

[9] Probably Private Cornelius Mills, 104th Foot.

[10] Either Vincemius Knox, ed., *Elegant Extracts: Being a Copious Selection of Instructive, Moral, and Entertaining Passages from the Most Eminent British Poets* (London, 1791) or *Elegant Extracts; or, the Literary Nosegay: Consisting of Selections in Prose, from Admired Authors* (London, 1814), both early and popular literary anthologies.

[11] A common nineteenth century British social institution, the assembly was a private dance held, at Kingston, in the ballroom of the British American Hotel. Its expenses were underwritten by its members who were wealthy men with marriageable daughters or sisters.

[12] HMS *Psyche*, frigate, 38 guns. Her frames were sent from England and she was assembled and launched in Kingston.

[13] Captain Henry Bowles, 81st Foot (b. 1788).

[14] Either Captain James Jackson, 1st Foot (1791-1868) or Captain John Jackson, 57th Foot.

[15] A reference to the action at Sandy Creek, 2 June 1814, see Journal entry for 4 June 1814.

[16] Possibly William Crawford, Assistant Deputy Paymaster General, Upper Canada.

[17] Robert Wilson, *The History of the British Expedition to Egypt* (London, 1802).

[18] "Quarter Master's Route." Military authorization to incur expenses on a march or journey.

[19] Given the words used by the farmer, such as *teufel* (or devil), it is likely that the family was German, not Dutch. It was common in North America at this time to

refer to all Germans as "Dutch," a corruption of *Deutsch*, the Germans' own word for their nationality.

[20] "Schiedam." Dutch gin.

[21] Lieutenant Philip Aubin, 57th Foot (1795-1863), a fellow Jerseyman.

[22] Le Couteur was mistaken about Mrs. De Rottenburg's age as she was only twenty-eight at this time. His reaction to her beauty, however, was typical. Born Julia Wilhelmina Carolina von Orelli, she was the daughter of a Swiss general in Neapolitan service and came to Canada with her much older husband in 1810. Mrs. De Rottenburg seems to have impressed almost every male who met her. Colonel Edward Baynes, Prevost's adjutant general, stated that Julia De Rottenburg "has made a complete conquest of all hearts" as she was "remarkably handsome, both in face and figure, and her manners uncommonly pleasing, graceful, and affable." See Baynes to Brock, 6 September 1810, Ferdinand Brock Tupper, ed., *The Life and Correspondence of Major General Sir Issac Brock* (London, 1845), 81.

[23] The Duke of York was the commander in chief of the British army.

# *Chapter Twelve*

## "IT WAS A DELIGHTFUL SEJOUR FOR A SOLDIER"
## Peacetime Garrison Life in Kingston and Montreal
## *April to December 1815*

***[March, 1815]***

The peace had made a Sudden and most agreeable change in the prices of many articles. Hay in one fortnight had fallen from 30, 25, to 14 dollars a ton. Oats at Kingston from Ten shillings to 3/9 the bushel. Butter from Four shillings to nine pence the pound and Provisions, meat & poultry, in proportion. These last had so enraged the Farmers that they applied to the General not to allow the Yankee farmers to bring their produce to Kingston — happily for poor Subs. — in vain.

I began now to long to meet once more at dear Old Belle Vue after all our dispersed wanderings. Montreal is a most agreeable quarter. I am very comfortable and in tolerable health, introduced to the genteelest circles: Sir John & Lady Johnson,[1] the Richardsons,[2] Forsythes,[3] Grants,[4] Algies, Caldwells,[5] Judge Ogdens,[6] Judge Foucher,[7] French Roman Catholics, among whom I found all sorts of entertainments, Balls, dinners & Country parties. A recommendation from Gen[era]l. & Mrs. Smyth to such a family as the Richardsons, noticed as I became by them, was a passport into every house in the North West company and many more.

A few days after I arrived, I visited the Richardsons to dinner. There was a ball in the Evening. I had resolved to make myself as acceptable as possible. Annie Ogden,[8] the eldest daughter, was a tall, Sylph-like, exquisitely fair girl. She was not beautiful but she was lovely! — a nice, open brow with long blue eyes of winning softness, a small Grecian nose, little mouth parted by smiling ruby lips which a row of well set pearls, small too but regular, beautiful flaxen locks fell over a swan-like neck supported by an easy graceful frame moving on light elastic springs.

What a very sweet person she was, every one felt, I among the number. This I found out soon but, on this first occasion, I had been introduced to two sisters, just of a height and dressed exactly alike. Never did two sisters differ more. When the dancing was to commence, I had engaged my fair friend for the first set. I walked up through a crowd. "Miss, Pl[ea]s[e] May I have the gratification of placing you in the dance?" "Sir!", with an eye of fire and a haughty toss of a nose *retroussé* I never forget: "I am not your partner!" It was an unpleasant rebuff to receive in a ball room. "I beg your pardon, Madam. I perceive it is not the Young Lady who so kindly consented to dance with me, the similarity of dress ..." "Oh, it was Annie, my Sister!" Gentle fair Annie it was.

Two or three days after this I was in the drawing room making violent puppy love to fair Annie, with all the fervour of a boy's heart at twenty. David Ogden[9] came up to me gently & tapping me on the shoulder: "Young Gentleman, You are making very ardent love to that young Lady, take care, You may singe Your heart!" "Why shouldn't I? Is it not a fair shrine?" "Aye, aye, very fair but I wish to save you from danger, she is all but my wife. She is engaged to be married to me." "Well that is both frank & kind", I exclaimed, "for I should certainly have lost my heart which I have not yet."

The Marquis of Tweeddale[10] gave a grand set-off to all the Gentry & neighbourhood of Montreal, a Masquerade Ball and Supper. Doctor Waring[11] and I, speaking French better than most, perhaps any, officers in the garrison, we agreed to go in the Costumes of a respectable Young Jean Baptiste[12] farmer and his wife. I got up my dress with care and a Young Lady's assistance, with Julia Le Mesurier's aid, in grand *Costume de fête*. A nice pair of stays, well-hauled as a Sailor would say, got rid of the military waist to a considerable degree. My face was well-whitened with a proper powder and the best rouge heightened the colour; the eye brows were well-darkened and a beautiful wig displayed a profusion of flowing curls under a lace cap decorated with gay ribbons. Bob Young,[13] as an Indian warrior, was our protector.

We went to the Richardsons. The dears were not allowed to go to such places, Mama being a little starchy. They did not know me, not in the least. I jabbered away French to Mr. & Mrs. & the Misses — no, not the least discovery. "Well, now I am safe", I said. Oh, the Screams of laughter that followed on discovering me.

What a delightful Ball. We had seven hundred persons, from the Devil to his darling, a Monk, dancing. Mazani as a Cock was Capital, his strutting up & pecking his way down to invite a partner to dance was delectable. He asked me to dance and Cocked Italian French to me thinking me a Girl all the while. My rather saucy manner tickled the men amazingly, several asked me to dance two or three times. "Comment, Monsieur, vous êtes trop pressant, Je vous assure, que J'ai des Parteners pour tout la soirée."[14] "Ah! Mademoiselle, mais ayez pitie dites que vous avez oublie -St[illegible] "Comment, que voulez vous donc."[15] My husband was obliged to remind me two or three times that I was his wife. At Supper, Mrs. De Rottenburg, who represented a lovely Squaw, was wild with glee when she was told who I was.

There was a beautiful Pandora's box in the Centre of the table which some lady was desired to open. She did so to distribute its favours or evils — when out flew a number of Canaries and other birds that flew at all the Candles and almost left us in darkness, charging and extinguishing them in succession. Such roars of laughter. I never was at a more lovely or elegant party. Health and long Life to our Noble and gallant Marquis. It was day when we got home.

### *April, 1815*

Soon after we got up plays in the Garrison but there were no Actresses to be had from the States and none in Canada. Que faire?[16] "Johnny, You played the Canadian girl so admirably, You must be our heroine." I Kicked, revolted — and played Carry Dot in "Who Wants a Guinea?"[17] but the Gentl[ema]n who played the woman's part did it so vilely that I was bullied into it. [I] Played Emily in the "Poor Gentleman"[18]; Peggy in "Raising the Wind"[19]; Lady Caroline Braymore in "John Bull"[20]; Grace Gaylove. Great fun behind the Scenes dressing in Women's clothes. We were half dressed by our servants and finished off, in the green room, by Milliners & hairdressers.

Who'd be a Manager with such a disorderly set, nevertheless Brampton[21] did get us into order and we feared Him — there was a gentlemanly tone of firmness about Him, that made us feel we were engaged in a business, and it must be done classically and well. It is a capital recreation for idle Young men — it gives them occupations, thoughts & Memory. It was said that we paid all expenses and gave £500 in charity. The Boxes, Pit & upper boxes were all at five shillings — crowded however....[22]

It was a delightful sejour for a Soldier, that city of Montreal. The little French I was master of made me pass for "un de la veille France"[23] with most Canadians who would have it that I was a Frenchman from My pronunciation, which no Frenchman would have said. I was messing with the 8th, or

*View of Montreal from the south bank of the St. Lawrence, 1803, by Richard Dillon. In 1815, Le Couteur spent a most enjoyable "sejour" in this, the largest city in Canada.* R. Dillon/National Archives of Canada/C-10537

King's Reg[imen]t., as an honorary Member — all that time they called me Le C. of ours, and were most brotherly and kind.

Major Billy Robinson[24] was the hero of that Corps, a most facetious, Clever Pat and Irish Falstaff in appearance, good humoured and witty. In the Camp at the Black Swamp, when we were all sadly out of spirits and low, at the sad havoc fever and dysentery were making among officers and men — that gay, heroic Spirit would place his broad back against a Monarch of the Forest while we crowded around Him. "Kape up yer Spirits boys and listen to me" — then roars of laughter would bring a lot of the men, creeping one after the other, to hear the brave and jolly Major rejoice our hearts. His was the best medicine in the world and joy and peace, I hope, attend Him with God's blessing for the light hearts He often made us feel in our sad hardships.

I think it was He who had Service read to us on Sunday, in God's own Temple for a Church. The Brigade was formed in a close column at ordered arms when the Clergyman read the service. It was the most solemn I had ever heard! There we stood in a dense primeval forest, surrounded by foul Miasma, the Enemy within half a mile of us, and our deadly crew ready with Sixty rounds of death-dealing Missiles at the Mens' backs.[25] The day previous [they were] skirmishing — perhaps even at that moment the double shots of the advanced Sentries might Summon us from the presence of the worship of the Almighty to wounds or death. I think that tears must have rolled down many a brave and rugged cheek at that awful thought. It was a grand, touching and pleasing act of duty. Nothing that I have seen since in forty years, no Cathedral service on earth was half so heart stirring! This was a back glance at a bygone day suggested by Major Robinson.

The men at Headquarters were in high dudgeon just now at being kept at Kingston. Major Hunter wrote to me that the Chiefs were "humbugging" the Regiment and that the state of uncertainty in which they remained was most irksome. [He said] That I must have had a fine time of it at Montreal, and my stirling ought to be pretty well run out, though He always said it was a long one, however not to come till I like; to look after any of our Pensioners who might come to Montreal; and to get them provided with great coats. Coates and the boys were as idle and thoughtless as ever and did nothing but growl, growl, growl. Coates wrote that he had given up hopes of moving. The 81st [Regiment of Foot] had made a Capital review, and their officers knew how to command. They moved in time admirably & formed *Square at the double quick* — new in those days. The 9th [Foot], a fine appearance but slow movements so so, and lost their distance and a *few other* trifling mistakes. The 104th did a great deal better than expected, the General expressing his approbation of them.

Then came the sore — We were to [do] no more garrison duty but two Captains, four Subalterns and two hundred Rank & file were to be placed in batteaux and to form a Marine Brigade "to conduct troops and stores" down to and from Fort Wellington. Later the Paymaster, Carmichael,[26] a most excellent friend of mine, wrote that the Reg[imen]t. had been cruelly and unaccountably treated, and the consequence began to appear in desertion to the amount of *sixteen* men besides several retaken, and if this pioneering system is maintained, as we expect it will, I shall not be surprised if one half the Reg[imen]t. march off, He adds.

### *19 May [1815]*

N.B. In this terrestial Paradise the ground is now covered with a luxuriant crop of snow.

### *24 May [1815]*

I came from a gay party at Grant's Island about 2 o'clock this morning and found a route on my table to rejoin the Regiment which it was decided at length should remain in Kingston. Paid my Small bills, picked up my Knapsack and Marched with a Sergeant and Eighteen Men, at 4 o'clock in the morning.

### *1 June [1815]*

Got to Prescott on the 1st of June where to my great Joy I found my friends.

### *20 June [1815]*

Cumming[27] and I took my Canoe and went up the lake to fish. I caught seventy-nine — Bass, [illegible] etc., etc. We got back by 9 o'clock when I had the happiness to receive a letter from my dear Mother, a month from Curaçao, informing me that my Father had applied for my appointment as his A.D.C.

### *22 June [1815]*

Had another day gunning with Mr. Weekes.[28] We had the misery to lose ourselves in the trackless forest for a considerable length of time — most uncomfortable sensation this. By carefully watching the general greater thickness of the moss, which is almost invariably on the *North Side* of the trees, You can pretty nearly, *as long as you can see*, steer in a particular direction but, if it is hazy or dark, it is all useless. You may wander for days and nights.

Lake fishing is very amusing. We used to catch forty or fifty fish constantly, enough for all the Flankers, but my night fishing with two Indians was the most exciting of all. While I was at McPherson's bay, one of the Chiefs offered Me an evening's sport of a very dark, still night. I was placed in the centre of their Canoe, a small short mast was placed in the bow, with a basket made of old iron hoops at top of it, in which was a quantity of pitch pine — this when lighted became a fine torch.

Away we started, one Nitchie astern, paddling and steering the water, the Young Indian in the bow erect, with his flexible well-shaped figure balanced in the canoe while his right hand held the unerring long fish spear, fastened to his wrist by a lengthy thong, the light glancing on his fine dark skin and single tuft of hair & feathers over the bald head, and his thin, yet sinewy, arm, now raised, now lowered, as the fish glanced by, with the low grunt, "Hununk, Hah!", right or left, to the steersman, was wildly exciting. I would have given worlds for a Salvator[29] or even a Hogarth's[30] pencil to have sketched his form.

Presently, off went the Spear with the speed of an arrow from a Yeoman's bow, up came a fine, large pickerel, a yard in length, then a Salmon and so none but precious fish — the vulgar herd were beneath his notice. He merely reversed his spear and the helmsman removed the fish and off again over the clear transparent water.

Pleasant fellows, nice safe companions, those same wild Indians, when they get attached to you. The Ottawa Chief, Black Bird, would have gone any length to serve me. He would have given me a pet scalp if I had asked for it but, as He said, it was but one which He would take to his Squaw, my *delicacy* forbade! So I have never owned a scalp though I have saved my own.

### *27 June [1815]*

Unwell from dysentery still hanging about me. A letter from my beloved Mother expresses alarm at the long continuance of my illness, and suspects it is something worse from my folly in not having named my complaint. Went to tea at Mrs. Robison's and beat Weekes at Chess. Dear sylphid, pretty Mrs. Weekes[31] say[s] she would give all she has that I fell desperately in love with a Yankee girl, as I call them. She herself might have turned my head, or any one else's, as I jokingly told her!

### *2 July [1815]*

Sunday. On returning from Church, found orders for the Regiment to move to Quebec on Friday next, on the arrival of De Watteville's Reg[imen]t.

### *6 July*

Thursday. Mr. & Mrs. Weekes left for *home*, Portland, U.S., to the great distress of the dear Old Lady from whom I took leave with a heavy heart on Friday Morn when the 104th left Kingston forever I suppose. The Colonel sent to me yesterday to say that He would require me to act as Quarter Master on the move as McDonald[32] was ill and must remain behind. I was very indignant at serving in a capacity below that of an officer[33] and said so to Moodie, adding that I thought it very hard for a Light Company officer to have to perform a duty He could know nothing of. He rejoined that He had selected, as was his duty, the Officer He thought the fittest for an emergency as some one must do the duty, and He would write to my Father to say that I objected to be useful when required. I answered that was quite unnecessary. The moment I saw He wished or insisted — I would do my best.

So instead of having to march, I took charge of all the women, children,[34] Sick, sorry, or lazy, besides all the heavy luggage of a strong Reg[imen]t. on a permanent move. Never was I so pestered. "Mr. Le C.", the Officers' wives imploring, some commanding, "See to my luggage. Do place an awning to the batteaux. See to my children. See to the Baby." Now, let no one imagine it was a pleasant duty, tho, I had some very nice women in my boat — the first in dignity, of course. Well, I did get an awning rigged in my own boat. We got down to Prescott delightfully. As I had charge, I took the light baggage and left my sub in charge of the heavy department.

The pull down this noble river was very delightful, the Banks being mostly wooded with noble trees to the river's edge. As you approach the Long Sault, the rapids increase in activity to a surprising degree. In the midst of them, the stream is like a sluice. One lady who fancied the batteau was going to strike the bank on the American side, actually rose to throw her child on to the land, through fright. I, happily being close to her, seized both Mother and child in my arms and implored her to sit still as our famous Canadian guide said there was no danger, if every one would sit still.

I confess that the danger did seem to me very great because I knew that three hundred Men of the 42nd Regiment had been drowned hereabouts in the last war owing to the want of proper batteaumen as guides.[35] I had three Canadian voyageurs in my batteau, young hands who guided me the "Long Sault" prosperously. However, they declined the responsibility of the rush down the "Cascades" to the Cedars, so that I had to engage a competent Pilot. At one point in this rush, You appear for a moment to be plunging down a short fall at a jump, on to a formidable rock exactly in the middle of the St. Lawrence but the steady Guide made nothing of it. One Lady gave a scream of alarm but I held her firmly as I had been forced to previously.

The next day when on shore and viewing a raft with timber coming down, several of us noticed that, though the wind was with the raft, she went by so much faster than the wind that her flag was flying *against* the wind. The La Chine rapids are very formidable but not near so alarming as those which we had passed. Hereabouts we had passed those rapids and that spot celebrated in Tom Moore's pretty Song, "Row Brothers, row, the Rapids are near" &c. and having run over the beautiful locality induced me to learn the song.[36]

The approach to Montreal is very lovely and I was heartily delighted to land my light baggage and my fair friends, the Ladies and women and chicks of the Regiment — leaving them I must say ungallantly to their own resources — and marching my detachment of men, as soon as I could obtain conveyance for the baggage, to the barracks.

I brought my *treasures regimental* very safely and got in the day before the Regiment but never did I behold such filthy barracks as we were to be quartered in — it was a real disgrace to the corps that had quitted. I set all my fatigue men to sweep the rooms and the women to wash the bed steads and rooms which I saw done thoroughly. When I visited the Kitchen, there was not a stove ready. What a towering rage old Bob Moodie would be in if his Men might not cook after their March.

Off I flew to the Barrack department. [I knew] Mr. Van Cortlandt,[37] the Barrack M[aste]r General. "See the stoves set apart for the 104th, let me have them directly." "Can't Sire. Must have the returns, receipts &c., can't have them today." "But my Men are starving and the Regiment marches in tomorrow." "Can't help it."

A thought struck me. "Are you sure the stoves are all right?" "Yes." "All there complete?" "Yes, Sir." "You've no one to send them?" No, Sir, I tell ye"', said the dry old Barrack sergeant. I saw He was alone — unprotected!! Off I went to the barracks, fell in my men in their fatigue Jackets, got some barrows, marched up to the barrack master yard and brought off all the Stoves chalked "104th Regt". The old Sergeant was away when this robbery, as He called it, took place. I put up my stoves snugly, lighted fires, fed My Men, women & children — without returns, receipts or orders.

But, in the interim, the Barrack Sergeant reported me to the Barrack

Master, the B.M. to the Superior, the Superior to the General, the General to my Colonel and the Colonel came to me. "What the Devil have you been at — walking off with gov[ermen]t. Stores without orders, returns, or receipts given. You are to be placed in arrest and will be tried by Court Martial." "That's what it is to make a Light Company officer a Quarter Master, Sir, and the first thing You told me on coming into the Barracks was 'Why Le C., how very nice and clean you have made the barracks and all the men's dinners ready. You are a smart fellow, and whatever *You undertake, You do well"*!', and now I'm to be tried by a Court Martial, at all events I shan't be broke upon your evidence, My dear Col[onel]." Then I told Him how I had been misled by My Zeal and meant to give all the Receipts when He arrived. Luckily, he was a personal friend of Mr. Van Cortlandt, a very amiable old Gentleman who at once excused me and withdrew his Reports, besides being personally very kind to me afterwards.

The Regiment left Montreal for Quebec. Col[onel]. Moodie left me in charge of a recruiting party. I was allowed to have my own System in this, as it was a duty to which I was averse. It was a decided favour shown me as I was my own Master with an agreeable brother Sub. under my orders. Coates and I were such old and dear friends that we thought ourselves very lucky after all.

I told my recruits the plain truth, pointing out to them the advantages of the Service, recommending them by no means to enlist unless they were resolved to continue in the army. By this System, I sent an excellent class of men to the corps.

It was an expensive affair, as the officer was only allowed five shillings for Stationery and expenses, where he received three Guineas per man during the war. He is responsible for any monies advanced — if his Recruit deserts *before* He is attested. Colonel Darling[38] was our Commandant at Montreal and was civil enough, though he did not recognize our Recruiting party till in G[enera]l. orders.

Montreal, 19th July, 1815

My Dearest Mama,[39]

The Regiment left this on its way to Quebec, its future quarter, on the 15th [of July] and the Colonel ordered me to remain here to recruit for the Reg[imen]t. It is a duty I by no means like, as to perform it as usual, officers have recourse to low tricks, I never can, or will, make use of. I mentioned to Col[onel]. Moodie it was a kind of duty I was not well calculated for, but since he wished it, I would undertake it for a short time and in case of my not succeeding, I am to be recalled. My orders to commence are not yet arrived from Sir G[ordon]. Drummond but I all ready have engaged two. I tell them the Plain truth as far as the *advantages* of the Service go, and recommend them not to enlist unless they intend remaining in the Service, etc., etc., all this is meant for my Father and not you. There is one thing which annoys me, which is my last trip to Montreal brought me in Debt with the P[ay].M[aster]. and this vile Service will only increase it. It is not now as formerly an officer only receives 5/ to cover Postage of letters, expense of Paper, pens etc., instead of Three Guineas which is great hardship on a recruiting officer, as he is answerable for all moneys advanced to recruits (who desert) if not finally approved.

I am anxiously looking out, for my order to join you, that will relieve my troubles at once. I shall have to draw on You, I believe, to provide myself with a Suit of Plain clothes, for travelling thro the States and with a suit of Uniforms as A.D.C., which can be made for me here, or in Quebec. I shall go there to settle with the Reg[imen]t. and to call on the Adj[utan]t. Gen[era]l. to receive the proper travelling allowances & to enable me to get on prosperously. I am vexed at being left here just now, as It is so much more expensive to live away from the Reg[imen]t. than with it. I am paying six Shillings a day for my board & Lodging, which is very hard on a Lieuts. Pay. No extra cash for amusements. I am heartily tired of a Subaltern's life.

To compleat [*sic*] my disagreeables, just now, on my arrival here I found every article of Linnen and Clothing wet, my Poor drawing box ruined, the colours well mixed, my Dresser case in Pieces, my books & papers spoiled, & my Desk full of water. The blockhead of an officer who came down with the heavy baggage, came down the tremendous rapids of the St. Lawrence with only one Guide to 15 batteaux, the Consequence is the boats were mostly filled with water, and it is providential they came down at all.

I had heard & seen (of course) of the Rapids, but never came down them myself till this last time, the Q[uarter].M[aster]. was absent and the Col[onel]. made me act for him. I came in charge of the Light baggage; one Cannot form an idea of what (sauter les rapides) is, the French word expresses it, as you actually jump down little falls but I was careful to have old Guides, the 42nd Reg[imen]t. lost 300 men here last war by attempting to go down them without Pilots. It is very fortunate our batteaux did not share the same fate and It is only that ours are such superior boatmen to the generality of troops, that they escaped being lost. I had Three Canadian Voyageurs in my boat, young hands, who guided me down the Long Saut, but they would not pass the Cascades and the Rapids, without experienced Guides, and in truth, tho' the latter ones were more dangerous, they did not appear so much so to me, the "batteaux" being steered by an able hand.

I hope the next post from Kingston will bring me the letter you mentioned having written, with the account of your adventures since you left Jamaica, I am quite in the dark about how or when you arrived. Once my leave arrives, I think I shall travel faster than my letters unless I am detained at New York for a Passage; I shall endeavour to learn where a vessel will sail soonest from, and there I shall travel to. I have no wish to be living at a Hotel for a length of time in the States, as their manners and customs are so different to ours, but I should assimilated myself to them as much as possible. Some of our high blooded Puppies, in travelling there, imagined they might take the same liberties at Yankee Inns as in England, and were quite surprised at having Insult returned for abuse.

The Fact is, in whatever country a man is, If he cannot assume the manners of it, He should at least gain respect by proper conduct, I have no patience with people who say and swear, "I'll make them do this and that, and tell 'em I'm an Englishman", and I believe there is not a country in the world, where the English name is less respected than in the States, particularly among the Lower classes, who teach their children to abuse and to hate us. An English gentleman, introduced to their society, is very much sought after and courted, and even that depends upon Himself. I shall judge impartially in passing thro' the States, and shall visit High & Low if I can. I must own I detest their familiar style, a Servant or any common fellow addresses you as he would his fellow, and you must answer him civilly, and listen to him patiently, or mischief will ensure. I have seen a good deal of them on Service, and in the Canadas, Montreal is full of them at present.

I must tell you Lady Johnson renewed her politeness, I dined with them last week, and as the Family are going to their country seat 9 miles hence, She told me, whenever I chose to come and stay there I should find a bed ready for me. Lady J[ohnson]. has been unwell these several days and they have not yet gone, but as I do not or rather cannot keep a horse, I don't believe I shall accept the invitation. I have, as a military man, given up all those comforts I had been accustomed to at home, but I shall know better, how to value them hereafter. It is at best a miserable life, tho' I am so used to it now I could never give it up, an officer's mode of life is different to every other I know of and service accepted one of the most Idle ones. It will be some time before I shall be at home, at my house, but I have become more accommodating in my disposition than formerly.

My Friend and brother Sub, Coates, the Col[onel]. left here, with me; we are going into a Lodging and intend living as on Service on our Rations, till we have Cash to spare, we find our present quarters too high, and it is disagreeable living with the people of the house. A vulgar old widow is Queen of the boarding house, and is very regular, tho' She has no trouble with us as It would be difficult to find two more steady Subs of Light Infantry than he & I. We have great trouble in finding one, I hope tomorrow we shall move. I am coming to an end with my letter, I believe I shall send it by New York to Mr. Graves, who I hope forwarded my last of the 22nd June. I am half uneasy about my order to Join you, Heaven defend me from a refusal, I should be miserable If I had to remain another winter here, I mean in America. I'd rather go to the army in Belgium Fifty times.

Adieu my Dearest Mama, I hope My Dear Father, Gordon and you are well, God keep you So, and grant me speedy conveyance to you, prays your ever affectionate Son.

John

### *[25 July 1815]*

The Col[onel]. wrote me from Quebec.

July the 25th, 1815

My dear Le Couteur

I have opened my letter of yesterday in consequence of the general orders of this day, which pointed out that Regiments allowed to recruit in North America are only to have parties at Montreal, Three Rivers and Quebec, so that in place of sending Coates to *L'Assomption*, You must send him to Three Rivers and its neighbourhood. You may however detach from *Your now to be* small party to L'Assomption or any where else you like, and *Coates* may do the same, taking care to apply to the Q[uarte]r. Master General's department for Transport whenever you wish to move from one place to another. This is agreeable to the General orders of this day.

I request you will keep all my letters as I may have occasion to call for them at some future period, and I have not time to have them copied. Adieu, let me know when you are tired of Montreal, or Coates of Three Rivers, and believe me,

Truly Yours,
signed/ R. Moodie

O[n].H[is].M[ajesty's].S[ervice].
Lieut[enant]. Le Couteur
104th Regiment
Montreal

My smart recruiting party of one Sub., One Sergeant, 2 Corporals and Thirteen men, was now reduced to Six. Lamery the Sergt. was a true recruiting Sergeant — a handsome, gay, chattering humbug. My men as clean and smart with ribbands as I could deck them, but no drunkenness.

Montreal, 26th July, 1815

My Dear Gordon,[40]

I have received your's and Mama's of the seventh February, and am much obliged to you for the very good account you give me of the Island. It conveyed to me a very dear Idea of it, and afforded me, a great deal of pleasure, your description is much clearer, and better than that given of the Island in the Gazetteer. I have got a little plan of the Island in a large chart, which I am copying and which I shall make you a present of when I arrive. I am sorry our Dear Father did not at first like his command, but as Mama's last letter mentions nothing farther about it, he is now reconciled to it. I was astonished to find the mean ways that had been formerly resorted to, by the Governors, in making money, but we may be proud, my Dear Gordon, that our excellent Father, will never deprive the poor and wretched, of their miserable pittances. Under his hand they will ever enjoy their rights and Privileges in peace and comfort, and their blessings will follow him and Us for it.

It will not be long, I hope, before I join you, and then I shall myself make the Tour of the Island. I am now inured to fatigues and hardships, and with my haversack and Bearskin, can live comfortably enough. The View of the Headlands of the Island, I have, make me imagine it a

Strange place, the Mountains are all sloping peaks, and must have a curious appearance from a distance. Yours and Mama's letters were enclosed in a war office cover, and from the size and thickness, I made sure it was my order to proceed to join you. I opened it with trembling hands, and was in truth partly disappointed tho' not much, as I hardly expected it so soon. The July mail I suppose will bring it, as I suppose my Father's application was made in May. I believe I shall send this by the Adj[utan]t. Gen[era]l. as I have not yet received an answer to mine from Mr. Graves of New York.

Adieu my Dear Gordon, God bless you, and keep you in health, prays you most affectionate Brother.

John

### *29 July [1815]*

Sat[urday]. I attended the funeral of the late Honourable Richard Cartwright of Kingston, a Member of Council and Colonel of a Militia Regiment, One of the most amicable, honourable and upright men in this country. The day before his death, He desired to see me, on purpose to tell me with what pleasure and hope of salvation, a Christian might die. It made a deep impression on my heart. He was a cheerful as ever, and although so enfeebled that He could not raise his hand to remove a fly that had settled on his face, which I did gently. He thanked me and smiled to think that He had no longer power to even hurt a fly. He gave me his blessing, as if I had been one of his family, and I esteemed a great honor to have been directed to attend the funeral of so excellent a person as Mourner.

Coates left me and wrote that He reached Sorel in eight hours in Batteau, after leaving me at Montreal, and reached Three Rivers in eight hours more the next day — very fair "Batteauxing", ninety miles in Sixteen hours. He had sent on our spare men to Quebec.

The Paymaster got a little alarmed at my gaiety in recruiting for He adds a P.S. to a letter: "I don't Know how the Devil Your fiddles and fifes are to paid for?" The fact was I allowed the men to give small dances, but no drinking, which answered well....[41]

### *October, 1815*

I had some very pleasant trips to St. Jean where Harry Le Mesurier[42] my Cousin was quartered in charge of the Commissariat department there. He became attached to a very sweet person, a Miss Guerute of St. Denys, the daughter of an old Norman Gentleman who settled in Canada, reputed to be very rich. His second daughter, Sophy, was a haughty beauty. Le Mesurier was much afraid that I should fall in love with Her. I found Her and Miss Amelia Caldwell, another sweeter and prettier girl, the Bridesmaids at their wedding which took place at St. Denys Oct[ober] 27 in Monsr. Guerate's fine old house, with great hospitality and French gaiety. Miss Caldwell introduced me afterwards to her Mother and Sister, Miss Mompesson, and nice little Sophy the youngest sister. Sophy married Jack Ashworth of the Commissariat.

With this family, who were the greatest friends the Le Mesuriers had there, I became very intimate. Mrs. Caldwell offered me her daughter but I said I had nothing beyond a Guinea a week and My Sub's pay which was quite out of Marrying conditions. Poor Le Mesurier was very annoyed when I told him of it and said I must gradually withdraw from too much intimacy because whatever I might feel Myself, I might be unsettling the peace of mind of a very sweet girl, who thought me very agreeable. Which of course I did, as cautiously as propriety would admit....

### *27 October [1815]*

I have been to Harry Le Mesurier's wedding which took place at St. Denys at the house of Monsieur Guerute, a French Protestant Gentleman from Rouen in Normandy. He is said to be very wealthy, lives in a fine large mansion and entertained us all very hospitably. The bride, Julia, his eldest daughter, is a very, sweet, sensible person, not handsome, but with a nice expression. Her next Sister, Sophy, is very pretty, She and Miss Caldwell make lovely bridesmaids. We remained four days at St. Denys very kindly welcomed by Madam and Monsieur G. who delighted in chatting French to me. (We), the happy Couple in one Carriage and the two fair girls and I in the other, left for St. Jeans, the future residence of the Le Mes[urie]rs. where I remained a few days.

St. Jean is a poor monotonous place, the country fertile but too level to be picturesque. Some of the 19th Light Dragoons are quartered here. One morning, they had got up some races among the dragoons and the Civilians — I went out with our party to see them.

Presently, in came a Yankee farmer, one of the long-haired, Slouch-hatted, monkey-tail-coated backwoodsmen, mounted on a lanky, ill-dressed, rough, long-legged looking Rosinante,[43] wicked looking enough in fine legs, a good chest & forearm and a fine neck and head, drooping however — her hind quarters were powerful too.

"What are the stakes? Maybe I should like to *inter* my meare." He was told: "Has your mare won any plates?" "Plates, noa. I guess we don't run for plates." "Can she gallop?" "Well, I calculate she can gallop a little, but what horses have She got to gallop against?" "Come and see!"

Well the dragoons were all delighted at the idea of doing Uncle Sam. "Well, I don't think as my Meare could gallop along with them horses." "Oh nonsense, My Man!" "Well, I s'pose You'll let a man ride without a saddle?" "Oh, yes, if that's all." They were so sure of doing Brother Jonathan that any concession was legitimate.

Off they went to the mounting stand, off went the *Meare's* saddle and she had hardly a bridle on. Off went Jonathan's hat & long Coat and, while the Jockeys were being lifted into their seats, Uncle Sam glided on to his Meare's back while she stood as if she was being loaded with a sack of flour at a Mill.

The Cavalry were neighing & prancing when "Off" went all. The Meare *did go along* with them sure enough, Jonathan streaming hair came glancing like a foul meteor while the Knowing ones felt silly. It was fairly won by a length or two by the *meare* while Jonathan had made a show of flogging without ever touching his dear *Meare*.

Bets against Her became shy and they began to hedge; there was some growling about his taking off his hat & coat but fair play was loudly called for and the second heat came off.

This time Uncle Sam whistled his *meare* on and She responded to his whistle like a Grey hound, distanced all the horses and there was loud growling but again the cry of Fair play prevailed. Jonathan pocketed the Stakes, calculated his *meare* could gallop on at times, mounted his *meare* and jogged off, butter & eggs, on his quiet *meare*. It was a regular *murmus* in those days, a *sell*[44] in later fashionable dialogue.

### *26 November [1815]*

I wrote to my Father pressing Him to get me removed to his Staff. My dear Mother seemed to fancy I might object going to a hot climate in the West Indies after our Canadian winters but all climates were alike to me so long as I might be with my family. My interest in this country abated with the declaration of peace.

I met an officer of the _____ who was at College with me in the same company, who passed a public examination with eclat and got his commission on the same day I did. I asked Him to dine with me, walked to his quarters, asked Him why He looked so ill, I could not say miserable. He burst into tears, avowed to me that dissipation and interference had so reduced Him ....[45]

*8 December [1815]*

Upon this I wrote to Colonel Moodie at Head Quarters and on the 8th I received a very kind letter from my friend Moore, the Adjutant, announcing that L[ieutenant]t. Considine (the same who was so badly wounded before Fort Erie) was coming up to relieve me. Moore added that He had bed and board for me. I had many leave takings to perform, with a grateful heart, to the Richardsons, Ogdens, Grants, Caldwells, Forsythes, McTavish,[46] Judge & Mrs. Reid,[47] a dear, sweet woman, and last, though not least, my very benevolent old friends, Sir John & Lady Johnson and charming Mrs. Bowes[48], Col[onel]. Heriot, my Country man, Judge & Mlle Fouché. I went down to Quebec to take leave of the Regiment, thinking never to see them again as a Corps and did so with a heavy heart. Started again and off by St. John's for the United States.

## Notes

[1] Sir John Johnson (1741-1830) and his wife Mary (d. 1815), see *DCB*, VI, 352-354. The son of Sir William Johnson, the Superintendent of Indians in the colony of New York, John Johnson raised and commanded a Loyalist regiment, the King's Royal Regiment of New York that fought throughout the Revolutionary War. Johnson reached the rank of brigadier general and was appointed Superientendent of Indians, succeeding his father. He worked hard to obtain compensation for white and Indian Loyalists and functioned as head of the British Indian Department in Canada. For a recent study, see Earle Thomas, *Sir John Johnson, Loyalist Baronet* (Toronto, 1986).

[2] John Richardson (1754-1831) and his wife Sarah Ann, see *DCB*, VI, 639-646. Richardson was a partner in the Forsyth, Richardson, trading company headquartered in Montreal and one of the wealthiest merchants in the city. A leader of the anglophone business community, he also occupied several political positions and was a staunch opponent of the francophone segment of the population. Richardson was a well-read, cultured man and both he and his wife were renowned for the high standard of their entertainment.

[3] John Forsyth (1762-1837) and his wife Margaret, see *DCB*, VII, 309-311. Forsyth was John Richardson's partner in the Forsyth, Richardson Company and was involved in the North West Fur Company. He was a wealthy and prominent leader of the Montreal anglophone business community.

[4] Charles William Grant, Baron de Longueuil (1782-1848). Grant was was a long standing member of the Legislative Council of Lower Canada and one of the leaders of society. His island, Grant's island, was the island of Longueuil, across from the city.

[5] Sir John Caldwell (1775-1842) and his wife, Jane, see *DCB*, VII, 133-136. Caldwell was the Receiver General for Lower Canada.

[6] Isaac Ogden (1739-1824). A Loyalist from a prominent New York family, Ogden was a judge of the Court of King's Bench at Montreal.

[7] Louis-Charles Fourcher or Fouché (1760-1829). Fouché was the judge of the court of King's Bench for Montreal and a supporter of the anglophone faction of Lower Canadian politics.

[8] Le Couteur is showing some confusion here as Ogden was Anne Richardson's married name.

[9] David Ogden was the son of Judge Isaac Ogden.

[10] Lieutenant Colonel George Hay, the Marquis of Tweeddale, commanded the 100th Foot during the Niagara campaign of 1814, see Chapter X above.

[11] Surgeon Charles Waring, 8th Foot (b. 1789).

[12] "Jean Baptiste." French-Canadian.

[13] Probably Lieutenant Colonel Robert Young, 8th Foot (1770-1815).

[14] "Comment, Monsieur, vous êtes trop pressant, Je vous assure, que J'ai des Parteners pour tout la soirée." Why, Monsieur, you are very pressing, I assure you that I have partners for the entire evening.

[15] "Ah! Mademoiselle, mais ayez pitie dites que vous avez oublie - St [illegible] Comment, que voulez vous donc." But, Mademoiselle, have mercy, say that you have forgotten [illegible] ... What would you have me do?

[16] "Que faire?" What to do.

[17] George Coleman, author, "Who Wants a Guinea?" first performed in 1805.

[18] George Coleman, author, "The Poor Gentleman," first performed 1802.

[19] James Kenney, author, "Raising the Wind," 1803 farce.

[20] George Coleman, author, "John Bull, or an Englishman's Fireside," first performed 1805.

[21] Ensign Samuel Brampton, Canadian Fencibles (d. 1830)

[22] In the original text, Le Couteur placed an event here that occurred in October 1815. This has been moved to its proper chronological order.

[23] "Un de la veille France." One from old France.

[24] A captain in the 8th Foot, William Robinson (1779-1828) was given a local promotion to lieutenant colonel train and command the Incorporated Militia Battalion of Upper Canada. A jovial Irishman with an irrepressible sense of humour, he was the perfect choice to turn a unit of raw civilians into a combat unit that performed well throughout the Niagara campaign of 1814. Like William Drummond of the 104th, Robinson was one of the "characters" of the British army in Canada during the war.

[25] "Sixty rounds of death-dealing Missiles at the Mens' backs." Each man carried 60 rounds of live ammunition in the cartridge box slung on his right hip.

[26] Paymaster Humphrey Henry Carmichael, 104th Foot (1780-1850). Carmichael settled in Fredericton after the war as Deputy Registrar of Deeds for York County. In 1834 he returned to the army as a captain in the 36th Foot.

[27] Lieutenant Francis Henry Cumming, 104th Foot (1786-1834).

[28] Mr. Lemuel Weekes of Portland, Maine, husband of Mrs. Robison's daughter, Eliza.

[29] Probably Salvator Rosa (1615-1673), an Italian artist and engraver known for his action-filled battle scenes and picturesque landscapes.

[30] William Hogarth (1697-1764), the English artist and engraver famous for his scenes of social commentary and satire.

[31] Eliza Weekes, daughter of Mrs. Robison and wife of Lemuel Weekes of Portland, Maine, whome she married in 1810.

[32] Quartermaster William McDonald, 104th Foot (1780-1857).

[33] "Capacity below that of an officer." Traditionally, the positions of quartermaster and paymaster in infantry battalions were reserved for men commissioned from the ranks and did not have same status as combat officers. Le Couteur resents being forced to take on what he regards as the work of an inferior.

[34] According to the Inspection Return of the 104th Foot dated May 1815, the regiment included on its ration strength 76 women, 45 male children and 67 female children. These were the spouses and children of the non-commissioned officers and men, those of the officers were not on ration strength. See PRO, WO 27, volume 133, Inspection Returns of the 104th Foot, May 1815.

[35] Le Couteur exaggerates here. Amherst lost eighty men by drowning while trying to pass the Long Sault in 1760. Only four men of the 42nd actually died in this incident.

[36] Thomas Moore (1779-1852) visited Canada in 1804 and later published *Canadian Boat Song. Epistle Odes and Other Poems* (London, 1816), a collection of Canadian folksongs and verse.

[37] Philip Van Cordtland (1766-1833), a former Loyalist officer and Barrack-Master General at Montreal.

[38] Lieutenant Colonel Henry Charles Darling, Nova Scotia Fencibles (1780-1845), Commandant of the Montreal District.

[39] This letter is part of the original text of the Journal.

[40] This letter is part of the original text of the Journal.

[41] The following passage was out of chronological order in the original manuscript and has been moved here.

[42] Harry LeMesurier (1791-1861), see *DCB*, IX, 462-463. LeMesurier entered the army in 1811 but lost his arm at the battle of Salamanca in 1812. Determined to stay in the military, he joined the Commissariat Department where he remained until 1818 when he went on half-pay. LeMesurier later became a successful merchant in Quebec City.

[43] "Rosinante" was the name of the hero's horse in Miguel Cervantes's famous novel, *Don Quixote*.

[44] "Sell." To cheat, trick, take in, or deceive.

[45] Several paragraphs of the original text become illegible at this point and only a scrap of the last sentence of a letter from his father that was placed here in the text, remains.

In his diary, Le Couteur wrote on 1 December 1815 that: "Joy! Joy! Received a letter this evening from my Dearest Father ... mentioning they know I am appointed ADC and they expect me at once to join them. My poor Mama says She hoped to embrace me on my Birthday, 21st Oct. last but I fear I shall not reach them before 1st January, New Year's Day."

[46] Members of the numerous McTavish clan (possibly John George McTavish, see *DCB*, VII, 577-578) who were the senior directors of the North West Company.

[47] James Reid (1769-1848), see *DCB*, IX, 655-656: Judge of the Court of King's Bench, Montreal, and later Chief Justice of Lower Canada.

[48] Sir John Johnson's daughter, Catherine Maria, who married Major General Bernard Bowes in 1805. Bowes was killed at the battle of Salamanca in 1812.

# *Chapter Thirteen*

"LEAVE THE BRITISHER ALONE!":
The United States and Curaçao
*January to March 1816*

***[January 1816]***
Washington Hotel [New York City]
We reached this beautiful city after our long journey of 350 miles through the United States, or rather the province of New York — what a province, longer than England. Englishmen setting out for this country just at the close of a hot war feel prejudiced against it, fancy the[y are going] to meet inconvenience and insult, but Burke[1] and I, who were both quiet fellows, found it very much otherwise. The people were familiar & gruff but civil, if used good humouredly.

At Sing Sing, we came in late, the table d'hote dinner was over. I went from the long room or dining room into the Kitchen to ask for some dinner. An Amazonian with dishevelled hair, saucepan in hand, and a toss of her head, said: "I guess you've come late, there's no dinner now so you'll have to wait for supper." "My dear Lady", I said in a soothing & very submissive tone, "it wasn't our fault really, part of our harness broke and the Coach could not come to time." "That wasn't My fault neither."

I saw a sweet looking girl about seventeen who, I fancied, seem to feel for me, so I made up to Her. "My dear Miss, do kindly give us a little help. We had breakfast at seven and it is past five and to wait till nine is a long while. Can't you kindly find some cold remains for the elderly Traveller & I. You look so kind, I am sure that you will not let us starve in the midst of plenty." "Mother, can't ye let these two men have summat to eat, I'll attend to 'em."

In this way we did get some cold turkey, Ham and etceteras, very like a cold dinner, till the enormous Supper was laid out — a dinner disguised — groaning with joints, roasted, boiled Turkey, fowls, vegetables, Pies, preserves, Spirits, Spruce beer — all for half a dollar.

But this was not the last grievance. There was only one spare bed, a small one, which of course I insisted Burke should take. The Yankee Landlord wished me to take half of it as a matter of course but I said: "we Britishers were *particular* on that *pint*." "Then", said mine host, "I guess if you don't *chuse* to take half a bed with some one, you'll jist sleep in a cheer[chair] or by the kitchen fire." "Well, landlord", I said, "since I may chuse", looking at some dozen Men in the room ....[2]

.... this I said in such a business like way, that mine host looked aghast and the Yankees burst into a roar of laughter: — "Well, I'm blowed, Landlord, if the Britisher aint done ye ....[3]

At another place I was sleeping in a smallish bed, in a long common bedroom, when I was waked by a great naked leg, coming into my bed. "What the Devil do you mean, my friend, this is not your bed!" "Oh, guess I didn't know — the help told me to get in here." "Leave the Britisher alone!", called another hospitable Yankee, "and come into bed here, don't be waking us all with your *noise*."

[At] Poughkeepsie, a large straggling town, the Inn was so crowded by a rush from the country round about to a grand ball & supper, that it was only by dint of persevering & coaxing that I secured beds and leave to sup with party at one o'clock. I then had a longing desire to see the Yankee beauties at the Ball and begged to know whether two British officers might be admitted. B[urke]. was in a horror at this, however, two of the Stewards came and politely invited us to the ball and supper. I opened my Portmanteau, dressed, and went in with old B[urke] like a sheep led to the slaughter.

"Will you dance, Sir?" "With pleasure, if you will be so good as to present me to a partner." A very nice, sprightly girl she proved. When the country dance was over, I remained for a few minutes chatting to Her but she whispered very nicely and politely: "Thank you for your attention, but you may not remain talking to me, it would be remarked, as it is not the custom." I thanked my fair friend for her kind inf[or]m[ation] and, bowing, retired.

Then indeed I understood why — the women were all drawn up in one line, on one side of the room, and the Males on the other — some of them as uncouth looking as any backwoodsmen need wish — no doubt, so soon after the war, looking at me as a very daring puppy to infringe a ball law of the Union.

After another dance, one of the Stewards, who we had not seen, took a Segar from his mouth and shouted: "If there is anyone here who is not invited, He had better retire." My old Major saddled up to me: "By Jove, Johnny, that's meant for us — let's go!" "Not an inch, My dear Major, the two who invited us are close by and must protect us ....[4]

.... in a few minutes Supper was announced. Our Friends told us to follow and to secure Seats without ceremony which reassured my old Major. There was a beautiful Turkey opposite me. "Johnny, a lady by me would like some Turkey." I cut a nice *equillette*[5] or two, pounce came a fork or two, off went the slices — as fast as I cut, vanish went the bit. At last I said: "Burke, stick your fork in the wing for your friend, while I cut it, or neither she nor you nor I will get a mouthful." So literally we had to stick our forks into the pieces we wanted in order to secure them — it was the greatest fun I ever saw. I laughed till old B[urke] was in a fit of fright.

There was plenty, plenty — joints, roast and boiled, Meat & Poultry, Pies, Tarts, Sweets a l'americaine, a l'Union, none [sic], Soufflets, meringues, or such French "*raffineries*[6]". Plenty of brandy & rum, Gin, Punch, Sling, Madeira, for those who wanted it.

About Two, we got to our room, a long one with but two unoccupied beds in it. I noticed a few shawls hung up at a distance but never gave them much thought, undressed, jumped into bed, said my prayers & [after] the travelling since daylight and the dancing — in a second nearly, was asleep in a jiffy.[7]

... methought I was in a dream. Several fair girls came skipping into the room, shut the door ... lots of giggling, laughing, chatting, talking of the ... Various and curious noises ... rustles and whispers ... reality I ... slowly.

It was not a dream, it was a growing reality & a small light at the distant end told the living truth. Laugh now, how dare I disturb the nymphs at their toilette & get shot through the head in the bargain. I crammed three of my knuckles into my mouth and bit them hard. I heard old B[urke] in the next bed giving a[n] "Ohh, Ohh", as if he were choking. I could not stand it, I roared out laughing, the girls shouted, screamed: "A Man! A Man!" — all vanished in a twinkling.

The travelling in New York [state] is delightful, the roads are level as a die, running along the River side for many miles. None of the horrid Caleches which you have in Lower Canada. There were not above three or four inches of snow on the roads, and that was so beaten down that it was travelling on ice, as it were. The Carriage was like a large Irish Car with Curtains — four Capital trotters brought us along at a rate of Ten miles an hour — a jolly pace.

They have handsome villages and Towns as you advance from the frontier, all along the whole 550 miles, the whole State through which we passed, seemed almost as clear as England and highly Cultivated we heard, the fields seemed well enclosed with wooden fences. I was surprised in this new Country to observe Schools at almost every two miles distance which accounts for their being so intelligent a people.

This [New York] is an admirably planned City. Broadway, which deserves its name, runs a mile and a half in a direct line through it, while the cross streets are at right angles to it, and other main streets parallel to it. At the extremity of those perpendicular to Broadway is the River Hudson on one side and the East River on the other. Capital wharfs and stores, with every accomodation for vessels of all sizes, close to the wharfs. Steam boats ply to and fro to the opposite shores, with a drop bridge to them, which forms a perfect bridge, by which to land or embark Carts, carriages & passengers.[8] The Battery is a beautiful, semi-circular fortification, looking on to the bay — a favourite, and no doubt very lovely, lounge in Summer time.

I had been most kindly received by John Boonan Graves Esq., a great Dutch Merchant, a man of grave, gentle, most kind habits who, when I was ushered into his presence, where He sat apart from a body of Clerks, took small notice of me till when I saw He had finished his letter. "Mr. Graves, I take the liberty to introduce myself and to express my deep gratitude to you for sending me letters during the war, from my dear Parents at Curaçao." "Oh, Mr. Le C., I beg your pardon, I thought it was some young person on business", taking me most kindly by the hand, "come with me into the drawing room, Mrs. Graves wishes to make your acquaintance. I will place you in her better care though I will offer you every service in My power."

Dear Mrs. Graves — what a nice specimen of the Ancient Dutch Gentlewomen she was, dressed all neatly in lace and starch, like one of Rembrandt's ladies — a sweet benevolent, round, laughing visage. [She was] so glad to see me that I almost think she [would have] kissed me, because I had written to Her so nicely about my Mother — then [also] my Father and Mother were so beloved in Curaçao where some of her relatives, the Bentners, resided.

She must send for her daughters to introduce them to me, which she did — nice rosy, merry girls — very soon at home with them all. A Ten days' daily acquaintance made me fancy one, a very dangerous, very sensible, very susceptible girl. Ten months instead of Ten days might have given me a Dutch wife and a better, more tidy, more exquisitely clean establishment than Mrs. Graves's, no English Gentleman could desire. At the Ruckers in London, such a crop I have seen, the most tidy in that great city perhaps?

Mr. Graves informed Me that a friend of his would freight a fine sloop of Ninety tons and load Her with Flour, and also give me a free passage if I would undertake to get Her leave to sell her cargo at Curaçao. I said I would pay the usual passage, that the vessel should enter if my Father was still Governor at Curaçao. I went to see the Sloop, she was a regular clipper. My Yankee Captain, a very civil fellow, was profuse in his attentions.

David Ogden had given me an introduction to Washington Irving,[9] afterwards so famous. He, unluckily for me, was away from New York but his friend, Brevoort,[10] who wrote [illegible] with Him, received me very kindly and took me to some of the first parties in New York — the Watts,[11] Gracies,[12] [and] Ogdens.[13] The dinners were very handsome, good, profuse, but hurried over, not the English social meal. The houses were superbly furnished — Damasks, India [illegible], papers and furniture, much plate glass which has a noble and dressy look a[t] night when brilliantly lit and filled with well-dressed women. The[ir] style [was] an attempt at French but a gauche imitation of it, the girls were not well got up.

I purchased stocks[14] for a fortnight's passage and sent it on board of the Yacht on the 18th, having now only to take leave of My dear friends the Graves and started on the 20th [of January 1816].

### *[January-February 1816]*

We had a delightful run to the Tropic of Cancer, our climate improving with a delicious warmth in this latitude.

I was alone on deck one morning, with the helmsman, there was not a breath of wind, the topsail was flapping on the mast, the large mainsail eased off as far as might be. The helmsman and I were chatting and wondering how long this Calm was to last, when all at once the Sloop gave a jump like a blood horse rearing, she seemed as if about to down astern. Yarmouth, the steady Steersman, put his helm down when, quicker far than I could speak, must less write it, the great spanker boom broke from the guy. I saw it coming like wrath and threw myself on the deck, shouting: "Down, Man!" The vessel reeled over, gunwale under, which saved Her. Up rushed the Captain and all the Crew. A white Squall had stricken us and the hardy mariner soon had his snug sail a trim close reefed, flying upon a wind over the yet smooth water.

A day or two after this, I was looking listlessly over the side, watching a lovely Nautilus which now and then would spread his rainbow Sail to the balmy air — itself the loveliest vessel that [sailed] the azure Sea — when lo, I lost my breath in wonder. A flight of birds rose from the water! I was so taken by surprise, so full of wonderment and admiration that I forgot all I had ever read of flying fish.

Presently another flight reminded me of my readings, yet the pleasure and delight of seeing these elegant creatures for the first time I shall never forget. Some of them gratified my extremest curiosity by dropping on board the Vessel — when they were examined with care and afterward tasted with avidity. It is a pretty fish like a long herring with a bright transparent wing [of] a shot azure satin, a bee's wing magnified. Not bad eating, either, when nicely fried, are the pretty critters. What a bolt the Dolphin, splendid fellow, makes at them and what a fly the covey make, the devil take the hindmost, sure enough in that case!

### *[February 1816]*

At length a fortnight is passed and we are in West Indian waters — passed some of the Islands which the Captain, indeed not a Soul, knew. One Morning the Captain said: "There, I believe, is Curaçao." I ran aloft to look out. "No, it is not Curaçao by my Views of it. There are hills there, but no peaks. Coming, as we do, from the Northwards, we should see ranges of high peaks." We stood on all day with a light breeze and became convinced that it was Aruba, a dependency of Curaçao. Presently, high, peaked points came to view. "There", said I, "are the Mountain peaks of our Island." It was provoking to be near, yet too far off to be able to run for a strange land at Night so we stood off and on till morning.

### *12 February [1816]*

At dawn, we ran for and along the Land till we got off the harbour & the Town of Williamsstad came in Sight, when a fine, long pilot boat, with a Black pilot in a white dress and Straw hat, hailed us. "Sloop Ahoy! Where from?" "New York", I shouted, "is General Le Couteur at Curaçao still?" "Aye, Aye, Sir! Stand by for a Rope! And up He came. "How are the General and my Mother?" "Oh dear, are you their Son, Sir? How anxious dey hab been for Ye, Sir." "I suppose You will let the American sloop enter the harbour, Pilot, that has brought me so safe?" "Oh Yes, Massa, Sir! You be de best passport!"

In a short time I was in the Court of Government house. My dearest Mother did not know My person but hearing my voice, flew to embrace me, looking young and really blooming with Colour. My dear Father looking strong & active but pale, and dear Gordon well. What a rush of joy to meet, all in health, after so many Scenes of War, Pestilence, climates and Storms! How merciful and gracious had Providence been to us All! My excited feelings prevented me from getting a wink of sleep all night — the Mosquitoes outside of my gauze curtains buzzed "Cousin, Cousin, Cousin" without being able to add misery at so long a want of sleep. Many hours did I lie in wakeful reflections at all the scenes I had passed thro' and the joyous expectations of soon revisiting Old Belle Vue.

I write from a letter of Gordon to me dated 20 Jan[uary] 1815.

> I like Curaçao much better than Jamaica. Although it is a very barren Spot, almost all solid rock, yet you would be astonished to see what fine Guinea corn grows here — also many fine trees, vegetables and fruits — out of a kind of stone. All the hills in this Country are made in this [picture] and they in general point to the North. I do most certainly think that this island was formed by a Convulsi[o]n of nature. You see rocks so oddly formed, they seem to me to be made of such stuff as I have read of in Volcanoes. We have been upwards of four months in this Island and I have not yet seen a stone like those at home, they are like honey Comb and very brittle. As for the large stones with which they build, they are impregnated with a quantity of salt which it requires twelve or fifteen years to wash away, before they are fit for use. They leave them out in the sun and rain, which at least cleanses them — if they do not do this, the walls are always damp.
>
> There are a great many pretty shells here. Mama and I pick them up on the Sea shore — I in general get them with their fish in them up on the Sea shore — I in general get them with their fish in them if I can, for they are much easier cleaned, by Mama. We have now a nice little collection which we mean to increase till we go away.
>
> Our house is about fifty yards from the Sea. It was built by Papa's predecessor, General Haydon, (the last Gov[erno]r. It is very large but not convenient for a family — there are a large hall, dining and drawing room below, four rooms up stairs. One is Papa's office, two bedrooms, and the other is where Mama and I sit, to work, but none of them lead one into the other, but through a beautiful piazza, or gallery, which goes round the house.
>
> The harbour here is one of the finest in the world. There are different lagoons, or saltwater lakes, which connect with one another so that if a storm blows from the South, a ship can go into a lagoon to the West where she is sheltered from it. As for the entrance which is deep enough

to admit the largest ship into the harbour, it is only about Forty yards broad and increases for half a mile then it opens into a large lagoon which could contain the whole fleet of England, sheltered by high hills all around.

On each side of the entrance to the harbour is situated the Town which is in three divisions. Williamsstad, the principal part, where Fort Amsterdam is the market and all the best shops but there are only two good streets in it. As for the others they are so narrow that, from the upper piazzas of the houses, You can step across from one to the other with ease. Curaçao is reckoned the Montpellier of the West Indies, there is a company of the 60th Regiment which has been three years here and they have not lost a man by fever. The climate is more settled than Jamaica — I think it is cooler although so much nearer the line, for there is almost always a constant Sea breeze.

I found my Father immersed in business, My Mother busy packing up. Shells, Coralines, beads, Basket work &c., the collections of years. Admiral Kikkert,[15] the Dutch Admiral who was to replace my Father, was a rough, pompous old Sailor. Very kind to us, with every seeming disposition nevertheless of taking full and despotic power over his New Government. He meant, He said, to relax no fees, fines, or privileges granted to the ancient Dutch Government, his predecessors, whatever the English governor may have done. I afterwards heard that He had kept his word.

There were large parties daily at Government house although we were on the move. My Father, Gordon & I generally rode out at 4 o'clock in the Morning, eight or ten miles. I had a nice pacer who took along in his namby pamby pace, two legs on a side together is a most agreeable way, after I had got over the hearty laugh I enjoyed at the brute's droll mode of progression.

### *22nd [February]*

Colonel/Captain Lewe Van Aduard,[16] the Commander of the *Prins Van Oranje*,[17] a Stately Dutch Eighty-Gun ship, to mount 104 Guns, gave General Le Couteur, Admir[a]l Kikkert and all the authorities a superb state dinner on board of the Liner. It was a superb turn out and very well done. The healths of the respective Sovereigns, and many more, warmed the hearts of the Orange people as well as the John Bulls. Hock[18] & Spa[19] is a splendid beverage in the Tropics or under the Line.[20]

*23 [February]*
Colonel Archy Maclaine,[21] He of Matagorda, gave us a farewell dinner at the Mess.

*24 [February]*
My Father gave his farewell dinner at Gov[ernmen]t house to the Admiral and his sister, the Members of the Council, Colonel Maclaine and the Staff.

*25 [February]*
The Admiral entertained us at dinner. Packing up.

*Friday, 1 March, 1816*
The General and I dined with Mr. Ming who had invited a large party to meet us. We left rather early as my Father gave a grand parting ball and supper to the Admiral, and to all the Inhabitants of Curaçao, who had universally been so kind to my Parents. Captain Williams[22] of the [7th West India Regiment], my brother ADC, Noel,[23] and I, with the Paymaster of the 7th West India,[24] acted as Masters of Ceremonies and a very gay affair it was. The Dutch beauties are plumper, not too rosy, but very frank and pleasant.

*2 [March]*
The Packet which arrived yesterday brought the warrant authorizing General Le Couteur to give up the Island of Curaçao and its dependencies to the King of the Netherlands. The General proceeded in State to Fort Amsterdam, passed in front of the Dutch and English troops from whom He received Salutes, proceeding to the Council Chamber to deliver the proclamation by which this Island is returned to the Netherlands. By this, the Gentlemen in British office and pay, up to this day, with all the inhabitants were absolved from their oath of allegiance to His Britannic Majesty.

As soon as the proclamation had been read, the General, then absolved Governor, and the Admiral, the New Governor, appeared together on the Balcony. Royal Salutes were fired from all the Forts, the British Union was lowered and the Dutch Tricolor waved aloft in its place. The flank companies of the 7th West Indian Regiment formed a street from the Fort to the point of embarkation and saluted as my Father left his command, the Band playing the National Anthem. We all went through the official ceremony of embarking, then landed to dine with Mr. and Mrs. Scates. The *Prins Van Oranje* saluted with yards Manned & colors flying in compliment.

### *Tuesday, 5 March*

I shall never forget the impression I received on witnessing the hearty feeling of real love and attachment which the poor blacks, especially, evinced on the departure of my Father and Mother. All classes testified their affection, many shed tears, which my Mother said appeared genuine. To hear and see the poor Negro race implore blessings on the head of their Massa Father, in the presence of the Dutch Governor, a Man of their own Country, as it were, while the ex-Governor being a Briton, was a testimonial never to be forgotten by a Son at least.

## Notes

[1] Probably Captain George Thew Burke, 99th (earlier 100th) Foot (c. 1776-1854), Deputy Assistant Adjutant General. Le Couteur describes him as a major and he may have had a brevet rank as such.

[2] Approximately nineteen to twenty words of the manuscript are illegible at this point.

[3] At this point, approximately twenty-five words of the manuscript are illegible. From the context, Le Couteur's reply probably read: " 'since I may chuse', looking at some dozen Men in the room [, "I choose you!"].

[4] At this point, approximately twenty words of the text are illegible.

[5] "Equillette." A long, thin, narrow slice of meat.

[6] "Raffineries." Fine delicacies.

[7] At this point in the text, Le Couteur's Journal contains many illegible paragraphs and sentences.

[8] Robert Fulton had constructed the first steam vessel to operate at New York in 1807 and by 1816 there was regular steamboat service to and from the harbour.

[9] Washington Irving (1783-1859). His recently published *Salmagundi* and *A History of New York* had established Irving as a rising young author. In 1815 he was absent from New York on an extensive journey in Europe.

[10] Henry Brevoort (1782-1848), friend and literary collaborator of Washington Irving.

[11] Probably John Watts (1749-1836) and his wife. Watts was Speaker of the New York State Assembly and Judge of Westchester County, NY.

[12] Archibald Gracie, prominent businessman and shipowner, who resided in a large country estate on the East River.

[13] Probably Thomas Ludlow Ogden (1773-1844) or his brother, David Ogden (1775-1849), both prominent New York lawyers and related to the Montreal Ogdens.

[14] At this point in the Journal, Le Couteur preserved a receipt dated 18 January 1814 for items bought from James Stuart. Among the items purchased were "1 1/2 Doz[en bottles]. Port wine, 2 Doz[en bottles]. English Porter, 1 Gall[on]. Brandy in bottles" as well as Souchong tea, chocolate, sugar, cheese, crackers, pepper, mustard, hams, oysters, and fowls.

[15] Admiral Albert Kikkert (1762-1819). Kikkert was to die on Curaçao.

[16] Colonel Captain Jan Evert Lewe van Aduard (1774-1832). Van Aduard reached flag rank in 1831 and was killed during the Belgian uprising the following year.

[17] HNMS *Prins van Oranje*, ship of the line, 80 guns, launched Antwerp, 1811, sold 1825.

[18] Hock is German white wine.

[19] Pure mineral water.

[20] "Under the line." Below the equator, in the tropics.

[21] Lieutenant Colonel Archibald Maclaine, 7th West India Regiment.

[22] Captain Roland E. Williams, 7th West India Regiment.

[23] Captain Etienne Noel, 7th West India Regiment.

[24] Paymaster Richard Allen, 7th West India Regiment.

# *Chapter Fourteen*

## "ADIEU TO ALL OTHER PROFESSIONS!"

An Ocean Voyage, Jersey and Canada

*March 1816 to June 1817*

***Wed[nesday], 6 March [1816]***

We left the kind and hospitable shore of Curaçao at 9 A.M., loaded with presents for the voyage from many families but, for the graphic account of the voyage, I refer to My dear Mother's own Journal which I affix here.[1]

> ***[6 March]***
>
> About 9 o'clock the Pilots came on board & we left the beautiful harbour of St. Ann. The *Prins Van Oranje*, like a Magnificent Castle, sweeping along side the houses of the Town of Amsterdam. Many persons had been apprehensive of so large a Vessel getting safe out of harbour, but we passed along the reefs in capital style & went on at the rate of 6 knots the hour.
>
> The Ship is Commanded by Colonel Captain Lewe Van Eduard; the Second in Command is Lieut[enant]. Colonel Captain Lucas,[2] reputed an excellent seaman. He was married the day before yesterday to Miss Elizabeth La Maison, daughter of Judge La Maison who came over from Holland with his Wife, Son & daughter in the *Prins Van Oranje*. They are an amiable well-informed family. Mrs. Lucas was particularly recommended to my protection by her Father & Mother, the parting with whom on both sides was truly affecting. She has been educated in England & has all the manners, & talks like an English woman.
>
> Colonel Lewe has had his handsome Cabin divided in two parts, one of which we occupy as a sitting room, besides the fore Cabins in which

the Quarter Gallery is, & a small room where the General's Cot is hung.

We breakfasted this morning in our own Cabin with Col[one]l. Lewe, Col[onel]. Maclaine who accompanies us to England, Captain Williams & Mr. De Vier, brother-in-law to Colonel Lewe who is on his passage to Holland.

We dined (the same party) & Col[onel]. Lucas, in the Captain's dining room & had an excellent dinner which I did not expect to partake of from sickness which I had in the morning. Gordon was sick & could not dine. Poor Mrs. Lucas was unable to appear. All the Officers' wives as well as many of themselves were miserably sick on deck. We had a fine wind & went on sometimes at the rate of ten knots per hour.

On Wednesday night about 12 o'clock, a storm of thunder, lightning & rain came on, it poured torrents until about 9 o'clock next morning, the water rushed in from all quarters. The Steward told me more rain had fallen in that short time than during their whole passage from Holland to Curaçao in the Winter Season.

***7th March. Thursday***

The party again breakfasted in our Cabin, as the Dining room was so filled with rain that we could not go into it. Gordon was still sick & all the ladies on board except myself. It cleared up in the afternoon & during part of the day we went at the rate of 14 knots per hour.

***8th March. Friday***

A fine morning. At 12 o'clock we were in Latitude 17. In the afternoon St. Domingo was very visible. The wind lessened towards evening & it was nearly calm during the night. I wrote to my brother Phil[ip]. Mrs. Lucas & Gordon dined at the table.

***9th March***

The vessel was opposite Cape Tiburon but it was nearly Calm & we went on very slowly during the day. The wind rose in the night & on the next morning.

***10th [March] Sunday***

At 6 o'clock we perceived Jamaica ahead, had a beautiful view of all the Eastern side of Jamaica round to the South East sailing very slow & when in sight of Kingston, it became a perfect Calm. Here we saw the Packet which left Curaçao twenty hours before us, completely becalmed a little to the head of us, as well as several other ships & small vessels. Pilots came on board about 8 o'clock A.M.

***Monday 11th [March]***

It was calm all night and continued until about 12 o'clock when a little breeze sprung up & brought us into the Harbour of Port Royal where we anchored about 5 o'clock in the afternoon. We had a beautiful view of the Fort & Harbour but the ship went too fast for me to take a proper sketch of it. Col[onel]. Lewe sent his long boat to take us to Kingston early on Monday morning.

***12th March***

We breakfasted at Bennet's Hotel, Mr. [illegible], Quartermaster, young De Quartel who commanded the boat as midshipman breakfasted with us.

The General & John paid visits to Gen[era]l. Fuller[3] & to Admiral Douglass.[4] The Admiral returned the visit the same day. Doctor Adolphus[5] & Captain Pratt called. We had no invitation to dinner & we dined at the Hotel & Captain Williams with us. John & Gordon went with Captain Williams to a Ball in the evening.

***13th March***

Gen[era]l. Fuller called, & Major Rumpler.[6] Colonel Lewe & two of his officers called us & we went together to dine at General Fuller's who sent his carriage for us, & received us in a most kind & hospitable manner. We were all enchanted with Mrs. Fuller, a most interesting young French woman without any of the levity of that nation & not appearing the least elevated by the high rank to which she has been suddenly raised from being in nearly a state of poverty. Her manners are modest, unassuming & extremely pleasing, She speaks English pretty well but does not like to speak it. She played on the Piano & sung several songs in the evening in a masterly style. Her little girl two months old is one of the finest babies I ever saw. So young a woman (about 20) married to a Man who is a grand Father & to whom she is the third wife cannot but excite a great deal interest in every feeling mind.

***14th March***

The Admiral sent us a closed carriage, a chaise & two gigs to take us & our party to dine at his Mess. Colonels Lewe & Lucas & Mrs. Lucas were most kindly received as well as ourselves.

*15th March*

The next morning Admiral Stewart called at Bennet's Tavern with two chaises to take Col[onel]. & Mrs. Lucas to see a little of the Country. They went as far as the Hope Plantation when they saw a black man 140 years of age, blind of one eye from an accident when quarrying but possessing all his faculties. He remembered perfectly the famous earthquake which destroyed Port Royal in the year 1693, also the names of all the Governors since that time. He walks occasionally to Kingston 5 miles & back again, but he told the Admiral this morning "Me go to Kingston when I want something but me not walk now, me creeps." He has been exempted from work on the plantation for 30 years past on account of his age. His eldest son died some time ago, aged 104, he has survived all his children, but he has many grand children. He was generally occupied in quarrying & has been a very strong man. He talks of the oldest men now living here & many that are dead as having seen them babies when he himself was a man. He is the only curiosity I regret not having seen in Jamaica.

We again dined with the Admiral & were as kindly received as the day before. We met today here Mrs. Fuller, the first time she had dined at the Admiral's. The Admiral, as the day before, sent carriages & sent us back. Col[onel]. & Mrs. Lucas slept at Bennet's Tavern.

*Saturday 16th March*

We got up at day break, hired a boat & called at Fort Augusta, the barracks of the 7th W[est]. I[ndia]. Reg[imen]t. on our way to the Ship *Prins Van Oranje*. We embarked about 9 o'clock and the Fort at Port Royal fired a Salute. I felt excessively fatigued. The General wrote to Gen[era]l. Fuller, recommended Capt[ain]. R.E. Williams & Scates.[7]

*Sunday 17th March*

The Pilot came on board at 4 o'clock in the morning. We sailed about 6, in company, or rather following, *The Carnation*,[8] Capt[ain]. Carter,[9] going to Havana. We had very little wind until about 1 o'clock when a strong sea breeze came, which not being favourable, gave a great deal of motion to the Ship. About 3 o'clock we split our main topmast which put us aback. It blew hard during the evening & during the Night. We were obliged to take an eastern course. I was seasick this day.

*18th [March]*
At 6 in the morning we had lost sight of land & continued steering toward the East, until 12 o'clock when the wind changed. We were obliged to tack & take a Northern course. The sailors were employed all day in replacing the main top mast & they made little sail.

*Tuesday 19th March*
The wind not favourable, went on very slow towards the windward passage.

*Wed[nesday]. 20th March*
Same wind. Steered North & N. West, a great swell, did not go more than two knots per hours, supposed ourselves between the two Islands of Jamaica & St. Domingo. Caught a Shark about 6 feet long & when pulled up as high as the quarter deck, the rope broke & it made its escape with the Hook in his Jaw. We passed the Morant Keys at 5 o'clock in the afternoon, & steered N.N.West.

*Thursday 21st [March]*
Mild weather during the night, tacked twice, wind the same. Squally & raining during the day, went on our course slowly through the windward passage. I did not feel well last night & took Rhubarb in the night.
Friday 22d March

Almost Calm, some showers, obliged to tack several times, made little way. Latitude this day 17 deg[rees]. 55 [minutes]. Morant Point still in view in the Evening.

*Sat. 23rd [March]*
About four in the morning a slight breeze sprung up & carried us about 16 miles to the Norward in four hours. At eight the breeze became less favourable, could see no land this morning. On taking the observation at 12 o'clock found we had only advanced 7 miles on our course since yesterday, being in Lat. 18 [degrees], 2 [minutes], Long[itude]: 75 [degrees]. At one o'clock, spoke the *Larat* of Liverpool bound for Jamaica.

*Sunday 24th. [March]*
At six in the morning, we were close to the little Island Narrows, a close to Cape Tiburon. A breeze sprang up & we went on a North & by West

course at the rate of 6 knots. The Vessel rolled very much. Latitude at 12 o'clock 18 [degrees], 58 [minutes]. About 10 o'clock, we perceived the Southern Coast of Cuba & at 5 P.M. it was perfectly visible, a fine high bold coast & mountainous. We went all day at the rate of 6 and 7 knots per hour, rather squally. Carried away our main topgallant sail. Went on very slow during the night. The Main Sail was torn & obliged to be taken down.

*Monday 25th [March]*
Cuba near us at 6 in the morning. The Main Sail was replaced about 11 o'clock. Little wind, went on slowly along the Coast of Cuba. Latitude 19 [degrees], 24 [minutes].

*Tuesday 26th [March]*
Made little or no latitude. A good breeze but a strong current against us threw us aback, & made us lose nearly all we gained in longitude. We thought we could see Port Maisi in the evening. Made little way in the night.

*Wed. 27th [March]*
Saw Cape St. Nicholas in St. Domingo on the South East of us in the morning but we went on very slow close to the wind all day and all night.

*Thurs. 28th [March]*
New moon. At 6 o'clock A.M., Cape St. Nicholas, St. Domingo on the East of us & Cape May in Cuba on the North. Went on very slow all day. Spoke a Merchant Ship bound for Halifax which left Jamaica four days before us, and which we left to leeward.

*Friday 29th [March]*
At five in the morning, close to Cape St. Nicholas & the Mole, St. Domingo. Tacked from it & steered North. At 12 o'clock we had weathered both, & also Cape Maisi in Cuba. Latitude 20 [degrees], 30 [minutes]. Got on from 5 to 6 knots all morning, lost sight of St. Domingo about 2 P.M. & of Cuba in the evening. Saw Inagua Island about 3 o'clock, came close to it at six. It is a curious low land extending at least 60 miles from West to East, appears uninhabited, & is not seen until you are close to it, expected to weather the Eastern point this evening but to our great disappointment, on

***Sat. 30th [March]***
Found ourselves very little forward & much deceived in the length of the Island which is not correctly stated in the Charts. Latitude this day only 20 [degrees], 40 minutes. At 5 o'clock tacked again for the night to the Southward to avoid the passage during the night leaving the Island of Inagua with innumerable hills or eminences to the East of it. It was fine cool weather all day with a good breeze. Dark night, made little way. In tacking, our main top yard broke in two.

***Sunday 31st March***
Put up a new yard. Went close to the East end of Inagua in hopes to weather it at half eleven A.M. within 3 miles of the beach, not being able to go round the point, attempted to tack, which the vessel could not effect & we were obliged to wear, but were so near a ridge of breakers close in shore that we expected to shipwreck here. I put money in my pocket & we filled the greatcoat pockets with biscuit in case of accident. Luckily, the Ship went round safe but I was much alarmed. Latitude 21 [degrees], 9 [minutes], little wind, attempted to tack again about 2, the ship would not turn, were obliged to wear, cleared the Eastern point of great Inagua & came in sight of little Inagua. Tacked from it at half past six towards the South East. A blowing night. At 12 the Ship tacked again & took a North course.

***1st April Monday***
At 8 o'clock we had completely weathered little Inagua to our great satisfaction. At 12 o'clock Latitude 21 [degrees], 56 [minutes]. Went upon the same tack all day. Saw the island of Mayaguana about 2 o'clock, were near it at 5 o'clock & tacked for the nigh towards the S. East. Nearly calm all night and tacked 3 times.

***2nd April Tuesday***
A calm close to Mayaguana. Latitude 22 [degrees], 9 [minutes], becalmed all the day, very warm & oppressive weather, the Sea like a looking glass.

***3 April***
The same calm, saw land all day. In the afternoon, a little breeze sprung up which took us to the Eastward, latitude the same as yesterday. At 11 o'clock at night tacked for the Norward very little wind.

***4th April, Thursday***
Land out of sight, light wind. Latitude 22 [degrees], 55 [minutes]. A squall came on about 1 o'clock & changed our course towards the N.West. Wind & Squally weather all night. The Main brace snapped in two.

***5th [April] Friday***
The same squally weather going close to the Wind, course North. Latitude at 12: 24 [degrees], 33 [minutes], longitude 72 [degrees], 17 [minutes]. The wind & weather more steady in the evening.

***6th [April]***
Course North, East, good weather, rather cold, latitude at 12 o'clock, 26 [degrees], 3 [minutes]. Put on my winter gown.

***7th [April] Sunday***
A calm came on about 12 o'clock, latitude 27 [degrees], 17 [minutes], longitude, 70 degrees. The Main Sail was brought down and another put up. Rather warm. Calm all night & warm. Great swell.

***8th [April] Monday***
Calm and small rain all day a great swell, it is likely a storm had very lately visited the Sea, very unpleasant weather. Wind right ahead, very little wind took us to the North West. In the evening it became a little more favourable & we got on very slowly all night rather to the Norward, the swell continuing.

***9th [April]***
The same swell, cloudy weather & foul wind, went only from 2 to 3 knots. Latitude at 12, 28 [degrees], 44 [minutes]. Great topping.

***10th [April]***
The wind rather more favourable. Went 5 knots. About 3 o'clock the wind came to the Southward, the sea smooth & we increased our course from 6 to 10 knots per hour. Went all night at the rate of 9 knots. Fine weather, wind southerly & moderate and no Sea.

***11th [April] Thursday***
Small rain, same wind. Studding and stay sails set, as well as yesterday. Cleared up, went at the rate of 9 & 10 knots. Smooth sea, Latitude 31 [degrees], 1 [minute]. Heavy sea in the night.

***12th [April] Friday***
Wind rather more westerly but little wind & more sea, latitude 31 [degrees], 48 minutes, longitude 62 [degrees], 18 minutes, went from 4 to 6 knots.

***13th [April] Sat***
I was almost deaf, syringed my ears. The same weather went 10 & 11 knots. Rather more sea than yesterday. The ship rolled terribly all night & went at the rate of from 10 to 12 knots.

***14th [April]***
Same weather, terrible sea & rolling could not keep the glasses & bottles on the table at dinner. I could scarce stand up. A great many glasses broke in ship. Went surprisingly fast with no other sails than the fore course & fore top sail all the afternoon & night. At dinnertime the main top sail broke & was obliged to be changed. My deafness continued but I contrived to sleep well at night notwithstanding the heavy rolling of the ships, & I was almost the only one who did so. Rains at night, went from 10 to 12 knots.

***Monday 15th [April]***
The wind & sea more moderate, went 9 knots. Latitude 35 [degrees], 11 [minutes], longitude, 49 [degrees]. I felt the cold severely & wore my cloth habits. At 12 o'clock this day, We had gone 493 miles during the last 48 hours. I took 4 grains of Calomel in the night.

***16th [April] Tuesday***
A Calm. Latitude 36 [degrees], 44 [minutes]. About 5 o'clock a breeze sprung up & we went from 6 to 9 knots all night, & we had a smooth sea.

***17th [April] Wednesday***
Wind on beam, smooth water which took us to the Eastward. Went 9 & 10 knots. Latitude 36 [degrees], 47 [minutes], Long[itude], 44 [degrees], 36 [minutes].

***18th [April] Thursday***
Almost calm, went only from 4 to 5 knots, the Ship rolled much. My deafness rather better. Latitude 38 [degrees], 5 [minutes]; Longitude 41 [degrees], 17 [minutes]. It was calm.

***19th [April] Friday***
Heavy weather, rather more wind & favourable. Went from 6 to 9 knots. Latitude 38 [degrees], 34 [minutes]. Rain in the afternoon.

***20th. [April]***
Hazy morning & rain. Went about 6 knots. Latitude 40 [degrees]. Very cold & very *ennuiyee*[10] in addition to my deafness.

***21st [April] Sunday***
It blew hard & heavy rain early in the morning & continued blowing a Gale with a rough sea till about 1 o'clock, when it moderated, cleared up & became nearly calm. We had gone from 8 to 9 knots all the morning. The night was squally, rain with thunder and lightning.

***22nd [April] Monday***
Heavy Sea, wind aft. Ship rolled terribly, went from 6 to 8 knots. Latitude 42 [degrees], 34 [minutes]. Longitude about 40 [degrees]. In the evening, a storm of Thunder, lightning & rain, which continued during intervals all night. Capt[ain]. Tooft, first Lieut[enant]., was of opinion it had not blown so strong for a century as it did for a short time a little before day light. The lightning & succeeding darkness was terrible. I could not help being alarmed & was very happy to see day light.

***23d [April] Tuesday***
The Squalls of wind & rain continued all the morning. We went at the rate of from 10 to 12 knots, without any sails set. Rough sea. Saw a Frigate which passed us towards the South East, she had lost her main top mast (probably during the night). Latitude at 12 o'clock (the Sun having shown himself for a short time) 43 [degrees] & long[itude], 38 [degrees], a fine afternoon.

***24th [April] Wednesday***
Went from 8 to 10 knots all last night, fair wind & fine weather, very cold. Latitude 44 [degrees], Long[itude], 25 [degrees]. It became nearly calm towards evening.

***25th [April] Thursday***
Almost a calm, very fine weather for *Land*, a delightful spring day *on shore* but not charming at sea.

***26th [April]***
Saw an English 40-gun Frigate going the same way with us, but we had the wind contrary & nearly calm. Latitude 45 degrees, 10 [degrees] Long. Calm continued all night.

***27th [April] Sat.***
Rain, and a fair breeze sprung up at day break, which continued increasing till 12 o'clock, when we went 8 knots per hour. Latitude 45 degrees, 54 [minutes]. Long[itude]: 22 [degrees], 5 [minutes]. Several ships in sight, the Frigate we saw yesterday kept the same course with us all night but we rather beat her this morning until about 12 o'clock when she altered her course to go more to the South East, we steered east. The breeze increased so that at dinner time we went at the rate of 10 knots & 11 before 6 o'clock. The ship was so steady that no more motion was perceived than if we had been at Anchor in Smooth water. At dinner no frame or stay for the dishes or glasses was used. It continued to rain all the afternoon & we lost sight of the Ships near us. The motion of the Ship scarce perceptible. Went all night from 8 to 10 knots.

***28th [April] Sunday***
Rain all the morning. Wind came round to the North West. Saw no Frigate this morning. Went about 6 knots. Latitude: 46 [degrees], 54 [minutes]. Long[itude], 17 [degrees]. Went on well all night.

***29th [April] Monday***
It rained about 7 o'clock, could not walk on deck. N. West Wind. Went at the rate of 7 & 8 knots all the morning. Latitude 47 [degrees], 19 [minutes]. Saw several ships. At 6 o'clock, hove the lead for the first time. The Seamen were divided in opinion, some thought they found bottom with 70 fathom, others that the lead did not reach the bottom. Hove the lead another time, no bottom found.

***30th [April]***
Fine weather but very cold. Saw several ships, and a Brig of War some took for the *Carnation* steering to the Northward of us. About 5 P.M. spoke a small Swedish brig — told us they saw the Lizard the evening before her Longitude was 8 [degrees].44 [minutes]. Latitude 40 [degrees]. 0 [minutes] agreeing nearly with ours.

### *May day, [1 May] 1816*[11]

I was getting up to dress for breakfast about 8 A.M. when, looking out of my Stern gallery window, in which I had a most snug berth, to my so great astonishment, I perceived land apparently about five miles off. That I rubbed my eyes to be sure that I was right — it seemed to me that I recognized Torteval church in *Guernsey*.[12] I flew to my Father's Cabin and told Him what I saw. He called it Nonsense but came out instantly and said: "It is it. Run up to Colonel Lewe or to Col[onel] Lucas and tell Him that the ship is in great danger, we are too near Guernsey."

I ran upon deck. Col[onel]. Lucas was there, when I called Him to look over the ship's side, *not a vestige of land was to be seen* — a thick fog lay like a shroud over the Sea. He scarcely believed me. He shouted to the Man at the Masthead: "Donder und Blizam", in Dutch, "don't you see the land ahead?" "Nothing but fog, your honor." While these words passed, the fog rose and Guernsey lay fair before us bearing SS East. About ship we went and soon after a fishing boat from Guernsey hailed us: "What are you doing so near Guernsey with a line of Battle ship? You would have been in great danger of low water!" and he piloted us off. We had evidently overrun our reckoning very considerably.

About six in the afternoon we made old England, our dear parent Country — tho' not the absolute place of our birth, the blessed land of our freedom.

Our noble ship gave and received a salute on anchoring at Spithead, when we soon after parted with our worthy host, afterwards Admiral Van Lewe killed at the Siege of Antwerp. Col[onel]. Lucas and Commander Tooft were very superior men, excellent officers, very pleasant companions.

Poor Tooft was unlucky one morning. He was giving orders and, making a flourish with his hand, his sleeve button caught in his watch chain and away flew a fifty Guinea watch by Barraud clear over the side to the treasures of the deep. I shall never forget the astonishment and vexation of his honest countenance on that occasion.

The discipline on board was very rigid, severe indeed. A midshipman for having disobeyed some order was *chained* to a gun and, though a tall, clever youth of seventeen or eighteen, would have been severely flogged but for the intercession of My Mother, through my brother, with whom He was on very friendly terms of intimacy.

The ship was undermanned, about five hundred [men] — her war complement would have been eight or about nine hundred. She was one of Bonaparte's Antwerp built ships, and still had the "N"[13] on all the stern *plate* glass windows. She was an admirable Sailer, outstripping everything we came near. One day in the Caribbean Sea, with a strong breeze on the quarter, all sails drawing & smooth water, she was running fourteen knots by log, which Col[onel]. Lucas held while I watched & My Father looked on. Give me a line of Battle ship for a Yacht, say I.

After a few days stay in London to enable my Father to settle his affairs with the Colonial Office and at the Horse Guards,[14] we left for dear little Jersey. I shall not attempt to described the greetings and heartfelt joy, reciprocally felt by us all and my beloved Grandfather, Uncles and Aunts. The best of everything, in words and deeds, was lavished upon a long-lost Family for perils by sea, pestilence by land and the accumulated horrors of war had menaced us all more or less in a four years' absence. Yet it pleased a Merciful Providence to reunite us all in our beloved circle and happy land, at old Belle Vue.

### *May, 1816*

In the short Six weeks I was allowed to continue on leave, I engaged my Cousin, Harriet Janvrin,[15] then only Eighteen, to become my wife whenever I became a Captain. This affair came off at a Pic Nic at Royal Manor, in the Arbour half way down in the wood — thus it is that Youths and Maidens at the inexperienced age of twenty-two and eighteen risk their earthly fate.

To my consternation, I was ordered to join my Reg[imen]t forthwith at Quebec owning, I afterwards learned, to a fresh rumour of War with America. I had applied to join the expedition to Algiers,[16] which also hastened my departure.

### *19 August [1816]*

Took my passage to Quebec in the *Starling*, Capt[ain]. Purse, a Clipper provided with everything but wine and bedding for £35. Received letters of introduction from Sir Thomas Saumarez to the Governor General of Canada, Sir John Sherbrooke, to Col[onel]. Addison.[17] Discussions as to quitting the army if I do not get my Company soon.[18]

Frank Janvrin[19] drove me in his spree gig and Grey thoroughbred to Richmond to see little LouLou Janvrin[20] at School — in a lonely situation. Heard that our Regiment had received a notification that it is to be disbanded.

My fellow passengers [are] two medical men and two Methodist parsons — expect to be sickened of physic and divinity by the time we arrive. I saw a cargo of pipes in the cabin, I shall be wretched if they smoke. I must devise some method of annoyance for the Smokers.

*Mary Le Couteur (née Dumaresq) (1774-1850), the mother of John Le Couteur.*

*Harriet Le Couteur (née Janvrin) (1798-1865), Le Couteur's wife.* Both portraits are by Fisher, dated 1850, and reproduced courtesy of Mrs. Nancy V. Agate, U.K.

### *23 August [1816]*

Gravesend. A nice country, should not mind to possess an estate within view of the River — the constant traffic on its bright bosom enlivens the picture. We passed the Downs with a small gale from the NW and until the day before yesterday with only two days of fair wind. I never wish to make another winter voyage in a small ship of three or four hundred tons tons besides not to say much of her lively motion, she is very like a constant shower bath, from being so sharp and fast. We are only 450 miles from the banks of Newfoundland — in twenty-six days with contrary winds.

I found Holmes, a fellow Collegian, on board [and] a nice Young Canadian Seigneur of Masquimonge, Atkinson. He had been travelling in France and was very companionable. The worthy Methodist parsons were originally Ship Carpenters but, having had a spiritual calling, turned from their evil ways, they said, became Preachers, gave up tea gardens, card playing, and such like iniquities. Our Cards they called the books of the Satan; our lively Songs, obscene — in short, till we *converted* them to our ways, [we] were thoroughly bemethodized.

One day whilst shaving, I had to endure a Sermon. Another day, when Seasick, blowing up a gale and three of us in bed with no means of defence and our retreat cut off, We heard Fourteen chapters, a sermon and some hymns which, with our Sickly responses, became ludicrous.

After six days of endurance and toleration, we shook off the yoke thus. I commenced reading Joe Miller[21] which annoyed them beyond measure. As soon as I was tired of reading & laughing, Atkinson continued, then Holmes went on. This completely silenced our antagonists. An Irish fellow passenger said "we were broths of boys" while the Captain and a French Roman Catholic thought it high fun.

However we made a treaty of peace and amity. Of a Sunday, they were to read part of our Service, part of their own prayers, and deliver a sermon — a convention which was duly adhered to, by the belligerent parties.

### *26 September [1816]*

A horrible gale. See my letter to come in here.[22]

*December,[23] 1816, Gale on the Banks of NewFoundland*

Our beautiful little ship was skipping over a lively sea with every Sail drawing. The Wind was about SE, we had studding sails, the sky was clear overhead with grayish murky look clouds, somewhat fleecy low down. We were all joyous and full of fun cracking our jokes at the idea of being so near to the North pole, and wondering whether the needle would really not vibrate toward the North, a wonder we heard of from our nice, intelligent Captain, who however, sometimes spun us a yarn out of mere mischief to sell the young Lobsters[24], that we hardly knew whether He was serious or not. The occasional blows which the Helmsman gave with a stick with a roll or kind of [illegible] at its end, to the compass made us feel that the Captain was not hoaxing him at any rate. He assured us that most of the unfortunate vessels that were lost in and about the Bay of Fundy and within the Capes was owing to their Captains not being aware of the secret derangement, the dip of the needle, which takes place as you approach the North pole.

The favorable wind at about 5 o'clock blew itself away at a breath, leaving not a sigh behind. It was calm, stark calm and still water. We all ran upon deck — where had the wind gone to so unkindly? To sleep? No, not a whit to refresh itself — aye — in five short minutes, with studding and other sails flapping on the masts. One of the mates shouted: "The ship will be taken aback,[25] Sir, the wind's running ahead like a race horse." The Captain stood by the wheel, gave the necessary words of command: "Helm a lee!" and the good ship laid over on the wind not till she had got some stern way, which the smooth sea did not make very dangerous, but away she staggered with her lower studding sail booms almost in the water. The studding sails and Royals were taken in with all speed but we were not a man of war and 18 men can not perform the work of 100, how good they are.

It came on to blow so fiercely and to increase so rapidly that it was perfectly astounding to us Landsmen. Some companion of Ulysses was on board in disguise and He opened the bag of winds [illegible] on a wind in ten minutes the storm was raging so that we, unlike Him, were driving right home.[26] "Bock again", as our Scotchman said, being forced to square the yards and scud before it. Night was closing as the gale increased, the gallant little Ship was plunging with the seas up to the Capstan bar, burying herself then lifting the Seas, which came sweeping aft. Everything was battened down and we could only peep occasionally from the top of the companion ladder.

Presently the sails began to tear into strips — by midnight every Sail, but the fore course and spanker, were in ribands, and after each roll, at each jerk of regained momentum to the opposite side, the strips of canvas being flicked like a Cartman's whip, in a quarrel with his team, the sound was like a rapid volley of musketry followed by the low surge of the Foresail, rising out of the calm trough of the Sea, which when on catching the gale filled with a noise of a Cannon. The gale had come so very fast that even the studding sail booms had not all been got in, and as to furling the sails that had been impossible, the men could not hold on in the rigging.

About midnight the storm was at its height and the wind blew down the seas, our worthy Methodist Parsons were on the[ir] knees praying devoutly while we no doubt did the same inwardly — suddenly the cry, "We've sprung a leak!" was heard. I exclaimed: "The Vessel has sprung a leak, we had better not be idle here doing nothing but go and offer to pump, we can do that I suppose at least." I started and others followed, when I got to the deck, I lost my footing. A sea came playing over me and I should have gone overboard if one of my friends had not dragged me down the Companion ladder head foremost I believe, for my thumb nail was half off, I was thoroughly drenched and bewildered with the awful noise on deck and the subsequent accident. The Captain sent us word by the Cook that the deck was no place for passengers, but to turn in. Which I did after stripping and saying my prayers in good earnest.

The Seas continued to curl over the main top while we were in the hollow, like a huge Cauliflower covering its stem, then she would creep gently up the next hill, catch the blast at the crest and plunge down the hill (for I call them hills, they were waves like hills) with the speed of an avalanche.

About one o'clock our black cook came in with the blessed intelligence: "Massa Gentleman, gale most choke, go sleep now." Sleep we all did soon, after real alarm. A general action is a joke to such a fearful hurricane, every other gale I have seen was but a capful of wind.

The next morning it was calm, long, soft looking undulating hills and valleys like some parts of Salisbury set afloat, green water instead of sward. Not a breath, the vile straps of canvas lashing in all directions like a thousand mad drummers, cat in hand. The tight little ship [was] a mere wreck, even the stiff jolly spanker had gone — not one sail whole. They were all day rigging & bending new sails, while we were catching codfish by the score.

### *20 October*

We were delighted to reach Quebec after being on short commons for a fortnight. The Regiment had gone to Montreal — a nicer quarter by far. Col[onel]. Addison was most kind. Col[onel]. Harvey gave me leave to remain at Quebec till Col[onel]. Moodie, who had gone to meet his wife at Kamouraska, should return. Sir John Sherbrooke, to whom He presented me, asked me to dinner & introduced me to Lady Sherbrooke, a fine young Woman. Colonel Harvey was as friendly to me as if I had been his Son.

### *4 November [1816]*

My friend and Chief, Col[onel]. Moodie, brought up Mrs. Moodie and Chicks from New Brunswick last week. He keeps me with Him to go up to Montreal in the Steamer[27] — My *first voyage by Steam*. He was quite surprised to see me and vexed that Major Hunter had not sold out to Jobling & Me who were both for purchase. He had not filled up my place in the Light Company in which I should certainly remain.

Sir John Sherbrooke was very courteous, conversed familiarly with me and took wine with me. Col[onel]. & Mrs. Taylor,[28] Com[missary] General Robinson,[29] the Melvins,[30] Atkinsons, were all most kind & hospitable. I dined out daily when I remained at Quebec.

The weather was very rainy and the Town filthy. It afforded me small opportunity to see the beauties of the neighbouring Country. My first fine day trip was to Cape Diamond which I described to my Mother. In clear weather, the view must be magnificent, You are several hundred feet above the water level, a grand and extensive scene. To your front, You have the rich and beautiful Island of Orleans by which the Noble St. Lawrence quietly glides, forming a strong contrast with the bold rocky shore to the right. A fine shelving Country is on the left, which runs into high distant mountains — the populace, villages and numerous houses entirely white, scattered about the Country, relieve the sight and enliven the somewhat sombre appearance of the woods.

The foreground on the left is very beautiful, as the Montmorency river which gives the name to, and causes the fine falls of which all have seen drawings, serpentines so much, as in some places to lose itself, then again suddenly breaks upon the view. The Banks are very fertile, many Gentlemens' seats add to the beauties of this extensive, glittering in the Sun, have a novel appearance, which it would not be easy to put upon paper, or indeed would such seem natural in drawing.

The background is more interesting than all, being where the battle of Quebec took place and where the never to be forgotten hero, *Wolfe*, fell. I am surprised that the inhabitants of this City have not erected a monument to his Memory. I imagine it is owing to the principal portion of the good folks being French and they very naturally can have no wish to erect a monument

*Street scene, Montreal, 1810, by John Lambert. Le Couteur had two spells of garrison duty in Montreal in 1815 and 1816-17, and thought it a "delightful" station for a soldier.* J. Lambert/National Archives of Canada/C-113741

to British valour, particularly when pointing out a triumph over French gallantry.

### *18 November [1816]*

Montreal. Got into my lodgings. The fine Old Baronet, Sir John Johnson, called desiring to see me. When I went to his house, he had left for the "Seigneurie"[31] but dear Mrs. Bowes, the sweet widow of Gen[era]l Bowes, who was killed at Salamanca, received me for her father & made me come to dine with Her. It was a great compliment, she told me, that Sir John had paid me for he never paid visits but I was a special favourite. George Pipon[32] & his wife were very kind so was his General, Widdringtons,[33] the Richardsons, Forsythes, Caldwells, Ogdens, Reids, [and] Grants were all most cordial and kind to me.

Major Goulbourn,[34] brother to the under Sec[retar]y of State,[35] a most elegant person of superior education and accomplishments had joined the Regiment. He lent me Jomini's works[36] to study. He had been in the 11th Light Dragoons at Waterloo, described the cavalry charges of the English or French light horse[37] to be ineffectual — the moment one charged, the other retreated.

### *11 January [1817]*

I heard with pleasure of my grandfather having resigned the office of Chief Magistrate of Jersey. My opinion then written to My Mother was:

> I am astonished at the proceedings of your Royal Court, they are of a tinct with those of the Manchester rioters,[38] most extraordinary, and I very much fear their well disposed persons whoever they may be may bring the attention of Ministers home to the Island, and that some change in the Court and Laws will follow, and the good people be surprised with hearing they will no longer have the privilege of choosing their Jurats,[39] since their choice is improperly fixed.

The Society of Montreal is excellent, the style of parties sumptuous. At all dinners, You are given Claret and Champagne, the former eight shillings the bottle, the latter from Ten to fifteen/. You see a quantity of plate, two or three courses, in short the style of four or five thousand pounds a year in England. There are bachelors' and other clubs weekly at a Noble hotel where every friend that is asked costs a Member Two pounds for his dinner — the entry for plate money is twenty-five guineas so that there must be a great deal of money in the place. My friend David Ogden, who may not be the first lawyer here, makes about Two thousand [pounds stirling] a year, and lives accordingly.

*27 February [1817]*

Captain Holland[40] called at my lodging and offered to sell his Company to me for Fifteen hundred pounds, to which I instantly acceded. Col[onel]. Moodie called soon after and helped me to write a Memorial for Holland and myself.[41]

*7 March [1817]*

I received a very kind letter from the Military Secretary, Col[onel]. Addison, stating that Sir John Sherbrooke had forwarded my papers with a strong recommendation but, as Capt[ain]. Holland had only been fourteen years an officer and did not purchase — "I hope it may succeed."[42]

*May [1817]*

The Regiment having received a notification that it was to be disbanded,[43] I obtained leave to proceed to England by New York and was allowed my passage money. I stayed a week at St. Johns with Harry Le Mesurier and his wife and reached New York on the 24th May. My first visit was to dear Mr. & Mrs. Graves — on hearing I was in the house she ran down stairs and absolutely embraced me, as if I had been her own Son. She told me much about Curaçao — the poor people sadly lamented the loss of my Father's government and the gentle English rule. They would readily surrender themselves back to England.

*23 June [1817]*

Landed once more in dear Old England and found Myself a Captain — *Adieu to all other professions*!

## Notes

[1] As Le Couteur intended, the diary of his mother for the period, March to May 1816, has been placed here. The original is located in the Lord Coutanche Library, Société Jersiaise, St. Helier, Jersey.

[2] Lieutenant Colonel Captain Lieutenant Engelburt Lucas (1785-1870): captain, 1825; rear admiral, 1838, vice admiral, 1844. From 1845 to 1851, Lucas was the Dutch Minister of the Navy.

[3] Lieutenant General Francis Fuller, Commander of the Forces in Jamaica.

[4] Rear Admiral Sir John Erskine Douglas, RN, Commander in Chief, Jamaica, 1815-1818.

[5] Surgeon Jacob Adolphus, Medical Department, British army.

[6] Probably Major Anthony Rumpler, 60th Foot.

[7] Captain John Scates, 7th West India Regiment.

[8] HMS *Carnation*, Brig-sloop, launched 1813, sold 1836.

[9] Captain Thomas Wren Carter, RN, lieutenant, 1805; commander, 1809, captain, 1815.

[10] "Ennuiyee." Bored.

[11] At this point, Le Couteur's Journal resumes the narrative.

[12] Torteval Church located in the southwest corner of Guernsey was probably the highest structure on the island in 1816.

[13] Having been built when Holland was part of the French Empire in 1811, the *Prins van Oranje* was marked with the Imperial "N" for the Emperor Napoleon.

[14] The Horse Guards was the headquarters in London of the British army in 1816 and took its name from the nearby Horse Guards parade ground.

[15] Harriet Janvrin (1798-1865), Le Couteur's first cousin and future wife.

[16] Increasing tension between Britain and the Dey of Algiers over the capture and enslavement of British nationals led to an Anglo-Dutch naval and military force being sent to Algiers in the summer of 1816.

[17] Lieutenant Colonel Thomas Fenn Addison (1773-1852), military secretary to the commander-in-chief, British North America.

[18] "If I did not get my Company soon." If I was not soon promoted to captain's rank.

[19] Frank Janvrin was Le Couteur's uncle by marriage and the husband of his mother's sister, Harriet.

[20] Louisa (LouLou) Janvrin, Le Couteur's cousin.

[21] James Ballantyne, *Old Joe Miller, by the Editor of the New Joe Miller* (3 vols., London, 1809), a humorous treatise.

[22] At this point, Le Couteur appended the following account of his experiences in a gale off Newfoundland which appears to be extracted from a letter written after his arrival in Canada.

[23] As Le Couteur was at sea in September, not December 1816, this may be either an error or the date of the letter in which this account first appeared.

[24] "Lobsters". A common nickname for British soldiers during this period was "lobster backs", derived from the frequent use of flogging as a punishment.

[25] "The ship will be taken aback." The ship would be running directly against the wind and would lose all headway.

[26] A classical illusion to an incident in the *Odyssey*, Book Ten, lines 1-79, when Aeolus, the god of winds, presents Ulysses with a bag containing the storm winds that might impede his homeward passage. Unfortunately, Ulysses does not inform his crew of the contents of the bag, which they open and let loose the winds which blow the ship back to Aeolus who refuses further assistance.

[27] A product of the entrepreneurial skills of the Montreal businessman, John Molson (1783-1836), steamboats began plying the St. Lawrence from Quebec to Montreal in 1810. By 1817, three craft, *Malsham, Lady Sherbrooke* and *Swiftsure*, were in regular service.

[28] Lieutenant Colonel George Taylor, 100th Foot and his wife. Taylor was the Inspecting Field Officer of militia in Lower Canada.

[29] Commissary General W.H. Robinson.

[30] Possibly Assistant Surgeon Alexander Melvin, 60th Foot and his wife.

[31] The "Seigneurie" was Johnson's country estate at Argenteuil.

[32] Lieutenant George Pipon, 26th Foot, and his wife.

[33] Major General David L. Widdrington, general officer commanding, Montreal district, 1816-1817.

[34] Major Frederick Goulbourn, 100th Foot, who joined the regiment in 1816.

[35] Henry Goulbourn (1784-1856), Lord Bathurst, the Secretary of State for War and the Colonies, 1812-1821.

[36] Antoine-Henri Jomini (1779-1869). Jomini served in the French and Russian armies during the Napoleonic wars and is remembered, with Clausewitz, as one of the great military thinkers of the nineteenth century. Jomini analyzed Napoleon's art of war through historical study and his *Traite des grandes operations militaires, ... avec un recueil des principes generaux de l'art de la guerre* (4 vols., Paris, 1811) was his first major work.

It would seem that, perhaps under Goulbourn's influence, Le Couteur was beginning to study his profession seriously. In his diary, 28 December 1817, he noted that he was reading Tielke. This was the German military writer, Johann Tielke (1731-1787), author of *An Account of some of the most remarkable events of the war ... from 1756 to 1763, and a treatise on several branches of the military art* (London, n.d.) and *The Military Engineer, or, Instructions upon every branch of field fortifications* (London, 1789).

[37] "Light horse." Light cavalry.

[38] Following the end of the Napoleonic wars in 1815, there was much economic and social unrest in Britain. In August 1819 a large crowd met in Manchester to hear speeches by reform politicians. The presiding magistrates in the city ordered the military to disperse the crowds and, in the resultant conflict, nine persons at least were killed. The so-called "battle of Peterloo", in reality a massacre, shocked Britain.

It is curious that Le Couteur, discussing a letter written to his mother in 1817, should mention in that letter an event that occurred in 1819. It would seem that Le Couteur has confused his chronology. He may be referring to the "March of the Blanketeers" in Manchester in March 1817 when the Riot Act was read a number of people arrested after a gathering at St. Peter's Field, the scene of the "battle of Peterloo" two years later.

[39] In 1816 the government of Jersey consisted of a lieutenant governor appointed by the crown, a bailiff and twelve "jurats" elected for life by those eligible to vote and a number of constables and deputies elected for a fixed term. As well as advising the lieutenant governor, the bailiff and the jurats constituted the Royal Court of Jersey, the only court on the island.

[40] Captain Edward Holland, 104th Foot. Holland enlisted in the army as a private soldier in 1798 and fought in Holland, Egypt and the West Indies before being granted an enseignancy in the New Brunswick Fencibles in 1803. See NAC, RG 8 I, vol. 1027, p. 3, Memorial of Captain Edward Holland, 27 February 1817.

[41] This memorial is contained in NAC, RG 8 I, vol. 1027, p. 3. On the same day (26 November 1816), Moodie wrote to Addison to inform him that Le Couteur was the most senior lieutenant in the 104th and that his claim to purchase a captaincy was "most justly grounded, for besides being an uncommonly fine young man whose invariable attention to his duty has always been conspicous, he was greatly disappointed in the purchase of the last Company sold on it owing to some unfortunate mistake at the money, altho' his Father Major General Le Couteur had written to say that it should be ready whenever required." See NAC, RG 8 I, vol. 1027, p. 1, Moodie to Addison, 26 February 1817.

Two days later Le Couteur wrote officially to Moodie requesting permission to purchase Holland's company and certifying "upon the word and honour, of an Officer and a Gentleman, that I will not either now, or at any future time, give by any means, or in any shape whatever, directly or indirectly, any more than the sum of Fifteen hundred Pounds, being the price limited by His Majesty's Regulation as the full value of the said commission." See NAC, RGRG 8 I, vol. 1027, p. 6, Le Couteur to Moodie, 28 February 1817.

The price Holland asked was in accordance with the *Regulations of the Army* which, on p. 32, listed an approved price of £1500 for a captaincy in line infantry regiments.

[42] On 7 March 1817, Sherbrooke wrote to the Adjutant General of the Army, Major General Torrens, requesting that Le Couteur's application be given favourable consideration. He added a private letter to Torrens pointing out that Le Couteur had been entitled in May 1816, to purchase the company being sold by Captain A.G. Armstrong and that his father had lodged the money with the agent for this purpose but that, through some mistake of the agent, the arrangement was not concluded. As a result, Le Couteur's father had complained to the Duke of York and received the assurance that his son would be promoted to the next eligible company. See PRO, WO 31, vol. 451, cont. (III), Sherbrooke to Torrens, 7 March 1817 and same to same (private) 7 March 1817.

[43] According to Squires, *The 104th Regiment*, 179-180, the General Order disbanding the 104th was dated at Quebec, 19 April 1817.

# Bibliography


## 1. Archival Sources

Archives of Ontario, Toronto
MU 2057, Memoir of the Niagara Campaign of 1813 by Sir John Harvey

National Archives of Canada, Ottawa
Colonial Office 42,
Record Group 8 I, British Military Records
Manuscript Group 24, F15
Correspondence of Colonel Hercules Scott, 103rd Foot
Micro M-8, Jacques Viger, "Ma Saberdache"

National Archives of the United States, Washington
Record Group 92, Commisary General of Purchases, Letterbook A

Public Record Office, London
War Office 17, Returns of the British Army
War Office 27, Inspection Reports
War Office 31, Correspondence of the Adjutant-General

Société Jersiaise, St. Helier, Jersey
Le Couteur-Sumners Papers
Finding Aid
M10 - Diary My Journal
M15 - Diary of Marie Le Couteur, 1816
Diaries of Sir John Le Coutuer No. 1, July 1815 to February 1818
Draft of "A Winter's March in Canada 1813"

## 2. Publications of Sir John Le Couteur and His Father

Colonel Sir John Le Couteur
"A Winter's March in Canada, 1813"
*The Albion*, New York, 26 November 1831

*On the rise, progress and present state of Agriculture in Jersey*
St. Helier, Jersey, 1852

*On the use of the Great or Jersey Plough, etc.*
London, 1842

*On the varieties, properties and classification of wheat.*
Jersey and London, 1836 and 1842; 2nd ed., London, 1872

*The Rifle; its effect on the war; on national military organization; and preparation for defence.* London, 1855

Lieutenant General John Le Couteur
*Letters, chiefly from India, giving an Account of the Military Transactions on the Coast of Malabar during the Late War* ... London, 1790

*Lettre d'un Officier du Centième Régiment*
Jersey, 1787

### 3. Period Newspapers

*Kingston Gazette*
April 1813 to July 1815

*Royal Gazette and New Brunswick Advertizer*, St. John, NB
July 1812 to February 1813

### 4. Published Memoirs, Correspondence & Documents

Cruikshank, Ernest A.
*Documentary History of the Campaigns on the Niagara Frontier in the Years 1812-1814*
Welland: Welland Tribune, 9 vols., 1898-1906

Dunlop, William
*Tiger Dunlop's Upper Canada*
Toronto: McClelland & Stewart, 1967

Ferguson, John Delancey, ed.
*The Letters of Robert Burns: 1790-1806*
Oxford: Clarendon Press, 1931

Gellner, John, ed.
*Recollections of the War of 1812. Three Eyewitness Accounts*
Toronto: Baxter Publishing, 1964

Klinck, Carl F. and James J. Talman, eds.
*The Journal of Major John Norton, 1816*
Toronto: Champlain Society, 1970

Finan, Patrick
*Journal of a Voyage to Quebec, in the Year 1825, with Recollections of Canada, during the late American War, in the Years 1812-1813*
Newry, U.K.: Alexander Peacock, 1828

Merritt, William H.
*Journal of Events Principally on the Detroit and Niagara Frontiers During the War of 1812*
St. Catharine's: Historical Society of British North America, 1863

Neilson, J.L.H., ed.
*Reminiscences of the War of 1812-1814. Being Portions of the Diary of a*

*Captain of the "Voltiguers Canadiens" While in Garrison at Kingston, etc.*
Kingston: privately published, 1885

Raymond, W.O., ed.
*Winslow Papers, A.D. 1776-1828*
St. John, NB: Sun Printing Co., 1891

Roach, Isaac
"Military Journal of the War of 1812"
*Pennsylvania Magazine of History and Biography* 17 (1893), 281-315

Temperley, Howard, ed.
*Lieutenant Colonel Joseph Gubbins. New Brunswick Journals of 1811 & 1813.*
Fredericton, NB: King's Landing Corporation, 1980

Wood, William H., ed.
*Select British Documents of the Canadian War of 1812*
Toronto: Champlain Society, 4 vols., 1920-1928

### *5. Biographical and Other Reference Works*

Adjutant-General's Office, London
*General Regulations and Orders for the Army, 1811*
London, 1811

———

*Rules and Regulations for the Cavalry*
London, 1795

Allaire, Jean-Baptiste Allaire, ed.
*Dictionnaire biographique du clergé canadian-française*
Montreal: Diocese of Quebec, 1910

Askwith, W.H.
*List of Officers of the Royal Regiment of Artillery from the Year 1716 to the Year 1899*
London: Royal Artillery Institution, 1900

Balleine, G.R.
*A Biographical Dictionary of Jersey*
London: The Staples Press, n.d. [c. 1948]

Brewer, E.C.
*The Reader's Handbook*
New York: Lippincott, 2 vols., 1899

Burn, Colonel
*A Naval and Military Technical Dictionary of the French Language*
London: John Murray, 4th ed., 1863

Charnock, John
*Biographia Navalis or, Impartial Memoirs of the Lives and Characters of the Officers of the Navy of Great Britain, from the Year 1660 to the Present Time ...*
London: R. Faulden, 4 vols., 1794

Colledge, James J.
*The Ships of the Royal Navy: An Historical Index*
Annapolis: Naval Institute Press, 2 vols., 1987-1988

Crone, John S.
*A Concise Dictionary of Irish Biography*
Dublin: The Talbot Press, 1928

Dubeau, Sharon
*New Brunswick Loyalists. A Bicentennial Salute*
Agincourt, Ont: Generation Press, 1983

Genest, John
*Some Account of the English Stage, From the Restoration in 1660 to 1830*
Bath: H.E. Carrington, 10 vols., 1832

[Grose, Francis]
*Lexicon Baliconitrum, or Dictionary of Buckish Slang, University Wit, and Pickpocket Eloquence*
London: C. Chapell, 1811

Halpenny, Francess G. and Jean Hamelin, eds.
*Dictionary of Canadian Biography*, vols. v - ix
Toronto: University of Toronto, 1983-1988

Harland, John
*Seamanship in the Age of Sail*
Baltimore: Naval Institute Press, 1984

Hart, H.G., ed.
*The New Annual Army List for 1847*
London: John Murray, 1847

Heitman, Francis B.
*Historical Register and Dictionary of the United States Army, 1789-1903*
Washington: Government Printing Office, 2 vols., 1903

Irving, Lukin Homfray
*Officers of the British Forces in Canada. War of 1812-15*
Toronto: Canadian Military Institute, 1908

James, Charles
*A New and Enlarged Military Dictionary, in French and English.*
London: 3rd ed., T. Egerton, 2 vols., 1810

———

*The Regimental Companion. Containing the Pay, Allowances and Relative Duties of Every Officer in the British Service*
London: T. Egerton, 2 vols., 1811

Johnson, Allen, ed.
*Dictionary of American Biography*
New York: Scribners, 23 vols., 1928

Marshall, John, ed.
*Royal Naval Biography; or Memoirs of the Services of all the Flag-Officers, Superannuated Rear Admirals, Retired-Captains, Post-Captains and Commanders*
London: Longman, Hurst, Rees, Orme & Bronw, 3 vols. and supplement, 1823

Mooney, James L., ed.
*Dictionary of American Naval Fighting Ships*
Washington: Government Printing Office, 8 vols., 1959-1981

Morgan, Henry J.
*Sketches of Celebrated Canadians and Persons Connected with Canada*
Quebec: Hunter & Rose, 1862

Nicoll, Allerdyce, ed.
*A History of English Drama, 1660-1900*
Cambridge: University Press, 6 vols., 1952-1959

O'Byrne, William R.
*A Naval Biographical Dictionary: Comprising the Life and Services of Every Living Officer in Her Majesty's Navy*
London: J. Murray, 1849

Partridge, Eric
*A Classical Dictionary of the Vulgar Tongue by Captain Francis Grose*
London: Routledge & Kegan Paul, 1963 [reprint of 1796 work]

———

*The Macmillan Dictionary of Historical Slang*
New York: MacMillan, 1974

Philippart, John, ed.
*The Royal Military Calendar*
London: T. Egerton, 2 vols., 1815

Smith, D.B., ed.
*The Commissioned Sea Officers of the Royal Navy, 1660-1815*
London: National Maritime Museu, 3 vols., 1854

Smith, George
*An Universal Military Dictionary*
London: J. Millan, 1779, reprinted Museum Restoration Service, Bloomfield, 1969

Stephen, Leslie, ed.
*Dictionary of National Biography*
London: Smith, Elder, 63 vols., 1885

Thorne, J.O., ed.
*Chamber's Biographical Dictionary*
Edinburgh: W. & R. Chambers, 1961

Van der Aa, A.J.
*Biographie Woordenboek der Nederlandern*
Haarlen, Netherlands: 1852, reprinted 1969

Wallace, W.S., ed.
*The Macmillan Dictionary of Canadian Biography*
Toronto: Macmillan, 4th ed., 1978

War Office
*Instructions to Regimental Surgeons, for regulating the concerns of the Sick and of the Hospitals*
London: 1808

———

*A List of All the Officers of the Army and Royal Marines on Full and Half-Pay* [1811-1816]
London: T. Egerton, 1811, 1812, 1813, 1814, 1815, 1816

Wilson, James G. and John Fiske, eds.
*Appleton's Encyclopaedia of American Biography*
New York: Appleton, 7 vols, 1888

## 6. Secondary Sources

### Books

Brenton, Edward B.
*Some Account of the Public Life of the Late Lieutenant-General Sir George Prevost*
London: T. Cadell & T. Egerton, 1823

Brett-James, Anthony
*Life in Wellington's Army*
London: George Allen & Unwin, 1972

Burne, Alfred
*The Noble Duke of York*
London: Staples Press, 1949

Clowes, William, ed.
*A Naval History of Great Britain from the Earliest Times to the Present, Volume VI*
London: William Clowes, 1901

Coggeshall, George
*History of the American Privateers and Letters-of-Marque, During Our War with England in the Years 1812, 13 and 14*
New York: author pub., 1861

Dalby, Isaac
*A Course of Mathematics Designed for the Use of the Officers and Cadets at the Royal Military College*
London: author pub., 2 vols., 1805

Duff, David
*Edward of Kent*
London: Muller, 1938, reprinted 1973

Edwards, R.David
*Tecumseh and the Quest for Indian Leadership*
Toronto: University of Toronto, 1984

FitzGibbon, Mary A.
*A Veteran of the War of 1812: the Life of James FitzGibbon*
Toronto: William Briggs, 1898

Fortescue, John
*History of the British Army*, vol. IV
London: Macmillan, 1913

Glover, Michael
*Wellington as Military Commander*
London: Sphere Books, 1973

———

*Wellington's Army in the Peninsula, 1808-1814*
New York: Hippocrene Books, 1977

Glover, Richard
*Peninsular Preparation. The Reform of the British Army, 1795-1809*
Cambridge: University Press, 1963

Graves, Donald E.
*The Battle of Lundy's Lane. On the Niagara in 1814*
Baltimore: Nautical and Aviation Press, 1993

Kirke, H.W.
*From the Gun Room to the Throne; being the life of Philip d'Auvergne, Duke of Bouillon*
London: Swann, Sonnenschein, 1904

Larpent, George, ed.
*Private Journal of Judge Alexander Larpent*
London: Bentley, 1854

McKenzie, Ruth
*Laura Secord, the Legend and the Lady*
Toronto: McClelland & Stewart, 1971

Mockler-Ferryman, Augustus
*Annals of Sandhurst*
London: Royal Military Academy, 1900

Oman, Charles
*Wellington's Army, 1809-1814*
London: Edward Arnold, 1912

Priestley, J.B.
*The Prince of Pleasure and His Regency, 1811-1820*
New York: Harper & Row, 1969

Pullen, Hugh F.
*The Shannon and the Chesapeake*
Toronto: McClelland & Stewart, 1970

Roosevelt, Theodore
*The Naval War of 1812*
New York: G.P. Putnam, 1882

Stevens, Joan
*Victorian Voices. An Introduction to the Papers of Sir John Le Couteur, Q.A.D.C., F.R.S.*
St. Helier: Société Jersiaise, 1969

Sugden, John
*Tecumseh's Last Stand*
Norman: University of Oklahoma, 1985

Saunders, A.C.
*Jersey in the 18th and 19th Centuries*
Jersey: J.T. Bigwood, 1930

Squires, W. Austin
*The 104th Regiment of Foot (The New Brunswick Regiment), 1803-1817*
Frederiction: Brunswick Press, 1962

Thomas, Earle
*Sir John Johnson, Loyalist Baronet*
Toronto: Dundurn Press, 1986

Thomas, Hugh
*The Story of Sandhurst*
London: Royal Military College, 1961

Thoumine, R.H.
*Scientific Soldier. A Life of General Le Marchant. 1766-1812*
London: Oxford University Press, 1968

Tupper, Ferdinand B., ed.
*The Life and Correspondence of Major-General Sir Isaac Brock*
London: Simpkin, Marshall, 1845

Whitehorne, Joseph A.
*While Washington Burned. The Battle of Fort Erie*
Baltimore: Nautical and Aviation Press, 1992

Winstock, Lewis
*Songs and Music of the Redcoats, 1642-1902*
London: Stackpole, 1970

**Articles**

Allen, Robert S., ed
"The Bisshopp Papers during the War of 1812," *Journal of the Society for Army Historical Research* 61 (1983), 22-29

Angus, Margaret
"The Old Stones of Queen's, 1842-1900," *Historic Kingston* 20 (1971) 7-21

Cruikshank, Ernest A.
"Record of the Services of Canadian Regiments in the War of 1812," *Canadian Military Institute, Selected Papers*
Part I, The Royal Newfoundland Regiment, 5 (1893-1894), 5-15
Part II, The Glengarry Light Infantry, 6 (1894-1895), 9-23
Part V, The Incorporated Militia, 9 (1897-1899), 70-80
Part VI, The Canadian Voltiguers, 10 (1899-1900), 9-21
Part VII, The Canadian Fencibles, 11 (1901), 9-22

Einstein, Lewis, ed.
"Recollections of the War of 1812 by George Hay, Eighth Marquis of Tweeddale," *American Historical Review* 32 (1926-1927) 69-78

Graves, Donald E.
"William Drummond and the Battle of Fort Erie," *Canadian Military History* I (1992) 25-44

Harrington, M. Eleanor
"Captain John Deserontyn and the Mohawk Settlement at Deseronto," *Queen's Quarterly* 29 (1921), 165-180

Martin, John P.
"The Regiment De Watteville: its Services and Settlement in Upper Canada," *Ontario History* 62 (1960), 17-30

Mullane, George
"Old Inns and Coffee Houses of Halifax, Nova Scotia," *Nova Scotia Historical Society, Collections* 22 (1933), 1-24

Patterson, William
"A Forgotten Hero in a Forgotten War," *Journal of the Society for Army Historical Research* 68 (1990), 7-20

Pope, Maurice A., ed.
"The March of the 104th Foot from Fredericton to Quebec in 1813," *Canadian Defence Quarterly* 7 (1930), 480-501

Roy, P.-G.
"Les Besserer de la province de Quebec," *Bulletin des recherches historiques (Lévis)* 23 (1917), 30-31

# Index

Note: The ranks and titles of all persons are as they were when Le Couteur met them. A listing, "215n", is a reference to a note on that page.

### *Part I - Places & Events*

## Part II - Persons

### A - British and Canadian Military and Naval Personnel

### *B - American and Other Military and Naval Personnel*



### *C - Civilians*

## *Part III - Military Units, Naval and Other Vessels*

### *A - British and Canadian Military Units*

***B - American and Other Military Units***



***C - British Warships***

**D -American and Private Warships**



**F -Civilian Vessels**